Charles S. Peirce
On Norms & Ideals

Charles S. Peirce
On Norms & Ideals

By Vincent G. Potter, S. J.

THE UNIVERSITY OF MASSACHUSETTS PRESS 1967

Copyright © 1967 by
The University of Massachusetts Press
All rights reserved
Library of Congress Catalog Card
Number 67-30845
Printed in the United States of America
by The Heffernan Press Inc.
Worcester, Massachusetts

In Memory of My Father

Foreword

CHARLES PEIRCE IS EMERGING, in the eyes of philosophers both here and abroad, as one of America's major thinkers. He is not likely, however, to become the founder of a philosophical tradition. Father Potter is correct in seeing that, unlike that of Aristotle, Aquinas, or Kant, Peirce's thought cannot be understood through some one principle or thesis that might be made into a "platform" for a school of thought. Although Peirce's philosophy actually possesses a greater unity than many would admit, the peculiar language, the often cryptic style, and the nonsystematic form in which he presented many of his ideas, stood in the way, and few of his contemporaries caught the main drift of his thought. Fortunately, the situation has changed. The high quality of his thought has not escaped notice; recent years have witnessed the efforts of philosophers and historical scholars alike to recover his works, to expound, to criticize, and to evaluate their import. In the end it will be discovered that Peirce accomplished something more important for the cause of philosophy than the founding of a tradition; through arresting questions and some most original answers he has forced us back to philosophical reflection about those basic issues that inevitably confront us as human beings, especially in an age of science. Peirce's concern for experience, for what is actually encountered, means that his philosophy, even in its most technical aspects, forms a reflective commentary on actual life and on the world in which it is lived. To read Peirce is to philosophize, for to follow his arguments it is necessary for the reader himself to be wrestling with the very problems Peirce envisaged.

Father Potter's fine study exhibits at one stroke both the originality of Peirce's thought and the kind of serious treatment now being given to his ideas. No part of Peirce's philosophy is bolder than his attempt to establish esthetics, ethics, and logic as the three normative sciences and, even more, to argue for the priority of esthetics among the trio. The author treats these ideas about the normative, the standards that structure and guide an activity, with clarity and good judgment, showing at the same time their connection with Peirce's pragmatism and his realism. As Father Potter makes clear, Peirce expressed views on the same topic at different times and he was not always consistent in these utterances. The present study, however, shows that Peirce did take seriously his trinity of normative sciences and that, at least on some occasions, he was convinced of the priority of the esthetic over the other two. Logic is said to be normative because it governs thought and aims at truth; ethics is normative because it analyzes the ends to which thought should be directed; esthetics is normative and fundamental because it considers what it means to be an end or something good in itself.

Father Potter brings to the accomplishment of his task two principal philosophical virtues; he combines sympathetic and informed exposition with straightforward criticism and he deals in a sensible way with the gaps and inconsistencies in Peirce's thought. The author always prefaces his critical commentary with a sustained effort to discover, by attending to all the relevant passages, exactly what Peirce was asserting on a given topic. Father Potter wisely stands with those who see in Peirce's many writings not a mere mélange of ideas but an original and generally consistent position which can survive some, if not all, of its incoherences. His study shows that Peirce was above all a cosmological and ontological thinker, one who combined science both as method and as result with a conception of reasonable action to form a comprehensive theory of reality. Peirce's pragmatism, although it has to do with "action" and the achievement of results, is not a glorification of action but rather a theory of the dynamic nature of things in which the "ideal" dimension of reality—laws, thoughts, tendencies, and ends—has genuine power for directing the cosmic order, including man, toward reasonable goals.

JOHN E. SMITH

Preface

STUDIES IN THE PHILOSOPHY of Charles Sanders Peirce which have appeared in increasing numbers over the last twenty-five or thirty years have won for him at last the recognition which, for the most part, he was denied during his lifetime. Everyone is now agreed that Peirce is one of America's truly original thinkers.[1] Indeed his contributions to logic alone would merit him that honor. Yet his writings cover such varied subjects as physics, history, cosmology, mathematics, metaphysics, and religion. They are very fragmentary and sometimes incomplete. Often they are merely outlines of projects to be undertaken. An important question, therefore, in determining Peirce's place in the history of philosophy is whether or not he succeeded in constructing his philosophy "architectonicly" (5.5). Did he, like Aristotle and Kant, succeed in laying broad and deep foundations on which to build? Is Peirce's philosophy *a* philosophy or merely a patchwork of incompatible tendencies?

Peircean scholars are divided on the issue. Not a few claim that there are two or more Peirces.[2] Others think that the very undertaking which he set himself—to construct a "scientific metaphysics"—is doomed from the outset because of the basic antagonism between the aims of science and those of metaphysics.[3] Still others argue that,

[1] For the best biographical sketch of Peirce, see P. Weiss, "Charles Sanders Peirce," *Dictionary of American Biography*, 14 (1934), pp. 398–403.

[2] E.g. T. A. Goudge, *The Thought of C. S. Peirce* (Toronto: University of Toronto Press, 1950), Ch. 1; R. S. Robin, "Peirce's Doctrine of the Normative Sciences," *Studies in the Philosophy of Charles Sanders Peirce*, Second Series, ed. E. C. Moore and R. S. Robin (Amherst: University of Massachusetts Press, 1964), p. 287; P. P. Wiener, "Peirce's Evolutionary Interpretations of the History of Science," *ibid.*, p. 143.

[3] E.g. R. Wells, "The True Nature of Peirce's Evolutionism," *ibid.*, pp. 304–305; E. Freeman, *The Categories of Charles Peirce* (Chicago: Open Court, 1934), pp. 4–6 (but Freeman thinks the major inconsistencies he has found can be resolved, cf. p. 3); M. G. Murphey, *The Development of Peirce's Philosophy* (Cambridge: Harvard University Press, 1961), p. 407 (Murphey thinks Peirce's "system" is an illusion).

despite the obviously fragmentary character of his papers, Peirce has outlined a genuine philosophical "system."[4] Yet another group feels that he has achieved a partial synthesis with gaps and inconsistencies, some of which at least can be remedied.[5]

Our own view tends to be something like this last. Peirce will never turn out to be the founder of a philosophical "school" as were Aristotle and Aquinas and Kant. He has left too much undone, too much in the form of promissory notes for that. Nevertheless, there will be "Peirceans" in the sense that men will be inspired by his ideals of inquiry and guided by his principles of logic. And perhaps one day some such "disciple" (or as Peirce himself might have thought, some such group of researchers) may achieve the sort of synthesis of which he dreamed. Peirce's work does show considerable unity and a good number of the alleged inconsistencies are only apparent. Large blocks of his work are remarkably interwoven and interdependent, so much so that one wonders whether or not Peirce's claims to have worked out certain problems, even though he never got around to putting the solutions on paper, are not worthy of belief. For example, the various formulations of the pragmatic maxim over the course of his career are basically consistent. His categories are not only consistent with his pragmatism but absolutely essential to understanding it. Again Peirce's extreme realism is, as he always claimed, the bedrock of pragmatism and synechism. A firm and definite line of thought does emerge from the tangle of his papers even though much of his work is incomplete and perhaps here and there inconsistent in details. It is

---

[4] E.g. P. Weiss, "The Essence of Peirce's System," *Journal of Philosophy*, 37 (1940), pp. 253–264; J. Feibleman, *An Introduction to Peirce's Philosophy, Interpreted as a System* (New York: Harper Bros., 1946), *passim;* W. D. Oliver, "The Final Cause and Agapasm in Peirce's Philosophy," *Studies*, Moore and Robin, pp. 289–290; R. Workman, "Pragmatism and Realism," *ibid.*, p. 242; H. Wennerberg, *The Pragmatism of C. S. Peirce: An Analytical Study* (Lund: C. W. K. Gleerup, and Copenhagen: E. Wunksgaard, 1962), pp. 25–28. Wennerberg's division of opinion concerning Peirce's consistency is an oversimplification; I do not see that Murphey should be listed as holding the same position on this matter as Feibleman.

[5] J. E. Smith, *The Spirit of American Philosophy* (New York: Oxford University Press, 1963), p. 5; T. S. Knight, *Charles Peirce* (New York: Washington Square Press, 1965), pp. 180–183.

simply too easy, therefore, to divide Peirce up neatly into "tendencies" which are incompatible.[6]

In the end perhaps we may disagree with Peirce, but first we must take him on his own terms, as sympathetically as possible. In that way we are more likely to understand him correctly and so our criticism will be the stronger. It is possible to defend Peirce's fundamental unity and coherence in large sectors of his writing and still not accept his position. The question of understanding a position from the "inside" is of course distinct from the question of that position's truth, or adequacy. Clearly, however, if it can be shown that a philosopher falls into contradiction again and again, it is a decisive point against him. On the other hand, to say that a philosopher is basically consistent is not necessarily to claim that his position is correct. We have a number of serious reservations and criticisms of Peirce, despite the position we are here defending, and we hope to have the opportunity one day to air them thoroughly.[7]

Our presentation is developed in three parts. Part I deals with the relation of the pragmatic maxim to the doctrine of the normative sciences. The 1903 version of that maxim was due in large measure to Peirce's realization of these sciences' role in human inquiry. Since the doctrine of the normative sciences was influenced by years of cosmological speculation, Part II takes up the doctrine of synechism. Peirce thought of his cosmology as proof of pragmatism. Pragmatism,

---

[6] Some commentators use James' distinction between the "tender-minded" and the "tough-minded" to characterize the "conflicting" elements of rationalism and empiricism in Peirce. They attach an evaluation to this terminology, approving of toughness and disapproving of tenderness. James did not mean to imply a value judgment. He merely meant to describe two temperaments, equally good and necessary in the search for the "whole truth." See W. James, *Pragmatism and Other Essays* (New York: Washington Square Press, 1963), pp. 5–21.

[7] For example, we have reservations about Peirce's extreme realism. Again there are problems concerning the status of the individual in Peirce's "system." We are not entirely convinced either that metaphysics can be collapsed into logic. Further, questions might be asked as to the legitimacy of assuming that the movement of history and evolution follows that of our reasoning. These are but some of the critical questions which might be addressed to Peirce.

he maintained, is a step in synechism. Yet there is no understanding of synechism without an appreciation of tychism and evolution. Indeed, there is no synechism at all without them. Hence Part III considers the doctrine of "evolutionary love." In a proper conception of the evolutionary process, Peirce believed, was to be found the *summum bonum*, the ultimate norm for man's thinking and acting. The title chosen by Philip Wiener for his edition of selections from Peirce, therefore, seems particularly appropriate since it sums up so well what Peirce's philosophy tries to discover—*Values in a Universe of Chance.* Throughout our presentation we have emphasized the key role habit is made to play in his thought. In a true sense it is the unifying thread which ties together the strands of realism, idealism, and pragmatism.

This thesis does not propose the last word on the subject of Peirce's "system." We think, however, that we have made a good case and that we have resolved some of the "inconsistencies" in his writings and have laid a foundation for the resolution of others. Perhaps more mature thought will lead us to modify or even abandon altogether the position we are here defending. For the moment, nonetheless, this is how we read Peirce. One thing is certain; we have begun to realize how much still remains to be done. This study has convinced us that his categories are truly at the heart of all Peirce's thought. We feel that an exhaustive study of them is very much needed, a study which will show them to be a great deal more complex than has generally been admitted. For example, a study should be made of the relation of the categories to the modes of being. Are they the same? If they are not, how precisely are they related? This study should emphasize the interrelation and mutual dependence of the categories and not be content with distinguishing them. Again, such a study ought to make clear how the application of the categories shifts and adapts to the various levels of analysis. At the moment, we are inclined to think that such a study in depth will support our general thesis.

We would like to point out that this work was originally submitted to the Department of Philosophy of Yale University as a doctoral dissertation under the title "Peirce's Ontological Pragmatism." The present version is substantially the same as that dissertation with the exception of some minor revisions and the addition of a footnote or two. The title has been changed at the suggestion of several associates as more appropriate to the work's central concern. The bibliography, of course, has also been brought up to date.

Finally, we wish to acknowledge our very great debt to Professor John E. Smith, who directed the dissertation at Yale, for the many hours he so generously gave us. Without his advice, suggestions, and encouragement we would have been utterly lost, and surely this book would never have appeared. We would also like to thank Mr. Richard Bernstein for his continued interest in our project. It was he who first introduced us in a formal way to Peircean studies and offered valuable criticism all along the way. The inadequacies and/or errors which remain are all the author's. We thank, too, the Philosophy Department of Harvard University for permission to use the Peirce manuscripts on deposit in the Houghton Library, and the library staff for their courtesy and assistance.

VINCENT G. POTTER, S.J.

Shrub Oak, New York
January, 1967

Acknowledgments

Permissions have been received from the publishers to quote from the following works:

The Collected Papers of Charles Sanders Peirce, vols. I–VI, eds. Charles Hartshorne and Paul Weiss (Cambridge: The Belknap Press of Harvard University, 1931–1935); vols. VII, VIII, ed. Arthur Burks (Cambridge: Harvard University Press, 1958). References to these *Collected Papers* will be by volume and paragraph number following the established convention. Thus (5.585) is to be interpreted to mean Volume V, Paragraph 585.

The Peirce Papers in the Houghton Library of Harvard University, the Philosophy Department of Harvard University.

Charles S. Peirce's Letters to Lady Welby, ed. I. C. Lieb (New Haven: Whitlock's, 1953).

In full the author's article, "Peirce's Analysis of Normative Science," *Transactions of the Charles S. Peirce Society*, II,1, pp. 5–32 (as Part I, Chapter 2).

In full the author's article, "Pragmatism and the Normative Sciences," *Journal of the History of Philosophy*, V, 1 (January 1967), pp. 41–53 (as Part I, Chapter 3).

Contents

I

Pragmatism &
the Normative Sciences

Introduction

IF ONE WERE ASKED to justify beginning a study of Peirce's pragmatism with a consideration of the normative sciences, perhaps the most simple and effective reply would be to point out that this is the way Peirce himself chose to expound pragmatism in his Harvard lectures of 1903. The first lecture was entitled "Pragmatism: The Normative Sciences." But why did Peirce elect to begin thus? Was it merely that he had to start somewhere, or did he think that the normative sciences in some way furnished the key to all that was to follow?

Although Peirce came to recognize the nature and role of the normative sciences only late in his career, still he was convinced that his own account of the hierarchical dependence of logic on ethics and of ethics on esthetics was a discovery of fundamental importance for a correct understanding of his system, and one which distinguished his "pragmaticism" from other less correct interpretations of his own famous maxim. It would be a basic mistake to think that because Peirce's exposition of that role was short and unsatisfactory, it is not an integral part of what he conceived to be his "architectonic" system. It would perhaps be more correct to say that Peirce's realization of the place of these sciences put in his hands the capstone which unified all that he had been trying to do more or less successfully for some forty years. At least Peirce himself seems to have looked at it in this way.[1]

In a letter to William James, dated November 25, 1902, Peirce remarks that many philosophers who call themselves pragmatists "miss the very point of it," and he tells us why:

> But I seem to myself to be the sole depositary at present
> of the completely developed system, which all hangs together

[1] Peirce was very conscious of his own development as a philosopher. He constantly refers to what he read and by whom he was influenced. He continually returned to what he had written to annotate and correct his opinions. Therefore, the most reliable and fruitful source for an appreciation of what he is trying to do is Peirce's remarks about himself.

and cannot receive any proper presentation in fragments. My own view in 1877 was crude. Even when I gave my Cambridge lectures I had not really got to the bottom of it or seen the unity of the whole thing. It was not until after that that I obtained the proof that logic must be founded on ethics, of which it is a higher development. Even then, I was for some time so stupid as not to see that ethics rests in the same manner on a foundation of esthetics—by which, it is needless to say, I don't mean milk and water and sugar. (8.255)

Other pragmatic positions, then, are only fragmentary.[2] They lack the unity provided by a theory of the normative sciences, and this deficiency has led those positions into error—the error of making action the be-all and the end-all of thought.[3] If other pragmatists had a correct view of the normative sciences, they would see how they are connected with Peirce's categories.

[2] But cf. 5.494 (*ca.* 1906) where Peirce sketches the differences between himself and James, Schiller, and Papini in a less polemical way.

[3] "It [calculation of probabilities] goes to show that the practical consequences are *much*, but not that they are *all* the meaning of a concept. A new argument must supplement the above. All the more active functions of animals are adaptive characters calculated to insure the continuance of the stock. Can there be the slightest hesitation in saying, then, that the human intellect is implanted in man, either by a creator or by a quasi-intentional effect of the struggle for existence, virtually in order, and solely in order, to insure the continuance of mankind? But how can it have such effect except by regulating human conduct? Shall we not conclude then that the conduct of men is the sole purpose and sense of thinking, and that if it be asked *why* should the human stock be continued, the only answer is that that is among the inscrutable purposes of God or the virtual purposes of nature which for the present remain secrets to us?

"So it would seem. But this conclusion is too vastly far-reaching to be admitted without further examination. Man seems to himself to have some glimmer of co-understanding with God, or with Nature. The fact that he has been able in some degree to predict how Nature will act, to formulate general 'laws' to which future events conform, seems to furnish inductive proof that man really penetrates in some measure the ideas that govern creation. Now man cannot believe that creation has not some ideal purpose. If so, it is not mere action, but the development of an idea which is the purpose of thought; and so a doubt is cast upon the ultra pragmatic notion that action is the *sole* end and purpose of thought." (8.211–212, letter to Mario Calderoni, *ca.* 1905.)

These three normative sciences correspond to my three categories, which in their psychological aspect, appear as Feeling, Reaction, Thought. I have advanced my understanding of these categories much since Cambridge days; and can now put them in a much clearer light and more convincingly. The true nature of pragmatism cannot be understood without them. It does not, as I seem to have thought at first, take Reaction as the be-all, but it takes the end-all as the be-all, and the End is something that gives its sanction to action. It is of the third category. (8.256)

Just how the normative sciences are connected with the categories we will have to examine in some detail. For the present, however, let us just note the fact, and Peirce's insistence thereon.[4] It was only when Peirce became aware of the connection that he fully realized how crude his first presentation of the pragmatic maxim was. In the 1878 papers ("How to Make Our Ideas Clear" and "The Fixation of Belief") he seemed to identify meaning with action-reaction[5] because he had not yet seen that action-reaction is to be understood only in terms of purpose and that purpose is essentially thought. Thought may well involve action, but it cannot be identical with it since Secondness and Thirdness are irreducible.[6] The acknowledgment of the role of ends in action is the insight into the role of the normative sciences, and this acknowledgment brought about Peirce's successive attempts to formulate the pragmatic maxim in a more sophisticated and adequate way. Meaning is the rational purport of a concept[7]—

[4] "Action is second, but conduct is third. Law as an active force is second, but order and legislation are third." (1.337, from an early fragment, *ca.* 1875, antedating the first published formulation of the pragmatic maxim. The distinction between action and conduct is essential to what follows.)

[5] Cf. 5.403 for the famous application of the maxim to the concept "hard" where Peirce went so far as to say that there would be no falsity in saying of a diamond that it was soft until someone tried to scratch it. But cf. 5.453 and 457 where Peirce changed his view (1905).

[6] Cf. 1.322–323; Peirce takes up the objection that law is essential to the notion of one thing acting upon another. Tychism develops the distinction.

[7] "In general, we may say that *meanings* are inexhaustible. We are too apt to think that what one *means* to do and the *meaning* of a word are quite unrelated meanings of the word 'meaning,' or that they are only con-

it is essentially a Third and not a Second even though a Second may
be involved in its recognition.

Peirce goes on to explain to James how the correct and systematic
understanding of pragmatism involves synechism, that is, the doctrine
of law in the cosmos.

> Only one must not take a nominalistic view of Thought as if
> it were something that a man had in his consciousness.
> Consciousness may mean any one of the three categories. But
> if it is to mean Thought it is more without us than within.
> It is we that are in it, rather than it in any of us. . . .
>   This then leads to synechism, which is the keystone of
> the arch. (8.256, 257)

The line of thought begins to become clearer: all action supposes
ends, but ends are in the mode of being of thought because they are
general. Thought, however, is not merely in consciousness but pervades everything so that consciousness is rather in thought. Generals,
then, are real and so authentic pragmatism is realistic. Elsewhere (in
the Pragmatism Lectures of 1903) Peirce explicitly suggests that the
normative sciences get us "upon the trail of the secret of pragmatism"
(5.129). Consequently, we may say that for Peirce the categories, the
normative sciences, pragmatism, synechism, and "scholastic realism"
are of a piece.[8]

nected by both referring to some actual operation of the mind. Professor
Royce especially in his great work *The World and the Individual* has done
much to break up this mistake. In truth the only difference is that when a
person *means* to do anything he is in some state in consequence of which
the brute reactions between things will be moulded [in] to conformity of
the form to which the man's mind is itself moulded, while the meaning of a
word really lies in the way in which it might, in a proper position in a
proposition believed, tend to mould the conduct of a person into conformity
to that to which it is itself moulded. Not only will meaning always, more or
less, in the long run, mould reactions to itself, but it is only in doing so that
its own being consists. For this reason I call this element of the phenomenon
or object of thought the element of Thirdness. It is that which is what it is
by virtue of imparting a quality to reactions in the future" (1.343).

[8] In a letter to Dewey, dated June 9, 1904, concerning a review of his
Studies in Logic about to appear in the September issue of *The Nation*,
Peirce deplores the way Dewey turns logic into a "natural history," instead
of pursuing it as a normative science "which in my judgment is the greatest
need of our age" (8.239).

The conclusion one must draw is that despite the relatively short time Peirce spent working out his conception of normative science, despite his many hesitations as to what ought to be included under that rubric, and despite the promissory character of the development which he left us, he had seen where and how the notion not only fitted into his view of philosophy, but he had also in some way united the whole thing, moulding his earlier attempts at formulating the pragmatic maxim into a comprehensive and highly subtle analysis of meaning.

1. The Categories & Normative Science

FOR PEIRCE, philosophy is a theoretical science of discovery. Since it is scientific it deals with fact. Philosophy, in short, is a positive science differing from the more familiar positive sciences (physics, chemistry, etc.) only in this: that the facts with which it deals do not require any special training or equipment in order to be observed. Philosophy deals with ordinary facts of man's everyday existence, open to all at any time to observe. Peirce subdivides philosophy into phenomenology, normative science, and metaphysics. Phenomenology takes inventory of what appears without passing any judgment upon what it observes. It says neither "true" or "false" nor "good" or "bad" about the phenomena.[1] One might say that, for Peirce, phenomenology merely observes and catalogs the contents of experience. Normative science evaluates and judges the data thus collected, while metaphysics tries to comprehend their reality. It is clear, therefore, that in some sense phenomenology is the most basic of the philosophical disciplines—the one without which the enterprise could not even begin. The categories which phenomenology provides will be the conceptual frame in which the other parts of philosophy will make their analyses and explanations. It is not surprising, therefore, that Peirce should tell James that the true nature of pragmatism cannot be understood without the categories (8.256), nor that Peirce himself employs them to elucidate his division of normative science (8.256, 1.121–124, 5.129). Since we are trying to understand the role of nor-

---

[1] An objection might be raised at the outset, namely, that the categories themselves are involved in the phenomenological analysis. Peirce would probably reply that some categories are supposed in any analysis, but they need not be the universal ones.

Peirce also distinguishes two stages in philosophy: the heuristic and the retrospective. The first he calls "coenoscopy," the second "synthetic philosophy." ("Charles S. Peirce Papers," Houghton Library, Harvard University, #283, pp. 13–15. These numbers are from R. S. Robin's *Annotated Catalogue*. Henceforth, references to the Peirce manuscripts will be as follows: Peirce Papers, #283, pp. 13–15.)

mative science in Peirce's pragmatism, we must consider briefly the relation of his categories to esthetics, ethics, and logic.[2]

To guide us in this rather intricate analysis, it would be well perhaps to anticipate one result of Peirce's phenomenological investigations, namely, his theory of how ideas may be separated, or to put it in more traditional terms, his theory of distinctions. According to him there are three grades of separability of one idea from another: (1) dissociation, (2) "prescission," and (3) distinction. By "dissociation" he means that one idea can be imagined without another, just as we can imagine the color red without imagining the color blue. By "prescission" he means that even when two ideas are so closely connected that we cannot imagine one without the other, we can sometimes suppose one without the other. Thus, for example, while one can neither imagine nor suppose color without space, one can suppose space without color even though our experience does not allow us to imagine uncolored space. In other words, although color and space are inseparable in our experientially-bound imagination, we can discern a logical priority of one over the other—in our example, that of the subject of inherence of a quality over the quality itself. By "distinction," Peirce means simply the power to discriminate between two ideas which cannot even be supposed one without the other, as for example, taller and shorter. The meanings here can be distinguished although not separated because they are strictly relative to one another. Peirce would probably also allow the nonmutual relation of quality to a subject of inherence as an example of what he means by "distinction" (cf. 1.549 n. 1) even though it might be argued that the foundation for the discrimination is really in the fact that the subject can be prescinded from the quality (1.353).[3]

In these terms, then, what is the relationship of normative science

---

[2] Cf. 5.39: "This science of Phenomenology, then, must be taken as the basis upon which normative science is to be erected . . . ."

[3] Peirce sometimes refers to prescission as abstraction (1.549), but in a long note, he pinpoints "prescission" as one type of abstraction. He quotes Scotus as his authority on this matter and yet nowhere takes up the much more sophisticated set of distinctions—one mostly Thomistic, the other Scotistic—current in the medieval schools. It turns out that in the theory of distinctions lie the basic differences in the philosophies of these two schools; or perhaps more accurately, the differences in the theory of distinctions result from metaphysical differences.

to phenomenology? They cannot be dissociated because normative science intrinsically depends upon phenomenology for its categorial structure. On the other hand, there is more than just a distinction between them, for phenomenology may be prescinded from normative science. The latter is a step beyond the former which perhaps need not be taken, but which cannot be taken without the former. Consequently, the categories precede normative science. But once normative science is investigated, it of course becomes part of the phenomena inventoried by phenomenology and so the categories must apply there too. In other words, while logical priority dictates that one begin with phenomenology and subsequently move on to normative science (and then to metaphysics), once normative science is born, there is a movement back again to phenomenology in order to classify (and so more fully to understand) the nature of the normative. This will become clearer as we proceed.

Let us begin then with a rapid description of Peirce's phenomenology, in order to get at his new categories. Peirce describes the role of this science as follows:

But before we can attack any normative science, any science which proposes to separate the sheep from the goats, it is plain that there must be a preliminary inquiry which shall justify the attempt to establish such dualism. This must be a science that does not draw any distinction of good and bad in any sense whatever, but just contemplates phenomena as they are, simply opens its eyes and describes what it sees; not what it sees in the real as distinguished from figment— not regarding any such dichotomy—but simply describing the object, as a phenomenon, and stating what it finds in all phenomena alike. This is the science which Hegel made his starting-point, under the name of the *Phänomenologie des Geistes*—although he considered it in a fatally narrow spirit, since he restricted himself to what *actually* forces itself on the mind and so colored his whole philosophy with the ignoration of the distinction of essence and existence and so gave it the nominalistic and I might say in a certain sense the *pragmatoidal* character in which the worst of the Hegelian errors have their origin. I will so far follow Hegel as to call

this science *Phenomenology* although I will not restrict it to
the observation and analysis of *experience* but extend it to
describing all the features that are common to whatever is
experienced or might conceivably be experienced or become
an object of study in any way direct or indirect. (5.37)

Although Peirce's phenomenological studies began under Kant's and
not Hegel's influence (cf. e.g. 4.3, 4.4), he found that his conclusions
and Hegel's were not so very different, at least in comparison with
those of other philosophers. Hegel was right in making phenomenology bring out clearly the categories of fundamental modes of reality.
He was again right in distinguishing between universal categories
(all of which apply to everything) and limited categories (limited to
various phases of evolution); it is with the former that we shall be
engaged.

In regard to these [universal categories], it appears to me
that Hegel is so nearly right that my own doctrine might very
well be taken for a variety of Hegelianism, although in point
of fact it was determined in my mind by considerations
entirely foreign to Hegel, at a time when my attitude toward
Hegelianism was one of contempt. There was no influence
upon me from Hegel unless it was of so occult a kind as to
entirely escape my ken; and if there was such an occult
influence, it strikes me as about as good an argument for the
essential truth of the doctrine, as is the coincidence that
Hegel and I arrived in quite independent ways substantially
to the same result. (5.38)

These universal categories, according to Peirce, are three in number, no more and no less, absolutely irreducible one to another yet
interdependent, and directly observable in elements of whatever is
at any time before the mind in any way. Firstness, Secondness, and
Thirdness roughly correspond to the modes of being: possibility, actuality, and law (1.23).[4]

---

[4] Cf. e.g., Peirce's letter to Lady Victoria Welby, Oct. 12, 1904 where
he defines and explains at length Firstness, Secondness, and Thirdness.
Charles S. Peirce's Letters to Lady Welby, ed. Irwin C. Lieb (New Haven:
Whitlock's, 1953), pp. 7–14.

The category most easily grasped is that of Secondness or actuality. It is typified in the experience of effort, of resistance, of struggle, of opposition. Actuality consists in a *then* and *there*, in a relation to other existents. Briefly, actuality is something *brute*—brute fact which shocks. There is no reason in it.

> I instance putting your shoulder against a door and trying to force it open against an unseen, silent, and unknown resistance. We have a two-sided consciousness of effort and resistance, which seems to me to come tolerably near to a pure sense of actuality. (1.24)

Secondness is the category of experience. The breaking of the night's silence by a piercing whistle—the shock and surprise in it—reveals a two-sided consciousness of an ego and a non-ego. This is what experience is—what the course of life *compels* one to think.[5] Firstness is characteristic of the mode of being which consists in its subject's being positively such as it is regardless of anything else (1.25).

> For as long as things do not act upon one another there is no sense or meaning in saying that they have any being, unless it be that they are such in themselves that they may perhaps come into relation with others. The mode of being a *redness*, before anything in the universe was yet red, was nevertheless a positive qualitative possibility. And redness in itself, even if it be embodied, is something positive and *sui generis*. (1.25)

Thirdness, on the other hand, characterizes the mode of being of laws governing future events. It manifests itself in experience through predictions which have a decided tendency to be fulfilled. If a prediction has a decided tendency to be fulfilled it must be that future events have a tendency to conform to a general rule. For Peirce, this can only mean that generals or laws or Thirds are real.

> "Oh," but say the nominalists, "this general rule is nothing but a mere word or couple of words!" I reply, "Nobody ever dreamed of denying that what is general is of the nature of a general sign; but the question is whether future events will

[5] *Letters to Welby*, p. 8–9.

conform to it or not. If they will, your adjective 'mere' seems
to be ill-placed." (1.26)

Thirdness *consists* in the fact that future facts of Secondness will take
on a determinate general character. It is clear, then, that Thirdness is
characterized by its mediating role. Law, governing events, mediates
between pure possibility (Firstness) and pure actuality (Secondness).
Put in logical terms, Thirdness is always and exclusively a triadic
relation.

> Analyze for instance the relation involved in 'A gives B to C'.
> Now what is giving? It does not consist in A's putting B
> away from him and C's subsequently taking B up. It is not
> necessary that any material transfer should take place. It
> consists in A's making C the possessor according to *Law*. . . .
> But now suppose that giving *did* consist merely in A's laying
> down the B which C subsequently picks up. That would be
> a degenerate form of thirdness in which the thirdness is
> externally appended. In A's putting away B, there is no
> thirdness. In C's taking B, there is no thirdness. But if you
> say that these two acts constitute a single operation by virtue
> of the identity of B, you transcend the mere brute fact, you
> introduce a mental element. (Letter to Lady Victoria Welby,
> Lieb's ed., p. 8)

But to be (or at least to involve) a triadic relation is to be "of the
nature of a general sign."[6] In psychological terms, then, we might
express the mediating role of Thirdness this way: Thirdness is the
category of thought, mediating between the Firstness of feeling and
the Secondness of reaction. Peirce gathers under Thirdness the following: triadic relations, thought, generals, and laws. They all involve
a mental element and yet are real, not just figments of someone's
mind. Therefore the mental or the realm of thought cannot be limited
to a man's "consciousness" (see 8.256). Thus it is that the category of
Thirdness leads Peirce to a form of objective idealism which he calls
synechism.

The above treatment, of course, is but the barest outline of

---

[6] Cf. *Letters to Welby*, pp. 9–14 for an extended development of the
theory of signs.

Peirce's categories. It will serve, however, to give us some idea of the schema. Now we must consider for a moment how Peirce conceives Firstness, Secondness, and Thirdness to be related to each other. On the one hand, it is clear that they are irreducible and omnipresent. They describe all phenomena. On the other hand, Peirce tells us explicitly that the categories are interdependent. In terms of the degrees of separability of ideas, Peirce explains that the categories *cannot be dissociated* in the imagination from each other, nor from other ideas. But one category *can be prescinded* from another in a definite order: Firstness can be prescinded from Secondness and Thirdness, Secondness can be prescinded from Thirdness, but Secondness cannot be prescinded from Firstness, nor Thirdness from Secondness. Of course, the categories *can* easily *be distinguished,* but still

> . . . it is extremely difficult accurately and sharply to
> distinguish each from other conceptions so as to hold it in its
> purity and yet in its full meaning. (1.353)

Perhaps what Peirce has in mind is the fact that a true appreciation of the categories would require a thorough study of the logic of relatives. Peirce develops his categories in two ways, from "without" and from "within." The former is through phenomenology, the latter through the logic of relations. The "logical" approach to the categories is through an analysis of what is *necessarily* involved in representations and triadic relations. A thorough appreciation of the categories requires *both*—experience and logic. The categories themselves must not be confused with the elements in the categories: a First is not to be confused with Firstness, nor a Second with Secondness, nor a Third with Thirdness. There can be various combinations of category with category, and of element with category. It becomes intricate indeed and requires no little logical skill. While it is not to our purpose to pursue this important point at great length it might be well to discuss some of these combinations briefly.

Peirce tells us that Secondness and Thirdness are conceptions of complexity, although they are not complex conceptions (because they are ultimate and irreducible categories of being) (1.525). Take Secondness for example. Secondness is the category of reaction and so naturally we think of two objects interacting, a First and a Second.

But it would be a logical mistake to look upon this dyadic relation as made up of *three* elements: the First, the Second, and their reaction. Secondness is not built up out of pieces; rather Secondness pervades the whole relationship. If an object is a Second, it is a Second precisely because it is in a dyadic relation to something else. It has an element of being what another makes it to be. *A fortiori* the same is true of the reaction itself. It is not another thing or object, but a fact *about* two objects (1.526). It follows, then, that one can talk about the Secondness of a Second and the Secondness of a First (where the First and Second are in a dyadic relation), and that the Secondness of the First need not be the same as the Secondness of the Second. Consider the Secondness of the relation of quality to the matter in which it inheres (Peirce's own illustration, 1.527). The quality in itself is a Firstness, a mere possibility. The relation of inherence does not change the quality in itself, but merely imparts to it existence. Its existence is nothing but the relation of inherence in matter. But the situation with regard to its matter is quite different. Matter has no being at all except as subject of qualities, that is to say, its relation to qualities constitutes its existence. Void of all qualities, matter would not only not exist, but it would have no definite possibility at all— it would be unreal—it would be nothing at all.

> Thus we have a division of seconds into those whose very being, or Firstness, it is to be seconds, and those whose Secondness is only an accretion. (1.528)

The reason is not difficult to find. Basically it is the same reason which allows one to prescind Firstness from Secondness and Thirdness, and Secondness from Thirdness: the very essence of those categories.

> This distinction springs out of the essential elements of Secondness. For Secondness involves Firstness. The concepts of the two kinds of Secondness are mixed concepts composed of Secondness and Firstness. One is the second whose very Firstness is Secondness. The other is a second whose Secondness is second to a Firstness. (1.528)

Peirce remarks that this way of mingling Firstness and Secondness is distinct from the ideas of Firstness and Secondness which it combines, and so seems to form a different series of categories which, however, in turn, depend upon Firstness, Secondness, and Thirdness as component parts.

> The idea of mingling Firstness and Secondness in this
> particular way is an idea distinct from the ideas of Firstness
> and Secondness which it combines. It appears to be a
> conception of an entirely different series of categories. At the
> same time, it is an idea of which Firstness, Secondness, and
> Thirdness are component parts, since the distinction depends
> on whether the two elements of Firstness and Secondness
> that are united are so united as to be one or whether they
> remain two. (1.528)

Thus arises Peirce's distinction between genuine and degenerate grades of Secondness. Genuine Secondness is the Secondness of genuine Seconds, or matters; degenerate Secondness is the Secondness of a Second whose mode of being *in se* is Firstness (quality, in our example). A similar analysis might be made of Thirdness, with the exception that it will be found to have two grades of degeneracy (1.529). Firstness, of course, cannot have such a distinction.

The categories themselves are capable of similar combinations, and that because of their very nature. Whenever you have a triplet, you have three pairs; where you have a pair, you have two units (1.530). This is why the categories are subject to "prescission" in a certain order (see above). Thus, for example, because Secondness is an essential part of Thirdness and Firstness is an essential part of both Secondness and Thirdness, there is a Firstness of Secondness and of Thirdness, and a Secondness of Thirdness, but there can be no Secondness of pure Firstness nor Thirdness of pure Firstness or Secondness.

> When you strive to get the purest conceptions you can of
> Firstness, Secondness, and Thirdness, thinking of quality,
> reaction, and mediation—what you are striving to apprehend
> is pure Firstness, the Firstness of Secondness—that is what
> Secondness is, of itself—and the Firstness of Thirdness. When
> you contrast the blind compulsion in an event of reaction
> considered as something which happens and which of its
> nature can never happen again . . . when, I say, you contrast

this compulsion with the logical necessitation of *meaning* considered as something that has no being at all except so far as it actually gets embodied in an event of thought, and you regard this logical necessitation as a sort of actual compulsion, since the meaning must actually be embodied, what you are thinking of is a Secondness involved in Thirdness. (1.530)

Thus we have the following combinations:
1) Firstness of Firstness—quality in itself, or "possibility" (Primity)
2) Firstness of Secondness—existence or actuality (Secundity)
3) Firstness of Thirdness—mentality (Tertiality)

Taking Secondness we find:
1) Secondness of Secondness—reaction
2) Secondness of Thirdness—law as actual compulsion

Finally Thirdness gives us:
1) Thirdness of Thirdness—generality, lawfulness, reasonableness.[7]

Since Thirdness is the most important category for a philosophical analysis and classification of sciences, let us consider it a little more closely. Wherever there is Thirdness, according to Peirce, there is a First, a Second and a Third (a triadic relation). The First is a positive qualitative possibility; the Second is an existent thing determined by that First; and the Third is a law, or concept, which determines the relation between the First and Second (1.536). But Thirdness has a genuine and two degenerate forms. In genuine thirdness, the First, the Second, and the Third are all of the nature of Thirds, or thought. They are First, Second, and Third only relatively to each: the First is thought in its capacity as mere possibility (*mind* capable of thinking);

---

[7] Of course these same divisions could be ordered in another way:

Firstness of Firstness	Firstness of Secondness	Firstness of Thirdness
	Secondness of Secondness	Secondness of Thirdness
		Thirdness of Thirdness

the Second is thought as an event (actual thinking *experience* or *information*); the Third is thought insofar as it brings information into the mind (informing thought or *cognition*) (1.537).

Peirce sees in this relationship between a First, a Second and a Third, the operation of a sign, and in terms of the elements in a sign he explains the two degenerate grades of Thirdness. First of all, a sign stands for something other than itself; but that other for which it stands can itself only be another sign. The reason is that if the sign is to be affected by the object, "the object must be able to convey thought, that is, must be of the nature of thought or of a sign" (1.538). Every thought is a sign. In the first degree of degeneracy, however, the Thirdness affects the object, whereas in genuine Thirdness the sign is only affected by the object. What happens is that the Third brings about a Secondness which it regards as nothing more than a fact. Peirce calls it the execution of an *intention*. In the last degree of degeneracy there is thought, "but no conveyance or embodiment of thought at all" (1.538). It is merely the apprehension of a fact according to a possible idea. Peirce calls it *instigation* without *prompting*.[8] He gives the example of one's saying "this object is red." If the speaker is asked to justify his judgment, he might say, "I *saw* it was red." But that is not accurate. What was seen was simply an image, with no subject or predicate in it, not in the least like a proposition. The image *instigated* the judgment owing to the possibility of thought.[9]

Peirce applied his categorial scheme to philosophy in general and to normative science in particular. For him, philosophy has a threefold division: phenomenology, which simply contemplates the universal phenomenon; normative science, which investigates the universal and necessary laws of the relation of phenomena to ends; and metaphysics, which endeavors to comprehend the reality of phenomena (cf. 5.121). Phenomenology is the Firstness of philosophy, since

[8] This looks very much like the "simple apprehension" of the older logicians.

[9] It can now be seen how the two degenerate forms of Thirdness are related to Secondness and to Firstness, respectively. The first degree involves the execution of an intention and hence a will act; the second degree involves only the origin of perceptual judgment in a quality of feeling.

it merely contemplates without judging; it merely looks at and records phenomena as they appear in themselves regardless of anything else. Normative science is the Secondness of philosophy, because it studies the dyadic relation of phenomena to ends and so enables one to form a basis for judging true and false, good and bad, beautiful and ugly. Metaphysics is the Thirdness of philosophy, because it mediates between phenomenology and normative science, between phenomena in themselves and in their relation to ends, by a study of the regularity, law, or efficient reasonableness therein involved.

> Reality is an affair of Thirdness as Thirdness, that is, in its mediation between Secondness and Firstness. . . . Metaphysics is the science of Reality. Reality consists in regularity. Real regularity is active law. Active law is efficient reasonableness, or in other words is truly reasonable reasonableness. Reasonable reasonableness is Thirdness as Thirdness. (5.121)

Peirce's division of philosophy, therefore, turns out to be according to his universal categories (5.121–124). And he tells us that if "Normative Science does not seem to be sufficiently described by saying that it treats of phenomena in their secondness, this is an indication that our conception of Normative Science is too narrow . . ." (5.125).

After a good deal of hesitation, Peirce's final opinion was that there are three normative sciences: esthetics, ethics (practics), and logic (1.573). This trio relates to feeling, action, and thought, and as such relates to the now familiar categories. Thus esthetics sets up norms concerning qualities of feeling or Firstnesses; ethics or practics sets up norms for judging conduct or Secondnesses; logic sets up norms for deciding what thoughts we should entertain and what arguments we should accept, what procedures we should adopt, that is, norms for Thirdnesses (1.574). Ethics or practics is what Peirce calls the mid-normative science. It is the normative science *par excellence*, since the phenomena which it examines are Secondnesses (action or conduct) considered in the dyadic relation they form with ends (another level of Secondness). Logic deals with Thirdnesses considered in their dyadic relation to ends (Secondnesses). Reasoning is but a special case of controlled action—controlled action dealing with Thirdnesses and not just with Secondnesses—and so logic is a special case of practics. Esthetics presented some difficulty, however, and caused Peirce to hesitate to include it among the normative sciences. How can there be any judgment as to the goodness or badness of a quality of feeling? A quality of feeling is just what it is without regard to anything else. In other words, how is it possible to get a Secondness from a Firstness? On the other hand, experience teaches that men do make evaluative judgments about qualities of feeling. A distinction is made between the esthetically good and the esthetically bad. Is it merely a matter of taste? When we consider in detail the development of Peirce's thinking about esthetics we will be in a better position to know whether these difficulties are resolvable. For the moment, let us just point out that Peirce's final position (and he claimed for it no more than an opinion) was that ethics or practics is a special case or species of esthetics, because somehow or other esthetics deals with the deliberate formation of habits of feeling which ultimately govern deliberate conduct (doing or thinking). It will turn out that while in one sense the phenomena with which esthetics deals are ultimately qualities of feeling (and so esthetics truly relates to Firstness), in another sense esthetics more proximately deals with the formation of *habits* of feeling (not just an isolated quality) and as such has something of Thirdness or generality about it. Isolated qualities of feeling can be judged good or bad precisely in terms of the habit, which in its turn can be altered, modified or rejected in terms of experience's shock.[10]

What do we have so far in Peirce's architectonic presentation of normative science? Philosophy as a positive science deals with facts —facts gotten from common, ordinary, everyday experience. These facts require no special apparatus to be observed; they are open to any one who will take the time and the effort to become aware of them. On the level of what one does with this data, philosophy divides in three: taking an inventory (phenomenology—Firstness of philosophy), evaluation (normative science—Secondness of philosophy), and comprehension (metaphysics—Thirdness of philosophy). Normative science, of course, is not itself the evaluation of phenomena, but more precisely the theory of such evaluation. It subdivides on another

[10] Cf. 5.113; see Part I, Chapter 2.

level according to the predominant characteristic of the phenomenon studied: quality of feeling (esthetics—Firstness of normative science), action (practics—Secondness of normative science), thought (logic —Thirdness of normative science).

Since, in Peirce's classification of the sciences, logic is again sub-divided into three parts and philosophy itself is a member of another trio, one would be led to expect that his universal categories apply to these divisions too. Consider logic. In one place he tells us:

> The term "logic" is unscientifically employed by me in two distinct senses. In its narrower sense, it is the science of the necessary conditions of the attainment of truth. In its broader sense, it is the science of the necessary laws of thought, or, still better (thought always taking place by means of signs), it is general semeiotic, treating not merely of truth, but also of the general conditions of signs being signs (which Duns Scotus called *grammatica speculativa*), also of the laws of the evolution of thought, which since it coincides with the study of the necessary conditions of the transmission of meaning by signs from mind to mind, and from one state of mind to another, ought, for the sake of taking advantage of an old association of terms, be called *rhetorica speculativa*, but which I content myself with inaccurately calling *objective logic,* because that conveys the correct idea that it is like Hegel's logic. (1.444)

In another place he says:

> We come, therefore, to this, that logic treats of the reference of symbols in general to their objects. In this view it is one of a trivium of conceivable sciences. The first would treat of the formal conditions of symbols having meaning, that is of the reference of symbols in general to their grounds or imputed characters, and this might be called formal grammar; the second, logic, would treat of the formal conditions of the truth of symbols; and the third would treat of the formal conditions of the force of symbols, or their power of appealing to a mind, that is, of their reference in general to interpretants, and this might be called formal rhetoric. (1.559)

Putting these two passages together, the division of "logic" might be sketched as follows:[11]

Logic in broad sense (normative logic)	Speculative or formal grammar, signs as signs
	Logic (in narrow sense), or critic, truth of signs
	Speculative or formal rhetoric, or objective logic, communication of signs

Though Peirce himself never applies his categories to this division (at least I found no such passage), it seems reasonably clear that he might have done so with success. Speculative or formal grammar is the Firstness of normative logic, since it deals with signs as signs regardless of anything else. Logic or critic is a plausible candidate for Secondness because it treats of signs as true or false, that is, in their relation to what they signify. Finally, speculative or formal rhetoric fits the category of Thirdness because it treats of signs as communicated, that is, not merely in their relation to what they signify, but for whom they signify.

Philosophy itself is one of the three theoretical sciences of discovery. The other two are mathematics and idioscopy. All three rest upon observation, but they are observational in very different senses (1.239). Mathematics does not undertake to ascertain any matter of fact, but simply posits hypotheses, and traces out their consequences. And yet it is observational

> . . . in so far as it makes constructions in the imagination according to abstract precepts, and then observes these imaginary objects, finding in them relations of parts not specified in the precept of construction. (1.240)

Philosophy deals with "positive truth," but its observations are "such as come within the range of every man's normal experience, and for the most part in every waking hour of his life" (1.241). Idioscopy, too, deals with "positive truth," but the special sciences which make it up depend upon special observation "which travel or other explora-

---

[11] Cf. also 3.430 ff.

tion, or some assistance to the senses, either instrumental or given by training, together with unusual diligence, has put within the power of its students" (1.242). On this basis, a reasonable case can be made that the categories apply at this level of classification of the sciences, as they should, since they are universal. What is required for the observations peculiar to mathematics? Nothing but the "observer's" creative imagination. Mathematics makes no assertions about the actual, existing world of experience, but rather explores the great world of possibility by means of hypothesis and deduction. Mathematics, then, does not logically require anything beyond itself—it is a First. Philosophy, on the other hand, makes categorical statements about reality which claim to be true or false. And according to Peirce its type of observation requires not only imagination, but also experience. Now experience is in the category of Secondness, and so one could say that philosophy is a Second. The special sciences, too, make assertions about the world, and they certainly depend upon experience for their observations. Yet their observations are always mediated. It is not a question of common ordinary experience which is available to all; it is not, so to speak, merely a question of ego confronting non-ego, of observer confronting phenomena. Rather the observer gets to his phenomena through something else—an instrument, a technique, etc. It may be argued, therefore, that the special sciences introduce a Third in their observational procedures, and so qualify as a type of Thirdness, perhaps only degenerate.

This tentative application of the categories to mathematics, philosophy, and idioscopy is at least plausible, and if it, or something like it, be admitted, there is a symmetry in Peirce's architectonic. We have considered the application of the categories only to those sciences with which we are dealing: to philosophy (relative to mathematics and special sciences), to normative science (relative to phenomenology and metaphysics), to the divisions of normative science, and finally to the subdivisions of logic. No doubt, a similar analysis could be made for the other triadic classifications in Peirce's alignment of the sciences. What we notice is that the categories are extremely supple, as indeed they must be if they are truly universal. They can bend or shift just enough to allow their application to different levels of analysis, and yet still keep their shape sufficiently to be readily recognized. They remind one of the act-potency categories of Aristotle as used in the scholastic systems where they are applied analogously to different levels of analysis.[12]

While no aspect of a phenomenon can be classified under two categories at the same level of analysis, that same aspect may receive a different classification at another level. Thus, for example, Peirce classifies normative science as Secondness (relative to the other divisions of philosophy); its own subdivisions exhibit all three of the categories. Hence, if one always keeps in mind the level of analysis, the perspective in which Peirce is viewing his subject matter, his use of the universal categories will be found to be more consistent than has sometimes been thought.

[12] Take for example their application in Thomistic metaphysics to the orders of existence, essence, and activity, respectively. Basically act means "perfection;" potency "limitation." In the order of existence, *esse* is act, while *essentia* is potency. In the order of essence, form is act, while matter is potency. In the order of activity, accident is act, while substance is potency. Nothing can be both act and potency *within* the same order, but one may well be act in one order and potency in another; e.g. substantial form is act in the order of essence, while essence (and hence substantial form too) is potency in the order of existence.

We are inclined to think that something like this is what Charles Hartshorne has in mind when he distinguishes the "relatively absolute" from the "absolutely absolute." Firsts and Seconds of experience are only "relatively absolute," relative to a context. Cf. "The Relativity of Nonrelativity," *Studies in the Philosophy of Charles Sanders Peirce,* ed. by Wiener and Young (Cambridge: Harvard University Press, 1952), pp. 219 ff. and "Charles Peirce's 'One Contribution to Philosophy' and His Most Serious Mistake," *Studies,* Moore and Robin, pp. 459 ff.

2. Analysis of Normative Science

NORMATIVE SCIENCE is the study of what ought to be (1.281), that is, it sets up norms or rules which need not but ought to be followed (2.156). "Ought" then excludes compulsion, coercion, and determinism. It is always possible to act contrary to the "ought." The "ought" rather implies ideals, ends, purposes which attract and guide (1.575) deliberate conduct. Peirce sometimes refers to normative science as the science "which investigates the universal and necessary laws of the relation of phenomena to *Ends* . . ." (5.121). Still, Peirce looks upon normative science as positive science, that is, as an inquiry which seeks for positive knowledge expressible in categorical propositions.

> By a *positive* science I mean an inquiry which seeks for
> positive knowledge; that is, for such knowledge as may
> conveniently be expressed in a *categorical proposition*. Logic
> and the other normative sciences, although they ask, not
> what *is* but what *ought to be*, nevertheless are positive
> sciences since it is by asserting positive, categorical truth that
> they are able to show that what they call good really is so;
> and the right reason, right effort, and right being, of which
> they treat, derive that character from positive categorical
> fact. (5.39)

The statements of normative science, then, make a truth claim. They are founded in experience—that same experience upon which philosophy in general is founded, namely, "which presses in upon every one of us daily and hourly" (5.120).[1]

It is understandable, therefore, why Peirce sometimes describes normative science as that which treats of phenomena in their Secondness (cf. 5.123, 125, 110, 111). As a positive science, it deals with fact,

---

[1] Yet in "Minute Logic" written shortly before the 1903 Harvard Lectures (that is, *ca.* 1902), Peirce seems to have held a different, and perhaps incompatible view. See Appendix I for discussion of this passage.

and fact is in the category of Secondness. Again, its proper and peculiar appreciations of the facts relate to the conformity of phenomena to ends (themselves not immanent in those phenomena) and this is another dyadic relation or Secondness (5.126). In terms of the relation of phenomena to ends, normative science enables one deliberately to approve or disapprove certain lines of conduct. Thus it is the science which separates the sheep from the goats, makes the dichotomy of good and bad (cf. 5.37, 110, 111). From every viewpoint normative science involves an "emphatic dualism" (cf. 5.551).

Since normative science deals with "ought," that is, with deliberate conduct, and since it allows one to make value judgments concerning such conduct, one might be tempted to look upon it as an art or a practical science. We have seen that for many years Peirce himself so considered ethics (cf. 5.111). Yet Peirce insists again and again that normative science is purely theoretical, indeed, "the very most purely theoretical of purely theoretical sciences" (1.282; cf. 1.575, 5.125). To say that knowledge of normative science would directly and in itself either help one to think more correctly or to live more decently or to create more artistically, would be like saying that a knowledge of the mechanics involved in a game of billiards would allow us to become a master player (cf. e.g. 2.3). A vast knowledge of physics does not make a good mechanic, nor is it so intended. Normative science looks primarily to an understanding of certain sets of conditions. Of course Peirce sees and explicitly says that normative science is closely related to art (1.575) and that there are "practical sciences of reasoning and investigation, of the conduct of life, and of the production of works of art" (5.125) which correspond to the normative sciences, "and may be probably expected to receive aid from them" (5.125).

> But they are not integrant parts of these sciences; and the reason that they are not so, thank you, is no mere formalism, but is this, that it will be in general quite different men— two knots of men not apt to consort the one with the other —who will conduct the two kinds of inquiry. (5.125)

Normative science, then, is theoretical, and according to Peirce that is precisely why it is called and must be called "normative" (1.281). Its business is analysis or definition (1.575).

Peirce feels obliged to emphasize that normative science is not a special science. It is a subdivision of philosophy and as such relies on data available to anyone at any time by reflection upon experience. It does not require specialized techniques or apparatus for its observations as do physics or chemistry or psychology. Furthermore, he insists that while now and then philosophy may make use of such special data it is not significantly aided thereby—not even by the results of psychology (5.125, 3.428). Thus, Peirce frequently argues, the science of logic, contrary to the opinion of the German school,[2] cannot be reduced to a matter of feeling. Ultimately, an argument cannot be judged valid because of some instinctive feeling that it is so, nor by any compulsion so to judge, nor by appeal to an intuition (cf. 2.155 ff., 2.19, 2.39–51, 3.432). In general, the psychological fact that men for the most part show a natural tendency to approve the same arguments which logic approves, the same acts which ethics approves, and the same works of art which esthetics approves is insufficient support for the conclusions of those sciences. And if one were to urge in a particular case, let us say, that something is logically sound, simply because men have a strong and imperious tendency to think so, one would be arguing fallaciously (5.125). It would be much like arguing for the truth of a proposition from the certitude which one has about it, instead of justifying one's certitude by establishing the truth of the proposition. Or to put the difficulty (and its solution) quite clearly in Peirce's own terms:

> By the theory of cognition is usually meant an explanation
> of the possibility of knowledge drawn from principles of
> psychology. Now, the only sound psychology being a special
> science, which ought itself to be based upon a well-grounded
> logic, it is indeed a vicious circle to make logic rest upon a
> theory of cognition so understood. But there is a much more
> general doctrine to which the name theory of cognition
> might be applied. Namely, it is that speculative grammar, or
> analysis of the nature of assertion, which rests upon

---

[2] E.g. Schröder, Sigwart, Wundt, Schuppe, Erdmann, Bergmann, Glogau, Husserl. Peirce opposes to this group the "English logicians," Boole, De Morgan, J. S. Mill, Venn (cf. "Why Study Logic"). And yet Peirce is very critical of J. S. Mill for "psychologizing" (cf. 2.39–51).

> observations, indeed, but upon observations of the rudest
> kind, open to the eye of every attentive person who is
> familiar with the use of language, and which, we may be
> sure, no rational being, able to converse at all with his fellows,
> and so to express a doubt of anything, will ever have any
> doubt. (3.432)

In a later paper (written *ca.* 1906) Peirce makes exactly the same
observations and adds a distinction which is quite to the purpose.
He says that those logicians who make logic rest on psychology
confound *psychical* truths with *psychological* truths (5.485). Of
course, logic rests upon the former since they are observational data
("of the rudest kind") with which speculative grammar deals. It is
such psychical truths which Peirce has in mind when he explicitly
admits that there is in a sense a compulsion at the base of logic, a
compulsion arising from positive observation of a factual situation,
not a compulsion of mere feeling, nor a compulsion based on the
principles of another theoretical science.

> But logic begins to be a positive science; since there are some
> things in regard to which the logician is not free to suppose
> that they are or are not; but acknowledges a compulsion
> upon him to assert the one and deny the other. Thus, the
> logician is forced by positive observation to admit that there
> is such a thing as doubt, that some propositions are false, etc.
> But with this compulsion comes a corresponding
> responsibility upon him not to admit anything which he is
> not forced to admit. (3.428)

The mistake of the psychologizing logicians is not so much to recognize the presence of compulsion of some sort, but to make logical
consequentiality consist in *"compulsion of thought"* (3.432).[3]

Peirce warned his reader that if he did not see that normative
science deals with phenomena in their Secondness, the reason lay in
a too narrow conception of that branch of philosophy (5.123). He

---

[3] See also 2.47–48 and cf. Richard J. Bernstein, "Peirce's Theory of
Perception" in *Studies*, Moore and Robin, pp. 165–189, for a thorough analysis of role of "compulsion" in authenticating perceptual judgments. Certitude
is not a sign of nor a guarantee of truth.

takes care to point out two ways in which modern philosophy generally misconstrues the nature of normative science. In the passages we are about to consider his references to these errors are exceedingly brief and so are enigmatic. A certain amount of explanation is necessary to understand why Peirce considers them so important and to realize in what ways they differ radically from his own views. The first mistake, according to Peirce, is to think that normative science's chief and only concern is to differentiate goodness and badness and to say to what degree a given phenomenon is good or bad. The error here is to think of normative science mathematically or quantitatively, instead of qualitatively. The distinctions which are of interest in normative science are those of kind, not of degree. Thus Peirce says that logic, in classifying arguments, recognizes different *kinds* of truth; ethics admits of qualities of good; and esthetics is so concerned with qualitative differences "that, [when they are] abstracted from, it is impossible to say that there is any appearance which is not esthetically good" (5.127). Briefly, the important question for normative science is not how good something is, but whether it is good at all. Peirce calls this "negative goodness" or "freedom from fault."

> I hardly need remind you that goodness, whether esthetic, moral, or logical, may either be *negative*—consisting in freedom from fault—or *quantitative*—consisting in the degree to which it attains. But in an inquiry, such as we are now engaged upon, the negative goodness is the important thing. (5.127).

Perhaps the reader is asking this question: why does Peirce consider it so important to mention a point which seems almost obvious? What is back of it? A tentative suggestion comes to mind: the doctrine of continuity. A quantitative treatment of goodness (or badness) would suppose that it comes in discrete packages, whereas in reality goodness is a continuum. In a certain sense goodness (or badness) does not admit of degrees. It is of the nature of a quality—of a Firstness—and is what it is without reference to anything else. To be sure, goodness involves a complex relation (e.g. between ends, means, intention, and circumstances), but the goodness *qua* goodness is an undifferentiated quality. Thus the old scholastic maxim: *bonum ex integra causa; malum ex quocumque defectu.* Nor does this insight into the continuity of goodness conflict with our use of comparative and the superlative degrees of the adjective "good," because they refer to a concrete subject participating or sharing in goodness and not to the quality itself. Again, Peirce would not deny that one might be able to set up a quantitative scale of measurement to indicate the degree in which a certain set of concrete subjects share in goodness, but he would insist that such a scale is always somewhat arbitrary and can never claim exactitude.

The second mistake of modern philosophy in this matter is to think that normative science relates exclusively to the human mind.

> The beautiful is conceived to be relative to human taste,
> right and wrong concern human conduct alone, logic deals
> with human reasoning. (5.128)

Peirce tells us that in the truest sense these sciences *are* sciences of mind, but that the mistake is to think of mind in the narrow Cartesian way as something which "resides" in the pineal gland.

> Everybody laughs at this nowadays, and yet everybody
> continues to think of mind in this same general way, as
> something within this person or that, belonging to him and
> correlative to the real world. A whole course of lectures
> would be required to expose this error. I can only hint that if
> you reflect upon it, without being dominated by preconceived
> ideas, you will soon begin to perceive that it is a very narrow
> view of mind. I should think it must appear so to anybody
> who was sufficiently soaked in the *Critic of the Pure Reason*.
> (5.128)

Indeed it would take "a whole course of lectures" to present Peirce's theory of mind. Clearly, however, Peirce is here making the same point he made in his letter to James (8.256) where he labeled as nominalistic (and hence erroneous) the notion that thought is in consciousness rather than consciousness in thought. Mind is thought, and thought is Thirdness, and Thirdness is ubiquitous. The human mind is only one manifestation of Mind, perhaps the highest because it has the greatest capacity for self-control, but not unique. Here again Peirce is insisting upon the continuity of reality. If mind is anywhere, it is everywhere in one form or another. It is true, however, that in his own usage of the term he is not always so careful as not to fall into the Cartesian usage.

Peirce accepted the traditional division of normative science into three disciplines: esthetics, ethics, and logic, but added his own meanings to them. This division was in his eyes by no means arbitrary. It had an inner logic dictated by the very process of reasoning itself. To appreciate fully the great importance Peirce attached to these three disciplines it is necessary to examine their close interrelation. It will become evident, too, that what Peirce means by esthetics, ethics, and logic is not exactly what had been traditionally meant. He tended to keep the terminology because it was close enough to his own conception to introduce the reader and direct his attention toward the general area he was to discuss.[4] It should become clear as we proceed that Peirce's early hesitation to call ethics a theoretical science and his persistent doubts about the nature of esthetics can be traced to a confusion in his own mind and in the literature he read as to what these subjects treat.

Let us begin, then, by examining at length one of Peirce's earliest presentations of the divisions of normative science and their interrelation. In his manuscript, "Minute Logic" (*ca.* 1902), he explains that after a study of phenomenology one must undertake "the logic of the normative sciences, of which logic itself is only the third, being preceded by Esthetics and Ethics" (2.197). He tells us that he had only recently come to realize the importance of esthetics in logical theory and that he is not completely clear about the matter yet himself (see above). He goes on to say, as we have seen, that for a long time he had looked upon ethics as an art and again that only recently had he come to appreciate its role as a theoretical science and its connection with logic (2.198). He had up till then not clearly distinguished ethics from morality. His mistake was to think ethics was correctly defined as the science of right and wrong. Only when he realized that these are themselves *ethical* conceptions did he see that they could not be used to define ethics.

---

[4] We have already remarked that Peirce did ultimately substitute the term "practics" for "ethics" and warned the reader repeatedly that his use of the terms "logic" and "esthetics" was peculiar. Evidently, he just could not think of better designations.

> We are too apt to define ethics to ourselves as the science of right and wrong. That cannot be correct, for the reason that right and wrong are ethical conceptions which it is the business of that science to develope and to justify. A science cannot have for its fundamental problem to distribute objects among categories of its own creation; for underlying that problem must be the task of establishing those categories. (2.198)

Ethics, then, is not concerned directly with pronouncing this course of action right and that wrong, but with determining what makes right right and wrong wrong. It has to do with norms or ideals in terms of which those categories have meaning. Peirce therefore came to see ethics as the science of ends.

> The fundamental problem of ethics is not, therefore, What is right, but, What am I prepared deliberately to accept as the statement of what I want to do, what am I to aim at, what am I after? . . . It is Ethics which defines that end. (2.198)

Now it becomes clear just what is the relation of ethics to logic. Logic deals with thinking and thinking is a kind of deliberate activity. It, therefore, has an end. But if ethics is the science which defines the end of any deliberate activity, it also defines the end of thinking. Logic is a study of the means of attaining that end, that is, the study of sound and valid reasoning.[5] The dependence of logic on ethics, therefore, is apparent. Thus Peirce concludes, "It is, therefore, impossible to be thoroughly and rationally logical except upon an ethical basis" (2.198).

A similar line of reasoning holds good for esthetics. Peirce began to appreciate its importance as a theoretical science and the foundation of ethics only when he began to realize that it should no more be defined in terms of beauty than ethics in terms of right. The reason is the same: the beautiful and the ugly are categories within esthetics. It is precisely these categories which esthetics must establish and

---

[5] Peirce later defines normative science as science of ends. Here he says logic is a science of means. Means, however, are themselves subordinate or partial ends. Thus reasoning has its own end, attaining truth, yet relative to action it is a means.

justify. Again esthetics, as a theoretical discipline, does not judge this or that to be beautiful or ugly, but tries to decide what makes the beautiful beautiful, and the ugly ugly. It has to do with norms and ideals in terms of which we can define and ultimately apply those categories. And so it is closely allied with ethics. Peirce reasons this way:

> Ethics asks to what end all effort shall be directed. That question obviously depends upon the question what it would be that, independently of the effort, we should like to experience. But in order to state the question of esthetics in its purity, we should eliminate from it, not merely all consideration of effort, but all consideration of action and reaction, including all consideration of our receiving pleasure, everything in short, belonging to the opposition of the *ego* and the *non-ego*. (2.199)

Esthetics, then, deals with ends (or more properly *the* end) in themselves. It studies the admirable *per se*, regardless of any other consideration. This is the ideal of ideals, the *summum bonum*.[6] As such it needs no justification, it is what it is and gives meaning to the rest. As such it belongs to the category of Firstness. English has no suitable word for it, Peirce observes, but the Greek *kalos* comes close. "Beautiful" will not do because *kalos* must include the unbeautiful as well. Whatever term may be chosen to express it, the question of esthetics is to determine what is admirable, and so desirable, in and for itself (2.199).

> Upon this question ethics must depend, just as logic must depend upon ethics. Esthetics, therefore, although I have terribly neglected it, appears to be possibly the first indispensable propedeutic to logic . . . . (2.199)

Peirce's position in this section of the "Minute Logic" is clear enough and makes good sense in terms of his revised notions of ethics

---

[6] The *summum bonum* ought not to be thought of as simply another member in a series of goods, not even the last member. Peirce is not always as clear as might be desired in the way he uses the term, but as we shall see as we continue our analysis he did not fall into that mistake. Cf. H. W. Schneider, "Fourthness," *Studies,* Wiener and Young, p. 211.

and esthetics. Human action is reasoned action; but reasoned action is deliberate and controlled. Deliberate and controlled action is action governed by ends; but ends themselves may be chosen and that choice, in order to be rational, must be deliberate and controlled. This ultimately requires the recognition of something admirable in itself. Logic, as the study of correct reasoning, is the science of the means of acting reasonably. Ethics aids and guides logic by analyzing the ends to which those means should be directed. Finally, esthetics guides ethics by defining what is an end in itself, and so admirable and desirable in any and all circumstances regardless of any other consideration whatsoever. As we shall see, Peirce concludes that this *summum bonum* is nothing else than reasoned and reasonable conduct. Ethics and logic are specifications of esthetics. Ethics proposes what goals man may reasonably choose in various circumstances, while logic proposes what means are available to pursue those ends.

A problem arises, however, as we read on in the "Minute Logic." Chapter 4 deals specifically with normative science and in it Peirce seems to contradict what he had said previously. There he seems to deny that pure ethics or esthetics are normative sciences at all. He seems to say that only logic is truly normative. Is there any way around the apparent inconsistency?

Peirce begins this chapter by enumerating various general positions concerning the number and nature of divisions of normative science. Everyone is agreed that logic is normative. The majority of writers also include esthetics and ethics, so that the division corresponds to the ancient triad of ideals: the true, the beautiful, and the good. Others, however, admit only two normative sciences, namely, logic and ethics. The former would consider the conformity of thought to being; the latter the conformity of being to thought. According to this position logic and ethics are normative precisely because nothing can be logically true or morally good without a purpose to be so. Thus the conformity therein involved is controlled and deliberate. But such control seems to be conspicuously lacking when it is a question of something being beautiful or ugly. It simply is beautiful or is ugly without any purpose so to be. Consequently, on this sort of analysis esthetics is excluded from the trio (1.575).

Finally, there seems to be some doubt as to whether ethics is truly normative. The subject matter of pure ethics is not "right and wrong" nor "duties and rights." These are practical matters which make "heavy drafts upon wisdom" (1.577). No, these questions are a superstructure raised upon the foundations of pure ethics. The question at the center of pure ethics is, "What is good?" and this is not normative, but pre-normative. The reason is, Peirce explains, that

> It does not ask for the conditions of fulfillment of a definitely accepted purpose, but asks what is to be sought, *not* for a reason, but back of every reason. Logic, as a true normative science, supposes the question of what is to be aimed at to be already answered before it could itself have been called into being. Pure ethics, philosophical ethics, is not normative, but pre-normative. (1.577)

It certainly seems that here Peirce makes logic the only true normative science. This is not to deny, however, that it depends on the answer which ethics gives to the pre-normative question, "What is good?" And there is no use objecting that logic already has its own object, truth, because in the final analysis logic must face the question "What is truth?" In other words, just what is it that logic seeks? And, of course, this involves the question of ethics in a particular context: truth is a good (1.578–579). Truth is nothing but a phase of the *summum bonum*, the subject of pure ethics (1.575).

There is a real difficulty in reconciling this chapter with the earlier one. The problem stems from Peirce's inability to decide clearly, once and for all, just what is to be included in the discipline called "ethics." He is searching in this work and will continue to search until near the very end of his career when he will discard that terminology altogether. The same is true of his presentation of esthetics, but his difficulty is more acute. The reader will have perhaps already remarked that in the passages just discussed what Peirce deems pure, pre-normative, ethics in Chapter 4 sounds very much like the esthetics he discussed in an earlier chapter. Nevertheless, the inconsistencies which one would expect to find in an original theory (at least in the first stages of articulation) are not destructive of the essential insight which Peirce is trying to express. Certain clear gains have been made and the line of thought is beginning to emerge. Furthermore, some remarks can be made which diminish somewhat the confusion these inconsistencies may cause.

In the first place, in reading the "Minute Logic," one must remember that it is a book on *logic*. Consequently, logic will be the center of attention and the main perspective from which the entire work will be developed. Thus, for example, in the section entitled "Why Study Logic?" Peirce says that he is to treat, not precisely the normative sciences, but *"the logic of the normative sciences"* (2.198, emphasis added). So too, when he points out the importance of esthetics as "propedeutic to logic" he concludes that *"the logic of esthetics"* ought not be omitted from the science of logic (2.199, emphasis added). This fact might help us to understand in part why Peirce, in Chapter 4, makes esthetics and ethics pre-normative. His main interest is logical; logic for certain is a "true normative science;" esthetics and ethics are necessary "propedeutics;" hence from that point of view one could think of them as in a sense pre-normative— that is, pre-logical. There is some textual evidence that Peirce was thinking of the topic in this way. Thus, after he reviewed the current opinions as to the number of normative sciences, he remarks:

> Those writers, however, who stand out for the trinity of
> normative sciences do so upon the ground that they
> correspond to three fundamental categories of objects of
> desire. As to that, the logician may be exempted from
> inquiring whether the beautiful is a distinct ideal or not; but
> he is bound to say how it may be with the true . . . . (1.575)

Peirce, then, writing as a logician, explicitly disclaims any responsibility for settling the question of the number of normative sciences. The only point he feels obliged to make is that the true is an aspect of the good and that therefore logic can be studied satisfactorily only once it has taken into consideration its purpose and end.

In the second place, Peirce identifies the usual tripartite division of normative science in his chapter on ethics with positions he had criticized earlier. This is clearly the case in his discussion of esthetics, and a case, less strong perhaps, might also be made for what he says about ethics. Remember that he said that the usual division of the normative sciences into logic, ethics, and esthetics makes their objects the true, the good, and the beautiful. Yet earlier he had said that esthetics had been seriously handicapped by its definition as the science of the beautiful. Now the apparent inconsistency with respect to what Peirce says about esthetics might be diminished if we look at it this way: those who (like Schleiermacher) would exclude esthetics from the normative sciences are correct if esthetics is taken to be concerned with the doctrine of the beautiful. The reason would be simply this: if the beautiful is the subject about which esthetics concerns itself and not merely a category within that science, it must be an ultimate, self-justifying category, and as such could be known only through intuition. There could be no argument about it; it could not be subjected to any criticism; there could be no legitimate and resolvable difference of opinion. One would see that X is beautiful or he would not. In other words, esthetics could not be a science which would allow one to decide and to judge that something is beautiful or not. It would not be normative at all; it would be only phenomenological. The beautiful would be a "non-natural quality" and any attempt to analyze it would be to fall into the "naturalistic fallacy." On this view, then, it would be correct to say that esthetics is not normative, but perhaps pre-normative. On the other hand, if, as Peirce did in the earlier section of the "Minute Logic," one defined esthetics as the science of the admirable *per se,* it could be considered normative precisely because it investigates the ideal, in terms of which one could separate the sheep from the goats, the beautiful from the ugly, and defend and justify that discriminatory judgment in terms of a norm. It is doubtful whether Peirce saw this distinction clearly here because in a later discussion he will still be struggling with the question of whether there can be such a thing as esthetic goodness and badness. Yet if it is admitted that this analysis could have been lurking just behind the clarity of consciousness, then all that would have been necessary for Peirce to avoid his apparent inconsistency would have been to state that he was discussing two different conceptions of esthetics.

A similar, although perhaps a less convincing, case might be made out for what he says about ethics. The difficulty here, however, is that the former mistake to which he objected was not in defining ethics as concerned with the good, but as concerned with right and wrong, duties and rights. Still, although he is not as explicit about it as in the case of esthetics, we think that his thinking is the same. For if one takes the good as the *object* of ethical study and not as a category within the science, again it becomes an ultimate, which cannot be judged but merely recognized. Such a study cannot be normative, but only pre-normative. It cannot justify the distinction of good and bad, it can only intuit it as a primitive given. Again we have the familiar notion of G. E. Moore. If Peirce had this in mind as the paradigm of theoretical ethics when he wrote the fourth chapter of the "Minute Logic," it is understandable why he looked upon ethics as pre-normative. On the other hand, if in the earlier section he was objecting to the indescribability of goodness, and rejecting at least implicitly the "naturalistic fallacy" as no fallacy at all, then he would be justified in making ethics a theoretical, normative science, a science of ends, in terms of which one might judge goodness and badness, in so far as goodness and badness were not "non-natural" properties but relations of conformity and disconformity to ends.[7]

In any case Peirce has made this significant gain: he has seen that truth and goodness are intimately connected. He will exploit this insight in his Pragmatism Lectures of 1903. There he will strive to show that logic, ethics, and esthetics deal with three kinds of goodness, and that this goodness is ultimately reasonableness manifesting

---

[7] We suspect that what Peirce is trying to express is something akin to the scholastic distinction between transcendental and predicamental categories. Traditionally the scholastics looked upon Oneness, Truth, and Goodness (some included Beauty) as the absolutely universal categories which attached to being as being independently of and thus cutting across all genera and species. These transcendental categories are not really distinct from being itself, but are merely three aspects of it, three ways in which man can consider it. When these transcendentals are predicated of this or that being they are so by analogy. Because these categories are transcendental, they can only be discovered by phenomenological analysis. The scholastics distinguished between these ultimate, absolutely universal categories and particular categories affine to the former. Thus, for example, they distinguished logical and moral truth from one another and from the universal category, ontological truth. Again they distinguished moral or ethical goodness from ontological goodness. The normative sciences of logic and ethics, in terms of the transcendental categories of truth and goodness, set up norms for deciding the logical truth or falsity of propositions and arguments, and for deciding the moral goodness or badness of such and such deliberate conduct. Perhaps Peirce was unconsciously sliding from one type of category to the other, and thus at one time saw ethics as prenormative and at another as normative.

itself in three different ways. Let us consider in some detail what he had to say in those famous lectures.

In the first lecture, "Pragmatism: The Normative Sciences," Peirce again tells us that traditionally the normative sciences have been numbered as three, logic, ethics, and esthetics, and that he will continue to employ those terms. He characterizes these sciences as those which distinguish good and bad in the representations of truth, in the efforts of the will, and in objects regarded simply in their presentation, respectively (5.36). Thus he begins to develop explicitly the notion that the sciences in question all deal with kinds of goodness.

The purpose of this first lecture was to sketch the connection between his form of pragmatism and the normative sciences. Although we will examine this essential point in detail later in this chapter, it is necessary for our understanding of the doctrine of normative science to consider how Peirce laid out his thought in this matter. After having expounded his maxim, he makes this important inference:

> For if, as pragmatism teaches us, what we think is to be
> interpreted in terms of what we are prepared to do, then
> surely *logic*, or the doctrine of what we ought to think, must
> be an application of the doctrine of what we deliberately
> choose to do, which is Ethics. (5.35)

Pragmatism is a doctrine of logic. It is a logical method helping us to know just what we think, just what we believe. Our thought's meaning is to be interpreted in terms of our willingness to act upon that thought—it is to be interpreted in terms of its conceived consequences. Peirce, then, sees a connection between thinking and doing, and so a connection between good thinking and good doing. What we are prepared to accept as proper conduct, good conduct, approvable conduct, as the interpretant of our thinking, must be the measure of proper, good, acceptable, *logical* thinking. Thus logic depends upon ethics. But in its turn ethics must depend upon something else. Conduct is approved or disapproved to the degree that it conforms or fails to conform to some purpose, but the question remains as to what purposes are to be adopted in the first place.

But we cannot get any clue to the secret of Ethics . . . until
we have first made up our formula for what it is that we are
prepared to admire. I do not care what doctrine of ethics be
embraced, it will always be so. (5.36)

To determine what we are prepared to admire, what is admirable
per se, is the task of esthetics.

It [Ethics] supposes that there is some ideal state of things
which, regardless of how it should be brought about and
independently of any ulterior reason whatsoever, is held to
be good or fine. In short, ethics must rest upon a doctrine
which, without at all considering what our conduct is to be,
divides ideally possible states of things into two classes,
those that would be admirable and those that would be
unadmirable, and undertakes to define what it is that
constitutes the admirableness of an ideal. (5.36)

Esthetics, then, attempts to analyze the *summum bonum,* the absolutely ideal state of things which is desirable in and for itself regardless of any other consideration whatsoever. Esthetics studies the ideal
in itself, ethics the relation of conduct to the ideal, and logic the
relation of thinking to approved conduct.[8]

In the following lectures in the series Peirce continues to hammer
home the key insight into the normative sciences: they all have to do
with goodness and badness, with approval and disapproval. Thus the
essence of logic is to criticize arguments, that is, to pronounce them
acceptable or not, good or bad (5.108). But to say that certain arguments are good or bad implies that they are subject to control. It

---

[8] It must not be imagined that esthetics and ethics do not involve
logic. They do because they are theoretical sciences. Therefore, it would be
incorrect to think that Peirce held for a purely emotive conception of ethics,
or a purely subjective conception of esthetics (not to be confused with mere
taste). All three normative sciences involve deliberate approval, and hence
are based on reasoning. The distinction to be kept in mind is that between
logica utens and *logica docens* which Peirce himself never tires of making.
Logic as a normative science is *docens*—a thinking about thinking wherever
it may occur. That Peirce was aware of the possibility of confusion on this
point is evidenced by his constant rebuttal of any type of hedonism as il-
logical and hence unreasonable.

supposes that in the future we can avoid using bad arguments and strive to use good ones. Indeed, the very notion of criticism implies the ability to control and to correct.

> Any operation which cannot be controlled, any conclusion which is not abandoned, not merely as soon as *criticism* has pronounced against it, but in the very act of pronouncing that decree, is not the nature of rational inference—is not reasoning. Reasoning as deliberate is essentially critical, and it is idle to criticize as good or bad that which cannot be controlled. Reasoning essentially involves *self-control;* so that the *logica utens* is a particular species of morality. (5.108)

The distinction between logical truth and falsity, then, is nothing but the distinction between logical goodness and badness, which in turn is only a special case of moral goodness and badness.

This is the very heart of the matter. It is the very heart of Peirce's logic and of his entire philosophical outlook. To make a normative judgment is to criticize; to criticize is to attempt to correct; to attempt to correct supposes a measure of control over what is criticized in the first place. Any other kind of criticism, any other conception of goodness and badness is idle (cf. 2.26). In this Peirce was directly opposed to almost all other schools of thought of his day.[9] Two of these positions Peirce considered to be of particular importance because their objections to his own position are serious and not easily answered. The first objection says that Peirce's position makes logic a question of psychology (5.110). This is J. S. Mill's view and one which Peirce criticized at length again and again (see e.g. 2.47–51). The principle on which Mill based his opinion is that to say how a man *ought to* think has to be based ultimately on how he *must* think. In the passage we are now examining Peirce does not take up a detailed reply. In like manner, we will content ourselves with Peirce's simple denial of the allegation.

> The first [objection] is that this [Peirce's position] is making logic a question of psychology. But this I deny. Logic does

---

[9] For Peirce's survey of opinions, 13 in all, see 2.19–78.

rest on certain facts of experience among which are facts
about men, but not upon any theory about the human mind
or any theory to explain facts. (5.110)

Psychology, like any science, theorizes about facts. In Peirce's view,
logic itself theorizes about facts and not about another theory. The
second objection is more serious and on Peirce's own admission de-
ceived him for many years (5.111). It argues that by making logic
dependent upon ethics, and ethics dependent upon esthetics, Peirce
in effect has fallen into the error of hedonism. What is more, such an
hierarchical arrangement of the normative sciences involves a basic
confusion of the categories of Firstness and Secondness (5.110).
Clearly this objection is a difficulty which Peirce proposed to himself
and which prevented him for a long time from seeing the importance
of normative science for his own thought. On the one hand, he had
been convinced from early in his career of the error of hedonism, and
on the other hand, he did not clearly see how to avoid an inconsistency in his doctrine of the categories if he accepted the traditional
triple division of normative science.[10] Let us consider in some detail,
then, how Peirce resolved this problem.

The answer came to him through a more penetrating analysis
of his categories. He began to realize that one can and does have a
representation of a Second or a First as well as of a Third. With this
new light it was clear to him that

To say that morality, in the last resort, comes to an esthetic
judgment is *not* hedonism—but is directly opposed to
hedonism. (5.111)

How is this so? Consider the phenomena of pleasure and pain to
which the hedonist appeals as the ultimate factors in a man's choice.
They are *not* mainly phenomena of feeling at all (5.112). Peirce says
that, despite his special training in recognizing qualities of feeling, he
cannot discover any such quality common to all *pains* (5.112). All
that careful observation reveals is that "there are certain states of mind,
especially among states of mind in which Feeling has a large share,

---

[10] The difficulty he felt was something like this: the three universal
categories are irreducible; but logic clearly deals with Thirds, ethics with
Seconds, and esthetics with Firsts. How then can one consistently seek the
source of a Third in a Second and the source of a Second in a First?

which we have an impulse to get rid of" (5.112). To add that such an impulse is excited by a common quality of feeling is a *theory*, not a fact. Hedonism, therefore, cannot claim to be a datum of experience although, like any other theory, it appeals to experience for confirmation. Furthermore, granting that the phenomena of pleasure and of pain are prominent only in those states of mind in which feeling is predominant, they do not consist in any common feeling-quality of pleasure or of pain (even supposing that there are such qualities) (5.113). If one analyzes the phenomenon of pain, he will see that it consists in "a Struggle to give a state of mind its *quietus*" (5.113). It is therefore, in essence, an event, an actuality, and not just a mere quality of feeling, or, in terms of the categories, pain is essentially a Second and not a First, although undoubtedly it is accompanied by a First. A similar analysis of pleasure will reveal that it consists in "a peculiar mode of consciousness allied to the consciousness of *making a generalization*, in which not Feeling, but rather Cognition is the principle constituent" (5.113). In other words, Peirce analyzes pleasure as a sort of Third—an affair of mind and not of mere conscious feeling.[11]

> ... and it seems to me that while in esthetic enjoyment we
> attend to the totality of Feeling—and especially to the total
> resultant Quality of Feeling presented in the work of art we
> are contemplating—yet it is a sort of intellectual sympathy,
> a sense that here is a Feeling that one can comprehend, a
> reasonable Feeling. I do not succeed in saying exactly *what*
> it is, but it is a consciousness belonging to the category of
> Representation, though representing something in the
> Category of Quality of Feeling. (5.113)

Thus, to make esthetics the science upon which the other two norma-

[11] For Peirce consciousness is merely a collection of qualities of feeling, or rather, qualities of feeling are the contents of consciousness.

"My taste must doubtless be excessively crude, because I have no esthetic education; but as I am at present advised the esthetic Quality appears to me to be the total unanalyzable impression of a reasonableness that has expressed itself in a creation. It is a pure Feeling but a feeling that is the impress of a Reasonableness that Creates. It is the Firstness that truly belongs to a Thirdness in its achievement of Secondness" (from the first draft of Lecture V of the Lectures on Pragmatism. Peirce Papers, #310).

tive sciences depend is not to subscribe to hedonism and is not to confuse the categories. The categories are not confused because esthetics deals with the representation (a Third) of a quality of feeling (a First), just as ethics deals with a representation (a Third) of an action (a Second) and logic with a representation of thought (a Third). Again hedonism is avoided because in this view pleasure consists in something intellectual; it is not the case that something is deliberately approved because it is pleasurable, but something is pleasurable (esthetically pleasing) because it is approved. Perhaps it would be more accurate to say that Peirce is saying that something is pleasurable because it is reasonable, and not *vice versa*.[12]

In the lectures on pragmatism, therefore, Peirce has once and for all linked logical truth and falsity to moral goodness and badness. He is still not absolutely sure that there is a science of esthetics (so that moral goodness and badness would be a species of esthetic goodness and badness), but he is inclined so to think and assumes that there is for the sake of developing his line of thought (5.129). It is essential to notice that Peirce at this point has made an important connection between goodness and badness and conformity or disconformity to an end or ideal. Normative science in general is the science of the laws of conformity of things to ends; normative sciences in particular are distinguished in terms of what sort of "things" one is considering in relation to their ends.

> . . . esthetics considers those things whose ends are to
> embody qualities of feeling, ethics those things whose ends
> lie in action, and logic those things whose end is to represent
> something. (5.129)[13]

The "things" he is talking about are more precisely aspects or modes of things corresponding to these three universal categories of Firstness, Secondness, and Thirdness. In scholastic terms we might say that Peirce distinguishes these sciences by their "formal objects." *Qua*

[12] Perhaps the reader sees in what direction this line of thinking will take Peirce: the admirable in itself is the growth of reasonableness in the world. Peirce develops this theme at length in a paper called "Ideals of Conduct" part of his Lowell Lectures of 1903 (1.591–615). We will have occasion to take it up in detail in another place.

[13] Cf. also 3.430 ff.

sciences, however, each normative science employs *representations* of its formal object, and these representations are of course Thirds. *Qua* normative each of these sciences treats its object in its Second-ness, precisely because it is engaged in judging good and bad within the phenomena considered.

In the remainder of the section we have been considering (5.130) Peirce argues in much the same way as he did before. Logic criticizes and classifies arguments. This criticism and classification implies *qualitative approval* (or disapproval) of the arguments so analyzed. In turn approval supposes control of what we approve. Hence infer-ence is a voluntary act. But approval of a voluntary act is a moral approval. Hence logic is a kind of moral conduct and so is subject to ethical norms. At this point, however, Peirce again mentions some lingering doubts about esthetics.

> Ethics—the genuine science of normative ethics, as
> contradistinguished from the branch of anthropology which
> in our day often passes under the name of ethics—this
> genuine ethics is the normative science *par excellence,*
> because an *end*—the essential object of normative science—
> is germane to a voluntary act in a primary way in which it is
> germane to nothing else. For that reason I have some
> lingering doubt as to there being any true normative science
> of the beautiful. (5.130)

The emphasis has shifted from that of the "Minute Logic." We have seen that there logic upstaged every other consideration to the point that Peirce called pure ethics "pre-normative." Here Peirce stresses the dependence of logic on ethics and he has come to see that ethics, not logic, is *the* normative science because reasoning in the last anal-ysis is a *voluntary* act. But precisely because of this insight he finds difficulty in fitting esthetics into the scheme. The problem is always the same: things seem to be beautiful or ugly independently of any purpose (cf. above and our remarks about "the beautiful" being the object of esthetics). Still, if by the "beautiful" we mean what is *kalos,* what is admirable in itself, Peirce feels that the only kind of good-ness such an ideal can have is esthetic, and so the morally good is a species of the esthetically good after all.

On the other hand, an ultimate end of action *deliberately*

adopted—that is to say, *reasonably* adopted—must be a state
of things that *reasonably recommends itself in itself* aside
from any ulterior consideration. It must be an *admirable
ideal,* having the only kind of goodness that such an ideal
can have; namely, esthetic goodness. From this point of view
the morally good appears as a particular species of the
esthetically good. (5.130)

But just what is the esthetically good? What is the admirable in
itself? In the first place, according to the doctrine of the categories, it
must be of the nature of a First. It must be some positive, simple,
immediate quality pervading a multitude of parts. It makes no difference what subjective effect that quality may produce in us; it is esthetically good.

> In the light of the doctrine of categories I should say that an
> object, to be esthetically good, must have a multitude of
> parts so related to one another as to impart a positive simple
> immediate quality to their totality; and whatever does this
> is, in so far, esthetically good, no matter what the particular
> quality of the total may be. If that quality be such as to
> nauseate us, to scare us, or otherwise disturb us to the point
> of throwing us out of the mood of esthetic enjoyment . . .
> then the object remains none the less esthetically good,
> although people in our condition are incapacitated from a
> calm esthetic contemplation of it. (5.132)

But from this account follow a number of startling and paradoxical
conclusions. In the first place, there is no such thing as positive esthetic badness. Everything is what it is, and as such has some quality
pervading its totality. Everything, then, to this extent is esthetically
good. (The scholastics called this ontological goodness.) In the second place, if one considers goodness and badness as relative terms,
then one might also correctly say that there is no such thing as esthetic goodness. This is the very conclusion that Peirce draws (5.132).
All that one has is various esthetic qualities, which are what they are.

> All there will be will be various esthetic qualities; that is,
> simple qualities of totalities not capable of full embodiment
> in the parts, which qualities may be more decided and strong

in one case than in another. But the very reduction of the
intensity may be an esthetic quality; nay, it *will* be so; and I
am seriously inclined to doubt there being any distinction of
pure esthetic betterness and worseness. My notion would
be that there are innumerable varieties of esthetic quality,
but no purely esthetic grade of excellence. (5.132)

What is back of Peirce's continual hesitation about esthetics is
perhaps becoming clearer. It seems to be this: normative science supposes criticism and control; but esthetic qualities seem to be just
what they are regardless of anything else and so are beyond criticism
and beyond control. The distinction of good and bad implies approval
and disapproval. But in what sense can one approve or disapprove
of something which is ultimate? In a way one can only recognize it
for what it is, unless one's approval of an aim makes it ultimate.
Peirce, however, cannot subscribe to that without reservation since
it would make the ultimate subjective and arbitrary.

Thus Peirce, in the following paragraph, considers another moment in the process of adopting ideals, namely, the instant when an
esthetic ideal is proposed as an ultimate end of action. Now it is no
longer simply a question of considering the ideal in itself, but a question of one's adopting or rejecting that ideal. Peirce talks in terms of
Kant's categorical imperative pronouncing for or against it with this
important difference, namely, that while for Kant that imperative is
itself beyond our control, for Peirce it is not. The imperative itself is
open to criticism and this is what makes it rational (5.133). At this
point, then, there is room for a distinction between good and bad
aims: a good aim is one that can be consistently pursued; a bad aim
is one that cannot. It follows, then, that a bad aim could not be ultimate.[14] A good aim, Peirce tells us, becomes ultimate once it is
unfalteringly adopted because then it is beyond criticism (5.133).

The question, therefore, is to ascertain what end or ends are
possible, that is, what end or ends can be consistently pursued under
all possible circumstances. This is the problem of the *summum bonum*.
The difficulty, however, is that here Peirce makes this inquiry a

[14] An ultimate aim is what would be pursued under all possible circumstances (5.134) and hence would not be disturbed by one's subsequent
experiences (5.136).

problem of ethics and not of esthetics as he had done in an earlier paper. Again, the general line of Peirce's thinking in this matter is clear enough, but he is having a great deal of trouble classifying the steps according to the traditional triad of normative sciences. Perhaps at this point it would be well to consider Peirce's final formulation of the normative sciences and see how he recognized and met these difficulties.

In the "Basis of Pragmatism" (1905–06), Peirce in his usual way shows that "the control of thinking with a view to its conformity to a standard or ideal is a special case of the control of action" (1.573). Thus the theory of controlled thinking, "logic," must be a special determination of the theory of controlled action—what he has up to now called "ethics." The theory of the control of conduct and action in general is the second of the trio of normative sciences and the one "in which the distinctive characters of normative science are most strongly marked." What should this science be called?

> Since the normative sciences are usually held to be three,
> Logic, Ethics, and [Esthetics], and since he [Peirce], too,
> makes them three, he would term the mid-normative science
> ethics if this did not seem to be forbidden by the received
> acception of that term. (1.573)

At last Peirce seems to have become aware of one of the obstacles in his earlier attempts to classify the "mid-portion of coenoscopy"—the usual way in which the term "ethics" had been used. Traditional treatises on ethics included much more than Peirce wanted to include in the mid-normative science. Thus, for instance, they included analyses of the ideal or *summum bonum* to which action was to conform. Peirce, however, wishes to make the mid-normative science only a theory of the conformity of action to an ideal, reserving the study of the ideal itself for another science, esthetics. This throws a good deal of light on the apparent confusion in Peirce's lectures on pragmatism discussed in the preceding paragraphs. There he was using the term "ethics" in its traditional sense and applying it to the mid-normative science. Hence what he included under "ethics" and "esthetics" overlapped. To make the distinction sharper he proposes new terminology.

> He [Peirce] accordingly proposes to name the mid-normative
> science, as such (whatever its content may be) *antethics,*

that is, that which is put in place of ethics, the usual second member of the trio. It is the writer's opinion that this *antethics* should be the theory of the conformity of action to an ideal. Its name, as such, will naturally be *practics*. Ethics is not practics . . . . (1.573)

Peirce's problem with esthetics had always been to make sense of goodness and badness applied to esthetic qualities since they seemed to be entirely beyond criticism and control. By the time he wrote the "Basis of Pragmatism" a number of considerations had helped him come to a satisfactory solution. The line of reasoning which would offer an answer seems evident. What is required is a distinction between esthetic qualities in themselves, that is, in their own intrinsic reality, and the conscious adoption of them as ideals to be pursued. Similarly, in the case of the ultimate aim, the *summum bonum*, a distinction needs to be made between its own objective reality and its conscious acceptance and approval. Armed with this sort of distinction one could argue that the business of esthetics is to seek out through reflective analysis (see 1.580) what end is ultimate (can be consistently pursued in any and all circumstances) and to use this as a norm in adopting any particular esthetic quality as an ideal. According to this account of esthetics there would be the necessary element of criticism and control even with respect to the *summum bonum*, not in the sense that the objective reality of that *bonum* would be affected, but in the sense that one would accept it and conform to it willingly and deliberately.[15] The only question is whether or not Peirce had such an explanation in mind.

There can be little real doubt that Peirce did come to this sort of solution, although a detailed proof would require many more pages of analysis than are available.[16] There is sufficient evidence for our

---

[15] One might refuse to recognize or to accept the ultimate good, but then that would be to act unreasonably and so to act without true liberty. Cf. 1.602: "My account of the facts, you will observe, leaves a man at full liberty, no matter if we grant all that the necessitarians ask. That is, the man *can*, or if you please is *compelled*, to *make his life more reasonable*. What other distinct idea than that, I should be glad to know, can be attached to the word liberty?" Cf. also 5.339 n.

[16] We think that such a proof would have to consider at least the following: (1) Peirce's distinction between motive and ideal, (2) his real-

immediate purpose in the following section from the 1906 paper, "Basis of Pragmatism":

> Every action has a motive; but an ideal only belongs to a line [of] conduct which is deliberate. To say that conduct is deliberate implies that each action, or each important action, is reviewed by the actor and that his judgment is passed upon it, as to whether he wishes his future conduct to be like that or not. His ideal is the kind of conduct which attracts him upon review. His self-criticism, followed by a more or less conscious resolution that in its turn excites a determination of his habit, will, with the aid of the sequelae, *modify* a future action; but it will not generally be a moving cause to action. It is an almost purely passive liking for a way of doing whatever he may be moved to do. Although it affects his own conduct, and nobody else's, yet the quality of feeling (for it is merely a quality of feeling) is just the same, whether his own conduct or that of another person, real or imaginary, is the object of the feeling; or whether it be connected with the thought of any action or not. If conduct is to be thoroughly deliberate, the ideal must be a habit of feeling which has grown up under the influence of a course of self-criticisms and of hetero-criticisms; and the theory of the deliberate formation of such habits of feeling is what ought to be meant by *esthetics*. (1.574)

The first thing to notice is that in this passage it is not a question of the ideal in itself, but rather the ideal as the agent's. It is a question of what attracts him upon review. Thus Peirce has shifted the emphasis from the admirable *per se* to a consideration of the habit of feeling in the agent in the presence of certain ends proposed as ideals. An end is made the agent's ideal through the mediation of habit, and in its turn habit, by its aspect of efficacious determination, will modify action in terms of the ideal so adopted. The second thing to remark is that the habits of feeling through which one makes an ideal one's own are subject to criticism and control. They develop; they are

ization that ideals can influence man's actions in different ways and in different degrees of awareness, and (3) the role of habit in deliberate conduct. We will have something to say about (3) in the course of this study.

modified; they are corrected. Consequently, the ideals which one adopts are subject to criticism and control—or, more precisely, the adoption of this or that ideal is subject to control. In the case of the ultimate ideal or *summum bonum,* of course, its deliberate adoption is conditioned only by its recognition, since refusal to make it one's own would involve the living contradiction of a rational man using his reason in order to be irrational. To put it another way, rejection of an ideal recognized as ultimate would be to refuse to accept the inevitable finality of human activity.[17] The recognition of the *summum bonum* is a question of comparing experience with the transcendental condition of such an ultimate, namely, that it is such that it can be pursued in any and every circumstance. Thus when the pursuit of an ideal is rendered impossible it cannot be ultimate (cf. 1.599 ff.). According to Peirce, then, habits of feeling and the adoption of ideals are subject to criticism and control, and indeed must be if they are to be called reasonable. Thus esthetics is truly a normative science if it be thought of as the science of the deliberate formation of such habits of feeling.

[17] This is perhaps possible for more or less long periods of time, but it seems to us that unless one abandon all thinking about the problem, he would sooner or later have to capitulate.

3. Pragmatism &
the Normative Sciences

EVEN AS A BOY Peirce was interested in the normative sciences. He recounts how he picked up his elder brother's textbook in logic and worked right through it on his own. Undoubtedly his mathematician father encouraged and directed this interest. Logic, however, was not the only normative science to which he early applied himself. He tells us that as an undergraduate at Harvard (*ca.* 1855) he expounded as best he could Schiller's *Aesthetische Briefe* to his friend Horatio Paine (2.197). Almost fifty years later he expressed regret that he had not seriously followed up this study, because he then saw how fundamental it was to a theory of knowledge (2.120, 2.197, 5.129 ff.).

Although logic received most of Peirce's attention throughout his long career, still he tells us that he had always been interested in ethical systems (2.198). Until the '80's, however, he considered ethics to be nothing more than an art or practical science which relied little upon theoretical principles. It should be remembered that the first formulation of the pragmatic maxim (which he later called "a rough approximation"—5.16) and his analysis of belief in terms of what one is willing to act upon appeared in the '70's. Peirce says that he first began to see the importance of ethical *theory* around 1882 (2.198). At that time he started to distinguish morality from "pure" ethics. As a result of this illumination he took up a serious study of the great moralists (5.111, 5.129) and began to suspect that there was some important connection between ethics and logic (5.111). It was only some ten years later (*ca.* 1894) that this suspicion became a firm conviction (2.198) and only in about 1899 was he ready to say that ethics is truly a normative science (5.129). Peirce's judgment in this matter, therefore, was certainly not hasty. Rather it was the result of long reflection during the height of his intellectual powers (in 1899 Peirce was only 58 years old). Finally in 1903 Peirce made public for the first time his conclusions in the Lowell Lectures (5.533). Yet even then he was not prepared to say apodictically that esthetics is a normative science and indeed *the* science upon which both ethics and logic ultimately rest. He is content with the modest proposal of an opinion and an hypothesis (5.129, 2.197).

In the Cambridge lectures of 1903 Peirce explicitly related his doctrine about the normative sciences to the correct understanding of pragmatism as he first used the term. He tells us that once one sees that the normative sciences in general examine the laws of conformity of things to ends, one begins "to get upon the trail of the secret of pragmatism" (5.130). What then was the development of the "pragmatic maxim" from about 1893 onward? Just how did Peirce's speculation concerning the normative sciences modify his thinking about the meaning of his 1878 statement (5.402)?

Peirce considered the first formulation of the maxim "crude" (8.255) and only approximate (5.16). His first emendation (5.402, n. 2) was made in 1893 at approximately the time he began to see a connection between logic and ethics. This note was meant to meet the objection that the maxim is "skeptical and materialistic."[1] Peirce defends himself by an appeal to a collective finality governing the "realization of ideas in man's consciousness and in his works." We must be on our guard, he warns us, against understanding the maxim in a too individualistic sense. The fruit borne by an individual's endeavors is not limited just to what he aims at; whether he knows it or not his efforts contribute to a collective result—a growth of reasonableness in the world.

> Individual action is a means and not our end. Individual
> pleasure is not our end; we are all putting our shoulders to
> the wheel for an end that none of us can catch more than a
> glimpse at—that which the generations are working out.
> But we can see that the development of embodied ideas is
> what it will consist in. (5.402, n. 2)

Three years later William James' *Will to Believe* pushed the pragmatic maxim "to such extremes as must tend to give us pause." Peirce interpreted his old friend's position to be that man's end is action and in an article[2] for Baldwin's *Dictionary of Philosophy and*

---

[1] Peirce has in mind those who would make his maxim "stoical." Cf. 5.3. For his analysis of classical Stoicism cf. 6.36.

[2] Under "Pragmatic and Pragmatism."

Psychology (1902) criticized James for not seeing that far from action being man's end, action itself supposes an end.[3]

> If it be admitted, on the contrary, that action wants an end,
> and that that end must be something of a general description,
> then the spirit of the maxim itself, which is that we must
> look to the upshot of our concepts in order rightly to
> apprehend them, would direct us towards something
> different from practical facts, namely, to general ideas, as the
> true interpreters of our thought. (5.3)

Action, then, cannot be the final logical interpretant of thought because it is not general while thought is.[4] Thought can only be interpreted in terms of Thirds; the general can only be understood in terms of the general. The meaning of a conception cannot be found in action, but in the end for which the action (resulting from the conception) is done.[5] Of course, the practical facts must not be overlooked or ignored. And if one chooses to call this necessary reference to the practical the "pragmatic maxim," then it should be applied in a thoroughgoing way indeed, but

> . . . when that has been done, and not before, a still higher
> grade of clearness of thought can be attained by
> remembering that the only ultimate good which the practical
> facts to which it directs attention can subserve is to further
> the development of concrete reasonableness; so that the
> meaning of the concept does not lie in any individual
> reactions at all, but in the manner in which those reactions
> contribute to that development. (5.3)

The meaning of a concept, therefore, is judged in terms of the contribution which the reactions it evokes make toward the realization of thought's ultimate end. In other words, Peirce introduces in the pragmatic maxim itself a normative function. The pragmatic maxim is a way of recognizing the reality of the objects of general ideas in their generality. But general ideas "govern" action; they are really

[3] Cf. letter to Calderoni (8.211–213).

[4] Peirce discusses interpretants at length in 5.475–493 and again in 4.536. See Appendix II for a summary of these texts.

[5] Cf. 1.343–344.

laws of growth; they are really final causes; they are really normative.

In this *Dictionary* article Peirce himself admits that his early formulation of the maxim did lend itself to the sort of interpretation given it by James and others, but he implies that he never meant it to be the "stoical maxim" that man's end is action. He explains:

> Indeed, in the article of 1878, above referred to, the writer practised better than he preached; for he applied the stoical maxim most unstoically, in such a sense as to insist upon the reality of the objects of general ideas in their generality. (5.3)

Now if one carefully rereads "How to Make Our Ideas Clear" in the light of subsequent clarification by Peirce, it will become clear that in truth he did not make action man's end, nor did he make action the end of man's thinking. Action, no doubt, is involved in thinking both in the sense that thinking is a form of action and that thinking normally results in action. Action is, therefore, certainly a criterion of thought. But he does not say that action is the purpose of thinking. Its purpose is the establishment of "a belief, a rule of action, a habit of thought."[6] A habit is not an action. It is in an entirely different category. A habit is general, an action is singular; a habit is a Third, and action is a Second. Still, although this is what Peirce meant and what he strictly said, a superficial reading of the paper could lead to misunderstanding especially if one were not acquainted with Peirce's subsequent development of the nature of habit as a general. Then, too, Peirce's examples of how the maxim is to be applied are misleading and betray perhaps a certain hesitation and lack of clarity in the new doctrine he was trying to work out for the first time. For example, he applies the maxim to elucidate the meaning of the term "hard":

> Suppose, then, that a diamond could be crystalized in the midst of a cushion of soft cotton, and should remain there until it was finally burned up. Would it be false to say that that diamond was soft? . . . We may, in the present case,

---

[6] Elsewhere, e.g. in a paper on the classification of the sciences (*ca.* 1902), Peirce distinguishes "purpose" from "final cause." Purpose is one kind of final cause, the one "most familiar to our experience." (1.211) But he is not always careful to observe the distinction. The point he is making is that final cause does not always require consciousness. (1.216)

> modify our question, and ask what prevents us from saying
> that all hard bodies remain perfectly soft until they are
> touched, when their hardness increases with the pressure
> until they are scratched . . . there would be no *falsity* in such
> modes of speech. They would involve a modification of our
> present usage of speech with regard to the word "hard" and
> "soft," but not their meanings. (5.403)

This certainly seems to be a rather strong expression of the very sort
of operationalism which Peirce branded nominalistic and hence erroneous because it reduces potentiality to actuality.[7] In another place
and at a later date (ca. 1905) he criticized and modified the misleading character of his illustration.[8] He regretted the infelicitous example
because it tended to obscure rather than to clarify what he had intended to say.

In any case, in 1903, Peirce decided to make pragmatism the
subject of a series of lectures at Harvard. This gave him the opportunity of comparing his doctrines with others of the same name but of
a different spirit. In those lectures he tells us that he has no particular
fault to find with the numerous definitions of pragmatism he had
lately come across, but "to say exactly what pragmatism is describes
pretty well what you and I have to puzzle out together" (5.16). Then
in a playfully ironic passage, he teases the "new pragmatists" for not
acknowledging their debt to him.

> To speak plainly, a considerable number of philosophers
> have lately written as they might have written in case they
> had been reading either what I wrote but were ashamed to
> confess it, or had been reading something that some reader of
> mine had read. For they seem quite disposed to adopt my
> term *pragmatism.* I shouldn't wonder if they were ashamed of
> me. What could be more humiliating than to confess that one
> had learned anything of a logician? (5.17)

Peirce is delighted to share the opinions of such a brilliant company
and has no complaint to make against them except that they are
"lively."

---

[7] But see 7.340, written in 1873, for a realistic interpretation of
"hardness."

[8] Cf. 5.403, n. 3; 1.615; 8.208.

The new pragmatists seem to be distinguished for their terse, vivid and concrete style of expression together with a certain buoyancy of tone as if they were conscious of carrying about them the master key to all the secrets of metaphysics. (5.17)

No doubt, Peirce has in mind "cocksureness" and not merely qualities of literary style when he chides this liveliness. One thing Peirce could not tolerate was a cocksure attitude. For him this was the very antithesis of the scientific attitude, humble "fallibilism" or willingness to learn.[9] Peirce clearly has in mind those who enthusiastically pushed the pragmatic maxim "to extremes." The maxim was not intended to be an open-sesame to all metaphysical problems nor a panacea for all intellectual ills. It was not proposed as a principle of speculative philosophy, but as a logical, or perhaps better, a semantic maxim which would guide all types of investigation.[10] Indeed Peirce recognized that

> . . . one of the faults that I think they [the new pragmatists] might find with me is that I make pragmatism to be a mere maxim of logic instead of a sublime principle of speculative philosophy. (5.18)

And, with tongue in cheek, he continues:

> In order to be admitted to better philosophical standing I have endeavored to put pragmatism as I understand it into the same form of a philosophical theorem. I have not succeeded any better than this:
> Pragmatism is the principle that every theoretical judgment expressible in a sentence in the indicative mood is a confused form of thought whose only meaning, if it has any, lies in its tendency to enforce a corresponding practical maxim expressible as a conditional sentence having its apodosis in the imperative mood. (5.18)

[9] Cf. 1.9 ff.; 1.55; 1.141.
[10] "I also want to say that after all pragmatism solves no real problem. It only shows that supposed problems are not real problems. . . . The effect of pragmatism here is simply to open our minds to receiving any evidence, not to furnish evidence." From a letter to James, March 7, 1904 (8.259); see also 5.13, n. 1.

Peirce managed to get his logical principle into the form of a philosophical theorem, but he immediately appends his original statement of the maxim thereby leaving his audience to judge whether the new form is really an improvement. In any case, he never used that form again. Still, there is one important point made in it: the pragmatic maxim must be interpreted in terms of conditionals. Indeed the burden of the Harvard lectures is to show that meaning is intimately bound up with real laws of nature, that is, with real potentialities in things expressible in conditional sentences. The conditional necessity of law is expressed not only by a "will-be" but also by a "would-be," because law deals with the realm of the possible—what *would be* the case whenever certain conditions are fulfilled. What the conditional expresses is not merely the juxtaposition of an antecedent and a consequent, but the *consequence* or connection between them. "If such and such *were* the case (or were done), then such and such *would* follow." When Peirce came to see this more clearly, he corrected what he had said about the relationship between the hardness of a diamond and scratching with carborundum. A diamond never scratched is nevertheless hard because if it *were* brought into contact with carborundum it *would be* scratched. Thus the meaning of hardness is not in an action but in an intention or "intellectual purport."

During this whole period (ca. 1896–1903), then, due to the sudden popularity of "pragmatism," Peirce was very much preoccupied with disassociating his views from those circulating. Again, in 1905, he felt that he ought to try once more to explain what his notion of pragmatism entailed and even went so far as to coin a new word for it, "pragmaticism," which was "ugly enough to be safe from kidnappers" (5.414). So he published a series of three articles in the *Monist*, which contain perhaps the clearest presentation of his case that he ever wrote.

In the first of these essays ("What Pragmatism Is") he re-expressed the maxim thus:

> Endeavoring, as a man of that type [a "laboratory-man"] naturally would, to formulate what he so approved, he framed the theory that a *conception*, that is, the rational purport of a word or other expression, lies exclusively in its conceivable bearing upon the conduct of life; so that, since

obviously nothing that might not result from experiment can have any direct bearing upon conduct, if one can define accurately all the conceivable experimental phenomena which the affirmation or denial of a concept would imply, one will have therein a complete definition of the concept, and *there is absolutely nothing more in it*. (5.412)

This formulation makes it clear that the maxim has very little indeed to do with the practical.[11] And Peirce explains that his awareness of this fact determined his choice of the name "pragmatism" or "pragmaticism" rather than "practicism" or "practicalism."

But for one who had learned philosophy out of Kant, as the writer, along with nineteen out of every twenty experimentalists who have turned to philosophy, had done, and who still thought in Kantian terms most readily, *praktisch* and *pragmatisch* were as far apart as the two poles, the former belonging in a region of thought where no mind of the experimentalist type can ever make sure of solid ground under his feet, the latter expressing relation to some definite human purpose. Now quite the most striking feature of the new theory was its recognition of an inseparable connection between rational cognition and rational purpose; and that consideration it was which determined the preference for the name *pragmatism*. (5.412)[12]

It is not, therefore, the practical consequences of a conception which make it true and meaningful. They are, of course, criteria of its truth and meaningfulness (since one might expect a true and meaningful concept to have consequences), but do not in some crude sense constitute truth and meaning. This is but another way of repudiating the notion that action is man's end and the purpose of man's thinking. The

---

[11] Cf. 5.197 where Peirce expounds pragmatism as the logic of abduction. He remarks that if pragmatism teaches that every conception is a conception of *conceivably* practical effects it makes conception reach far beyond the practical, since it allows any flight of imagination which will ultimately alight upon a possible practical effect. Cf. also 5.538–545.

[12] Cf. Kant, *Anthropologie in pragmatischer Hinsicht* (Leipzig: Modes und Baumann, 1839), Vorrede. See Smith, *op. cit.*, pp. 13–16, for an excellent discussion of Peirce's use of the term "practical."

key to meaning and to truth is the relation of a conception "to some definite human purpose," to some end which governs actions in the same way Thirds govern Seconds. Rational cognition is in the category of Thirdness and must be interpreted in terms of some other Third. For Peirce this is nothing other than rational purpose. The pragmatic maxim, then, is but a way of expressing this relation. Once again we see that Peirce intends meaning to be identical with rational purport and not with action alone. Of course, Peirce realizes that a *proof* that this is so would require a sustained exposition of his entire philosophy of logic, cosmology, and metaphysics, or, in his words, "the establishment of the truth of synechism" (5.415).

In the same article Peirce tries to answer certain objections to his positions in the form of a little dialog. It is particularly enlightening because it indicates as clearly as anyone could wish the connection he saw, or at least thought he saw, between pragmaticism and the normative sciences. It is objected, first, that according to the pragmatic position nothing enters into the meaning of a concept but an experiment; yet an experiment in itself cannot reveal anything more than a constant conjunction of antecedent and consequent (5.424). This typically Humean objection, Peirce observes, betrays a misunderstanding of pragmaticism's fundamental point. In the first place, the objection raised misrepresents what is involved in an experiment. An experiment is not an isolated, "atomic" event, but always forms a part of connected series or system. An experiment essentially requires the following ingredients: 1) an experimenter, 2) a verifiable hypothesis concerning the experimenter's environment, and 3) a sincere doubt in the experimenter's mind about the hypothesis' truth. The experimenter, by an act of choice, must single out certain identifiable objects on which to operate. Then by an external (or quasi-external) act he modifies those objects. Next comes a reaction of the world upon the experimenter through perception. Finally, he must recognize what the experiment teaches him. While the chief elements in the *event* of the experiment are action and reaction, the *unity of essence of the experiment,* what makes the experiment an experiment, lies in its *purpose and plan* (5.424).

In the second place, this sort of objection fails to catch the pragmaticist's attitude of mind. Rational meaning does not consist in an experiment, but in *experimental phenomena.* These phenomena, to which the pragmaticist refers, are not particular events that have already happened to someone or to something in the dead past, but are "what *surely will* happen to everybody in the living future who shall fulfill certain conditions" (5.425). Essential to experimental phenomena is that they have been predicted.

> The phenomenon consists in the fact that when an experimentalist shall come to *act* according to a certain scheme that he has in mind, then will something else happen, and shatter the doubts of sceptics, like the celestial fire upon the altar of Elijah. (5.425)

In the third place, this objection that an experiment can only show constant conjunction of antecedent and consequent overlooks in a very nominalistic way the fact that the experimenter is not interested in this single experiment or in that single experimental phenomenon. He is interested in *general kinds* of experimental phenomena, for what is conditionally true *in futuro* can only be general. In other words, experimental method implicitly at least affirms the reality of generals (5.426).

It is just at this point that the connection between pragmaticism and the normative sciences becomes unmistakable. Peirce asks how it is that the relational meaning of a proposition lies in the future. The reason is that according to his theory the meaning of a proposition is precisely that form in which it becomes applicable to human conduct, "not in these or those special circumstances, nor when one entertains this or that special design, but that form which is most directly applicable to self-control under every situation, and to every purpose" (5.427). Future conduct is the only kind that is subject to self-control, and, in order that the form of the proposition might apply to every situation and purpose upon which it has any bearing, "it must be simply the general description of all the experimental phenomena which the assertion of the proposition virtually predicts" (5.427). Therefore, according to pragmaticism, the meaning of a proposition is attained when it is grasped as capable of governing future action through the exercise of self-control. That is its "rational purport."

The next objection which Peirce raises against his own theory is that pragmaticism is a thoroughgoing phenomenalism. He answers it briefly by denying the allegation in the light of what had just been said about "rational purport." The following objection, however, is the really crucial one in Peirce's view and the one involving James' fundamental mistake.

> QUESTIONER: Well, if you choose so to make Doing the Be-all and the End-all of human life, why do you not make meaning to consist simply in doing? Doing has to be done at a certain time upon a certain object. Individual objects and single events cover all reality, as everybody knows, and as a practicalist ought to be the first to insist. Yet, your meaning, as you have described it, is *general*. Thus, it is of the nature of a mere word and not a reality. (5.429)

The objection is just about as clearly and as forcibly put as it can be. And for Peirce it touches the very heart of the matter because it points out the basic choice that all philosophers must make between nominalism and realism. The objection is powerful because it involves so many things that must be admitted, and Peirce clears away the ground immediately by conceding what he must.

> It must be admitted, in the first place, that if pragmaticism really made Doing to be the Be-all and the End-all of life, that would be its death. For to say that we live for the sake of action, as action, regardless of the thought it carries out, would be to say that there is no such thing as rational purport. Secondly, it must be admitted that every proposition professes to be true of a certain real individual object, often the environing universe. Thirdly, it must be admitted that pragmaticism fails to furnish any translation or meaning of a proper name, or other designation of an individual object. Fourthly, the pragmaticistic meaning is undoubtedly general; and it is equally indisputable that the general is of the nature of the word or sign. Fifthly, it must be admitted that individuals alone exist; and sixthly, it may be admitted that the very meaning of a word or significant object ought to be the very essence of reality of what it signifies. (5.429)

These admissions come down to this: pragmaticism holds that meaning or rational purport, since it is necessarily general, can only belong to the category of Thirdness, and consequently, cannot be reduced to action-reaction or to individual existence which belong to the category of Secondness. Of course, a general is of the nature of a word or sign precisely because it cannot be exhausted by any singular individual instance. While it is true that generals do not *exist*, it does not follow that they are not *real*. They have the reality of *types* or *forms* to which objects conform but which none of them can exactly be (5.429). The type or form abstractly considered is an ideal which the instances embody to a greater or less degree, and as an ideal the type or form plays a normative role with respect to its concrete instances, to our knowledge of them (by natural classification), and to expression of that knowledge in terms of abstract definition.[13]

It would take us too far afield to discuss in detail Peirce's notion of reality and his adaptation of "scholastic realism." Yet from what we have seen thus far their connection with pragmaticism is evident. A brief word, however, may not be out of place. For the pragmaticist, "that is *real* which has such and such characters, whether anybody thinks it to have those characters or not" (5.430). Thus anything is real which is not a mental fiction. On the other hand, reality is that ultimate state of things which will be believed in the ultimate opinion of the community of inquirers. The ultimate opinion, however, seems to be for Peirce a theoretical limit toward which the community of inquirers converge but which is never quite attained, for no opinion is ultimate in the sense that no further questions may be asked about the subject matter of that opinion. There will always be more to learn. There is convergence in the sense that independent inquirers will tend to accept as established certain propositions about their subject matter. Peirce's view seems to be that both the external world and man's knowledge of that world are evolving. On the one hand, since man's knowledge of the world is dependent upon experience, since he does not create the objects of knowledge, and since the world he experiences is constantly growing, there will always be a lag in his knowledge of the world. Man's knowledge of the world is constantly corrected by experience and so, given an indefinitely long time, man's opinion about the world will tend to become uniform. Taught by

[13] Cf. 1.222. An abstract definition does not constitute necessarily a "natural" or "real" class. What constitutes such a class is a common final cause. An abstract definition expresses, or attempts to express, the class already constituted.

nature herself, man would come to know through experience what to expect from nature. This does not mean that he would ever have finished his lessons, for nature will always exhibit "sporting," but he would have come to understand the process in terms of its general direction and purpose—the growth of concrete reasonableness.

> Now, just as conduct controlled by ethical reason tends
> toward fixing certain habits of conduct, the nature of which
> . . . does not depend upon any accidental circumstances, and
> *in that sense* may be said to be *destined;* so, thought,
> controlled by a rational experimental logic, tends to the
> fixation of certain opinions, equally destined, the nature of
> which will be the same in the end, however the perversity
> of thought of whole generations may cause the postponement
> of the ultimate fixation. If this be so, as every man of us
> virtually assumes that it is, in regard to each matter the truth
> of which he seriously discusses, then, according to the
> adopted definition of "real," the state of things which will be
> believed in that ultimate opinion is real. But, for the most
> part, such opinions will be general. Consequently, *some*
> general obects are real. (Of course, nobody ever thought that
> *all* generals were real . . .) (5.430)

Some generals, then, are real and have a real efficacy in just the way common sense acknowledges an efficacy in human purposes. Human actions are controlled in terms of human purposes; they are specified and determined by certain ends and goals. So, too, real generals specify and determine human knowledge. Real generals are what constitute the cosmos as ordered and intelligible. They are both the condition of possibility of any rationality whatsoever and the normative principles of that sort of rationality (human) which is continually dependent upon the shock of experience. "Individual existence or actuality without any regularity whatever is a nullity. Chaos is pure nothing" (5.431).

According to Peirce, if this "scholastic realism" is put in the form of a general conditional proposition about the future such that it is calculated to influence human conduct, one has the pragmatic maxim. True pragmatism, therefore, does not make action the *summum bonum.* The growth of concrete reasonableness in the world of existents is that ultimate good. As evolution progresses, human intelligence plays a greater and greater role in that development through its characteristic power of self-control. There is an interaction between human rationality and the evolutionary process.[14] In the beginning the human mind emerged from that process, according to Peirce's view, but once emerged it can and does influence the course of evolution through deliberate conduct. In effect human rationality becomes one of nature's agents in the process. Nature's objective regularity specifies man's knowledge, and man guides his own activity toward and in nature accordingly. Even if, through some perversity, some men, even over long periods of time, should choose to counteract nature's directives, to swim against the tide, in the long run man will be forced by experience to recognize her as growing in rationality despite him and as guiding him in his own quest for reason.[15]

Peirce concludes this informative *Monist* article by insisting upon the utter inadequacy of action (Secondness) to account for the generality (Thirdness) of meaning (5.436). To understand all that is involved in this contention one would have to undertake a serious study of continuity which "is simply what generality becomes in the logic of relatives, and thus, like generality, is an affair of thought, and is the essence of thought." Peirce tells us why he alludes to the theory of continuity here: to emphasize what is absolutely essential to pragmaticism, namely, that

> . . . the third category—the category of thought,
> representation, triadic relation, mediation, genuine thirdness,
> thirdness as such—is an essential ingredient of reality, yet
> does not by itself constitute reality, since this category . . .
> can have no concrete being without action, as a separate
> object on which to work its government, just as action cannot

[14] Cf. W. D. Oliver, "The Final Cause and Agapasm in Peirce's Philosophy," *Studies,* Moore and Robin, pp. 294–295.

[15] "Accordingly, the pragmaticist does not make the *summum bonum* to consist in action, but makes it to consist in that process of evolution whereby the existent comes more and more to embody those generals which were just now said to be *destined,* which is what we strive to express in calling them *reasonable.* In its higher stages, evolution takes place more and more largely through self-control, and this gives the pragmaticist a sort of justification for making the rational purport to be general." (5.433)

exist without the immediate being of feeling on which to act. (5.436)

Almost fifteen years earlier (*ca.* 1892) Peirce had said, "My philosophy resuscitates Hegel . . . in a strange costume" (1.42). Hegel too had seen the importance of continuity and indeed the "Secret of Hegel" was just that he discovered that the universe is everywhere permeated with continuous growth (1.40–41). Peirce's pragmaticism, then, is "closely allied to Hegelian absolute idealism" with this important difference: Thirdness alone is not enough to make the world. Hegel's fundamental mistake was to dismiss Firstness and Secondness (5.436).[16]

The second article of this *Monist* series also appeared in 1905 under the title "Issues of Pragmaticism." Peirce remarks that in the 1878 formulation of the pragmatic maxim, contrary to his wont, he used five derivates of the same word, *concipere.* He did so for two reasons: 1) to show that he was speaking of meaning "in no other sense than that of *intellectual purport,*" and 2) "to avoid all danger of being understood as attempting to explain a concept by percepts, images, schemata, or by anything but concepts." The point is, of course, that only something in the category of Thirdness can constitute meaning. Action is like the finale of a symphony, but nobody would say that the finale was the purpose of the symphony; it is rather its upshot (5.430, n. 3). Of course, pragmaticism recognizes a connection between thought and action.[17] Ultimately it makes thought apply to action, and indeed it is thought which distinguishes *conduct* from mere activity. Yet this is quite different from saying either that thought *consists in* action or that thought's ultimate *purpose* is action.

> Pragmaticism makes thinking to consist in the living
> inferential metaboly of symbols whose purport lies in
> conditional general resolutions to act. As for the ultimate
> purpose of thought, which must be the purpose of everything,
> it is beyond human comprehension; but according to the

---

[16] Cf. also 5.79, 5.37 ff.

[17] Cf. 5.491. Peirce's way of looking at this connection has marked similarity to the scholastic maxim "*agere sequitur esse.*" J. Boler points this out too in *Charles Peirce and Scholastic Realism* (Seattle: University of Washington Press, 1963), p. 102.

stage or approach my thought has made of it . . . it is by the indefinite replication of self-control upon self-control that the *vir* is begotten, and by action, through thought, he grows an esthetic ideal . . . as the share which God permits him to have in the work of creation. (5.403, n. 3)

II

Synechism & Law

Introduction

PEIRCE FREQUENTLY REMARKED that his pragmaticism was intimately related to synechism or the doctrine of continuity. In a letter to William James he says that his own version of pragmatism leads to synechism (8.257). In another place Peirce remarks that a thoroughgoing proof of pragmaticism's truth "would essentially involve the establishment of the truth of synechism" (5.415). In still another place he says that synechism "is not opposed to pragmatism in the manner in which C. S. Peirce applied it, but includes that procedure as a step" (5.4).[1] Peirce spent the better part of twenty years working out his synechistic cosmology. This period (from about 1880 to 1900), it will be noticed, fills in the gap between Peirce's first formulation of the pragmatic maxim and the later reworking of it. It should also be pointed out that this period coincides with his awakening to the place of the normative sciences in philosophy. This was not all by accident. Peirce's appreciation of the connection between logic, practics, and esthetics came out of his cosmological studies. He undertook and pursued the inquiry into the nature of the cosmos under the guidance of his pragmatic principle. As this inquiry progressed he gained greater insight into the meaning of this principle itself. In a very real sense Peirce drew out what was implicit in his early essay by putting the maxim to work. In other words, Peirce's cosmological speculations form the bridge between the 1878 and 1903 versions of pragmaticism.

Just what, then, is this synechism which Peirce considers so essential to this thought? His popular presentation of the notion in Baldwin's *Dictionary of Philosophy and Psychology* will serve our present purposes. In the first place, it is not "an ultimate and absolute

---

[1] The main features of synechism were developed after the first formulation of the pragmatic maxim in 1877 and its subsequent revision in the light of the doctrine of normative science (*ca.* 1903). No doubt it was Peirce's work with synechism which led him to see the relevance of normative science for pragmatism. Cf. M. Thompson, *The Pragmatic Philosophy of C. S. Peirce* (Chicago: Phoenix Books, 1963), p. 103.

metaphysical doctrine," but like the pragmatic maxim itself "is a regulative principle of logic" (6.173). While this renowned maxim deals with the meaning of concepts, the synechistic principle prescribes "what sort of hypothesis is fit to be entertained and examined" (6.173).[2] In general, it seeks to exclude any hypothesis which would block the road of inquiry.

> The general motive is to avoid the hypothesis that this or that is inexplicable. For the synechist maintains that the only possible justification for so much as entertaining a hypothesis is that it affords an explanation of the phenomena. Now, to suppose a thing inexplicable is not only to fail to explain it, and so to make an unjustifiable hypothesis, but, much worse, it is to set up a barrier across the road of science, and to forbid all attempt to understand the phenomenon. (6.171)

Thus, Peirce tells us, synechism as a logical principle forbids one to consider any inexplicability as a possible explanation, and this is nothing more or less than the assumption behind the scientific enterprise as such, namely, that the world is knowable.

The synechistic principle does not deny that there is an element of the inexplicable and of the ultimate and brute in the world. That would be to deny that there is such a thing as experience. Experience is what is forced upon one *will he, nill he*. It is the element of shock and surprise which counters expectation, engenders doubt, and so stimulates further inquiry. In short, there is a sort of compulsion which in the very act is inexplicable and so ultimate. There is brute fact, or Secondness. This does not block the road of inquiry, but rather stimulates one to generalize from the experience, to form new hypotheses, because he is convinced that the facts can be understood —that they manifest another mode of being other than brutishness, namely, obedience to rationality and to law.

> It would, therefore, be most contrary to his own principle for the synechist not to generalize from that which

[2] In his Harvard Lectures of 1903, Peirce says that pragmatism is nothing but the logic of abduction, that is, it proposes a rule for the admissibility of hypotheses to rank as hypotheses (5.196). It must be, then, an expression or summary of synechism.

experience forces upon him, especially since it is only so far
as facts can be generalized that they can be understood;
and the very reality, in his way of looking at the matter, is
nothing else than the way in which facts must ultimately
come to be understood. (6.173)

It is clear, then, that an understanding of synechism as a principle of
inquiry is closely bound up with an understanding of the interdependence of the categories of Secondness and Thirdness. What Peirce
has in mind is much like Aristotle's distinction between the fact and
the reasoned fact. Every phenomenon insofar as it is an event has
something brute about it. If that event happens contrary to our expectations, that bruteness manifests itself as struggle and shock. But
insofar as that event is a *kind of* phenomenon, it can be understood,
and our expectations can be altered to include its like in the future.
Therefore, the ultimacy of fact is not the last word—it is not something to be looked upon as absolutely realized.

For science, therefore, and so for synechism, facts cannot be
looked upon as being, in the last analysis, atomic and unrelated. They
cannot be considered incapable of generalization. They must be seen
in a system (cf. e.g. 1.424) where they are related and grouped
according to general laws. Peirce thinks of this relatedness of facts as
a continuum.

A true continuum is something whose possibilities of
determination no multitude of individuals can exhaust . . .
(6.170). True generality is, in fact, nothing but a rudimentary
form of true continuity. Continuity is nothing but perfect
generality of a law of relationship. (6.172)

Atomic, isolated facts would be ultimate in the objectionable sense
of being inexplicable and unintelligible. They would be examples of
pure Secondness—uninterpretable and so unknowable. They would
be Kantian "things-in-themselves." In short, they would not have any
reality—at any rate not for us.

In short, synechism amounts to the principle that
inexplicabilities are not to be considered as possible
explanations; that whatever is supposed to be ultimate is
supposed to be inexplicable; that continuity is the absence

of ultimate parts in that which is divisible; and that the
form under which alone anything can be understood is the
form of generality, which is the same thing as continuity.
(6.173)[3]

By now the reader undoubtedly suspects that, despite Peirce's
apparent disclaimer concerning synechism's metaphysical pretensions,
this regulative logical principle does indeed involve an ontology
and a metaphysics. And these suspicions are justified, for Peirce himself in several places tells us that metaphysics consists in the acceptance of logical principles as principles of being (1.487; 1.624–625).[4]
But if any doubt remains, Peirce dispels it when he writes:

Synechism is founded on the notion that the coalescence,
the becoming continuous, the becoming governed by laws,
the becoming instinct with general ideas, are but phases
of one and the same process of the growth of reasonableness.
This is first shown to be true with mathematical exactitude

[3] Peirce, of course, was much influenced by Kant. He cut his philosophical teeth on the *Critique of Pure Reason* and had it almost by heart.
A passing remark made in his famous rejoinder to Prof. Carus indicates that
the doctrine of synechism was fashioned with Kant in mind—that is, to
bridge the gap between the inner and outer worlds. Discussing the view
that Kant's *a priori* is a universal objective, as opposed to subjective, condition of cognition, Peirce declares: "It is a weak conception, unless the whole
distinction between the inward and the outward world be reformed in the
light of agapastic and synechistic ontology. For to deny that the *a priori* is
subjective is to remove its essential character; and to make it both subjective
and objective (otherwise than in the sense in which Kant himself makes it
objective) is uncalled for, and is cut off by Ockham's razor. But when synechism has united the two worlds, this view gains new life" (6.590).
[4] Here again Kant's influence is apparent. The *Critique of Pure Reason*
concluded that metaphysics as an empirical science was impossible because
the *a priori* source of necessity and universality is a subjective condition
of knowledge only. Knowledge itself, or in any case, empirical knowledge
requires a synthesis of the manifold of sense. In other words, for Kant, empirical knowledge is limited by experience. When Peirce says that his
synechism unites Kant's "two worlds," he means that the transcendental
conditions of knowledge should not be confined merely to the subject, but
must also be in the object. In other words, the object of knowledge itself is
intelligible, has a rational structure.

in the field of logic, and is thence inferred to hold good
metaphysically. (5.4)

In the second place, then, synechism is a metaphysical position (even
though not "ultimate and absolute") precisely because it is a regulative logical principle.[5] Although one cannot separate logical from
metaphysical considerations in Peirce (for the reasons just adduced),
insofar as they can be distinguished our interest will be confined to
the metaphysical. Thus we must undertake a close examination of
"becoming governed by law" as a phase in the "process of the growth
of reasonableness."

[5] It may be well to reproduce this Peircean description of metaphysics:
"Metaphysics consists in the results of the absolute acceptance of logical principles not merely as regulatively valid, but as truths of being. Accordingly,
it is to be assumed that the universe has an explanation, the function of which,
like that of every logical explanation, is to unify its observed variety. It follows that the root of all being is One; and so far as different subjects have a
common character they partake of an identical being. This, or something like
this, is the monadic clause of the law. Second, drawing a general induction
from all observed facts, we find all realization of existence lies in opposition,
such as attractions, repulsions, visibilities, and centres of potentiality generally. . . . This is, or is a part of, a dyadic clause of the law. Under the third
clause, we have, as a deduction from the principle that thought is the mirror
of being, the law that the end of being and highest reality is the living im-
personation of the idea that evolution generates" (1.487). As always Peirce
uses his universal categories to characterize whatever discipline he wishes to
describe.

1. Synechism & Metaphysical Realism

PRAGMATISM IS A STEP in the general procedure of synechism because the correct formation of hypotheses supposes a correct understanding of the concepts so employed. Both pragmatism and synechism are built upon the bedrock of realism,[1] that position which Peirce tells us he espoused so very early in his career and to which he ever remained faithful through all the vagaries of his speculations.[2] In Part I of this essay we indicated how "scholastic realism" is essentially involved in Peirce's understanding of the pragmatic maxim. Since the truth of pragmatism essentially requires the truth of synechism, we must consider in some detail the relation between synechism and realism, and to do that we must present a more careful analysis of the issue under debate in the realism-nominalism controversy.

Let us begin by eliminating what is not at stake. It is not a question of just epistemological realism, that is, a question of the existence of a real "external" world. Peirce never considered that to be a genuine problem. It is rather a fact of everyday experience, doubts about which could be easily dispelled unless one is blinded by some irrational scruple about the kind of evidence required or prejudiced by a preconceived theory. In this sort of realism all medieval thinkers were agreed, even the nominalists. It is little more than what common sense requires—to recognize that we cannot

---

[1] "Now whoever cares to know what pragmaticism is should understand that on its metaphysical side it is an attempt to solve the problem: In what way can a general be unaffected by any thought about it? Hence before we treat of the evidences of pragmaticism, it will be needful to weigh the pros and cons of scholastic realism. For pragmaticism could hardly have entered a head that was not already convinced that there are real generals" (5.503).

[2] See, e.g. 6.605. Writing in 1891 he says, "Yet be it known that never, during the thirty years in which I have been writing on philosophical questions, have I failed in my allegiance to realistic opinions and to certain Scotistic ideas . . . ."

think whatever we want and that wishing will not necessarily make it so. Still there are some passages in which Peirce addresses himself to this question, usually when he is expounding his "Critical Common-sensism" (e.g. 5.439) or elucidating the meaning of truth (e.g. 2.153[3]). Thus, for example, in the "Logic of 1873" Peirce writes this very curious passage:

> The question is, "Whether corresponding to our thoughts
> and sensations, and represented in some sense by them,
> there are realities, which are not only independent of the
> thought of you, and me, and any number of men, but which
> are absolutely independent of thought altogether." The
> objective final opinion is independent of thoughts of any
> particular men, but is not independent of thought *in general*.
> (7.336)

The passage is curious because on the one hand it declares for epistemological realism, and on the other for objective idealism (cf. 2.153). To understand how the two are compatible we must examine the problem of metaphysical realism and the solution Peirce adopted.

Peirce continually insisted that he held "scholastic realism" as against nominalism in all its forms. Further, he insisted that he opted for one particular style of that realism, namely, that of John Duns Scotus. Exceptionally well acquainted with medieval philosophy, he knew that the great issue of the day concerned the ontological status of "universals" and that even among the realists there were a variety of opinions.

> In the days of which I am speaking, the age of Robert of
> Lincoln, Roger Bacon, St. Thomas Aquinas, and Duns
> Scotus, the question of nominalism and realism was
> regarded as definitively and conclusively settled in favor of
> realism. You know what the question was. It was whether
> laws and general *types* are figments of the mind or are real.
> If this be understood to mean whether there really are any
> laws and types, it is strictly speaking a question of
> metaphysics and not of logic. (1.16)

[3] Yet cf. 8.218 ff. where he criticizes Royce for failing to understand the realist position.

But in accord with his general conviction that logic and metaphysics are intimately related, nay, that metaphysics is objectified logic, he says immediately:

> But as a first step toward its solution, it is proper to ask whether, granting that our common-sense beliefs are true, the analysis of the meaning of those beliefs shows that, according to those beliefs, laws and types are objective or subjective. This is a question of logic rather than of metaphysics — and as soon as this is answered the reply to the other question immediately follows after. (1.16)

Peirce wrote this in 1903. A few years earlier, in 1898, he formulated the same question in a way which emphasizes its relevance to Peirce's synechist theory of law.

> Now what was the question of realism and nominalism? I see no objection to defining it as the question of which is the best, the laws or the facts under those laws. It is true that it was not stated in this way. As stated, the question was whether *universals*, such as the Horse, the Ass, the Zebra, and so forth, were *in re* or *in rerum natura*. . . . in using the word law, or regularity, we bring into prominence the kind of universals to which modern science pays most attention. Roughly speaking, the nominalists conceived the *general* element of cognition to be merely a convenience for understanding this and that fact and to amount to nothing except for cognition, while the realists, still more roughly speaking, looked upon the general, not only as the end and aim of knowledge, but also as the most important element of being. Such was and is the question. (4.1)[4]

---

[4] "The facts which the abstract nouns such as hardness, sweetness, etc. are used to express are really and truly *so*. But there are in the physical universe no existing, that is *reacting*, things hardness, sweetness. They have their being only in the discourse of our minds with themselves and in our speech to others. Hence they are called *entia rationis*, or beings of Reason. Some men say they are *real*, meaning that they serve to express what is really so. Others say that they are not 'real,' meaning that there are no such reacting things called hardness, sweetness, etc. The former writers use the word 'real' in the precise sense which it was invented to signify; and re-

The question, then, was not whether there is an external world which we can know to some degree, but what is included in that world's reality which enables us to understand it to some degree. Is generality, rationality, lawfulness, Thirdness a real mode of the world's being? If it is not, then the world is not in itself intelligible and does not exhibit any structure. It does not reveal itself to man upon diligent investigation, but rather presents itself as a mad puzzle into which man must *introduce* order from without, as it were. If it is a real mode, then scientific inquiry seeks to discover the world's order and rationality by careful attention to correct reasoning and by docility to experience, the world's own great revealer and teacher. If the nominalists are right, then we do not strictly speaking *know* the world or anything about it. We may encounter it in brutal shock, but that encounter does not reveal anything about what is encountered. It might be thought that on the nominalistic view one might be able to say that he knows *that* there is an external world "out there" but it would remain opaque as to what it is. It would be unknown and unknowable in this sense, and it would be a short step indeed to denying even knowledge of the *that*. Whatever is known is categorized and generalized. It is set in relation to other things, objects, and experiences. And if *it* is known, *it* must warrant such generalization. To do that, Peirce argues, *it* must have a real mode of generality as part of its structure and being. To be actually known implies to be know*able*, while to be does not in any way imply to be actually known. In another place, discussing the weak evasive tactics of the conceptualists (the fainthearted nominalists), Peirce formulates the issue once again in a way which clearly brings out the point.

> The question was whether all properties, laws of nature, and predicates of more than an actually existent subject are, without exception, mere figments or not. The conceptualists seek to wedge in a third position. . . . They say, "Those universals are real, indeed; but they are only real thoughts."

member this: To use a precise word in a wrong sense is a sin, because it tends to make human thought, which is the only really valuable ingredient of human nature, to be confused. The latter writers are apt to think that it is only what actually *has happened* that is true, while in fact what *would surely happen* under described circumstances is as true and more important, because it guides our conduct more directly" (Peirce Papers, #48, p. 11).

... The great realists had brought out all the truth there
is in that much more distinctly long before modern
conceptualism appeared in the world. They showed that
the general is not capable of full actualization in the world
of action and reaction but is of the nature of what is
thought, but that our thinking only apprehends and does
not create thought, and that that thought may and does as
much govern outward things as it does our thinking. ...
The conceptualist doctrine is an undisputed truism about
thinking, while the question between nominalists and
realists relates to *thoughts*, that is, to the objects which
thinking enables us to know. (1.27)

Peirce was not content merely to declare for "scholastic realism"
in general. He is very careful to specify the particular brand he
chose. Peirce claims Scotus as his inspiration, and this insistence is
not without great significance in understanding his synechistic version of metaphysical realism (cf. e.g. 1.6, 4.50, 5.77, n. 1, 5.312, etc.).
Thomism and Scotism are the two great rivals among the scholastic
realisms. Both schools were equally antagonistic to nominalism on
the one hand and to platonizing or "extreme" realism on the other. In
common they held that all concrete existents are singular, while our
knowledge of them is in terms of universal concepts. But since our
knowledge is objective, there must be some sort of ground in the
singular for the universal. Both schools agreed in a general way that
the *fundamentum universalitatis* had to be something really and objectively common (*natura communis*) to all individuals of which the
universal is predicable. This was the logical aspect of the problem.
The distinction often used to express this position is between *that
which* a universal concept represents (*id quod conceptus representat*)
that is, the common nature, and the *way in which* (*modus quo*) that
content is real in the concrete singular of which it is objectively predicated and in the intelligence which so predicates it. Thus far, Scotists
and Thomists agree. But as to the question of the ontological status
of that *natura communis* and to that of how such a nature is individuated, they part company.[5] While Aquinas held for a unique

[5] Cf. 5.107; Peirce recognized that the relation of law to "a blind reacting thing" (of Thirdness to Secondness) involved "the great problem of

substantial form accounting for the unity of the species and for signate matter (*materia quantitate signata*) as its individuating principle, Scotus thought that there were a plurality of forms ingredient in any individual (one to account for each essential property of the species to which it belonged, as, for example, in a man, a form of bodiness, a form of life, a form of mixture, etc.) and that these forms were made concrete, singular and actual by *haecceity* or "thisness," itself not another form, but an entitative perfection effecting the passage from specific unity to individual unity.[6] Thus in Scotus' view the concrete individual in a species is made up of a common nature in virtue of which it is a member of the species and *haecceity* in virtue of which it is this individual. The common nature itself is made up of a plurality of forms, each corresponding to a note (essential or accidental) in that nature's description. These forms are not really distinct from one another, nor are they merely rationally distinct in the sense of being mere fictions, but rather between them is a formal distinction. The same is true of the relation between common nature and *haecceity*. As Scotus sometimes puts it, the formal distinction is between *realitas et realitas*, but not between *res et res*.

It is instructive to notice that the most frequent criticism of Scotism by Thomists is that it tends toward, if it is not really, a form of extreme realism. The Thomists criticize *haecceitas* as a mere *deus ex machina* to escape making the individual a mere bundle of concrete universals (platonizing), not to mention the fact that despite the Scotists' protestations it looks very much like another formality, if not the airiest of abstractions. Again the formalities, according to the

the *principle of individuation* which the scholastic doctors after a century of the closest possible analysis were obliged to confess was quite incomprehensible to them."

[6] E. Bettoni, O.F.M., *Duns Scotus: The Basic Principles of his Philosophy*, trans. by B. Bonansea, O.F.M. (Washington, D.C.: Cath. U. of Amer. Press, 1961), p. 61, sums up the notion of *haecceity* as follows: "In other words, the haecceity is not just a perfection added to the form and within the form, but a new mode of being that affects matter, form, and the composite, i.e., the whole common nature, which is thereby contracted and forced to come out of that sort of indetermination which is proper to the specific nature. It is on the plane of act, and therefore a real principle, without being a formal element."

Thomists, are either really or only rationally distinct. They do not see that any halfway house is possible. If they are only rationally distinct then Scotism has not answered the nominalist position, while if they are really distinct, then the realism is extreme. And yet, Peirce criticizes Scotus for not having been an extreme enough realist and, therefore, accuses him of having to a degree fallen into nominalism (cf. e.g. 1.560, 6.175, 8.11). Thus he says of himself, "I should call myself an Aristotelian of the scholastic wing, approaching Scotism, but going much farther in the direction of scholastic realism" (5.77, n. 1) and "I am myself a scholastic realist of a somewhat extreme stripe" (5.470). Peirce, therefore, opts for extreme realism—that type of realism which Scotism would be without the theory of individuation. And Peirce does in places insist that such a theory must be abandoned.[7] Nor does Peirce seem to think that this extreme realism would leave him open to the charge of reifying universals. He feels that his new logic of relatives allows him to escape this sort of error.[8] Thus, he prefers to phrase his realism in terms of the objective reality of laws rather than in terms of universals (see 4.1). Laws are formulations of relations, not "things."[9] So all properties are in the end laws expressed in subjunctive conditionals (see e.g. 5.545). It is hardly necessary to point out that this sort of position is not without very serious difficulties especially in regard to the status of the concrete, singular individual. And while a logic of relatives may escape the charge of platonizing in the grand old style, it may not be so successful in escaping latter-day platonizing à la Hegel (despite Peirce's many protests to the contrary).

The extreme metaphysical realism which puts universality for-

----

[7] "Even Duns Scotus is too nominalistic when he says that universals are contracted to the mode of individuality in singulars, meaning, as he does, by singulars, ordinary existing things. The pragmaticist cannot admit that. I myself went too far in the direction of nominalism when I said that it was a mere question of convenience of speech whether we say that a diamond is hard when it is not pressed upon. I *now* say that experiment will prove that the diamond is hard, as a positive fact. That is, it is a real fact that it *would* resist pressure, which amounts to extreme scholastic realism." (8.208, from a letter to Mario Calderoni, Italian pragmatist, *ca.* 1905)

[8] Cf. Peirce's paper "The Logic of Relatives," *Monist*, 7 (1897) 3.456 ff. esp. 3.458–463.

[9] Cf. Boler, *op. cit.*, pp. 102–103 and W. B. Gallie, *Peirce and Pragmatism* (Penguin Books, 1952), pp. 153–156.

mally (not just *radicaliter*) in things themselves and not in the mind
of the knower, avoided by Scotus through his doctrine of formal distinction and *haecceity*, is defended by Peirce. That is why he can call
his doctrine *objective idealism*.[10] It is a form of idealism because of
the close affinity he posits between knower and object known; it is objective because he recognizes that it is the object known which governs
our knowledge and not vice versa, that is, the object known has such
and such characteristics independent of any particular person's knowledge, though not independent of thought in general. But objective
idealism, interpreted in terms of the synechistic principle of investigation, leads to a form of *monism* or what Peirce preferred to call neutralism (6.24). Synechism requires that reality be looked upon as continuous, or as Leibniz says *"natura non facit saltus."* The only
differences in nature, therefore, are those of degree and not of kind.
As we shall see more clearly in our discussion of law and determinism,
Peirce rejects mechanistic monism as a false theory. Accordingly, "the
one intelligible theory of the universe is that of objective idealism, that
matter is effete mind, inveterate habits becoming physical laws" (6.25).

It is not unusual, then, that Peirce should criticize the scholastics
for their "matter-of-fact" dualism. It was because of this dualistic position that their formulation of the realist-nominalist controversy in
terms of universals rather than in terms of laws is not altogether satisfactory. It was their dualistic assumption which led to a variety of
answers to the problem (rather than a simple yes or no) and to its
division into various parts (4.1). The belief that mind and matter are
two ultimate and irreducible ingredients of reality caused the scholastics to exaggerate, in Peirce's view, the opposition between universals
and individuals and so for some of them to regard the one or the other
as "more real." Again, this belief raised the perplexing question of how
matter can act on mind and of how the concrete can be transformed
into the universal. To answer this sort of problem required a breaking down of the question into logical, psychological, and metaphysical
questions, the first dealing with predication, the second with the
origin of ideas, and the third with the ground of objectivity. The scholastic theory of abstraction as a psychological process by which the

---

[10] Cf. e.g. 6.25, 6.158, 6.339, 5.310, 8.151. In 5.121 Peirce identifies
"reality" with regularity or active law which is Thirdness.

mind sorted out the intelligible structure of sense data through the action of the agent intellect was designed especially to bridge the gap between mind and matter. This, of course, Peirce's idealism could dispense with. Thus, when he talks of precisive abstraction, he is not concerned with a psychological process but with a type of logical distinction between concepts. We have already remarked that metaphysics is for him only objectified logic. And so the problems which were distinct for the scholastics are for Peirce really only one because in virtue of his extreme realism he applied without qualification the principle: whatever is needed to explicate reality must be granted a place within reality[11] (1.351).

It is not possible here to present in any complete way the arguments which Peirce adduces for his metaphysical realism. Such a presentation would require a detailed study of his theory of inquiry, philosophy of logic, and entire metaphysics. Of course, as we proceed, certain of Peirce's reasons will be analyzed, but for the moment we would content ourselves with a brief sketch of some of the more important arguments, positive and negative. The strongest positive argument in favor of realism is that the very enterprise of science requires it (cf. e.g. 1.351, 7.186). Thus, Peirce more than once refers to the work of his friend Dr. F. E. Abbot, *Scientific Theism*, as having convinced him that "science has always been at heart realistic, and always must be so" (1.20, 5.12, 5.423). Basically this is so because science necessarily makes *predictions* which in the majority of cases are fulfilled in the event (cf. e.g. 1.26, 1.343, 5.96, 8.212, etc.). A prediction is essentially general and as such can never be completely fulfilled. It says what would be the case whenever certain conditions are fulfilled. No series of actual cases, however long, will exhaust the prediction. But when a prediction shows a definite tendency to be fulfilled, that decided tendency can only be due to the fact that the future events are governed by a law, not by sheer chance.

If a pair of dice turns up sixes five times running, that is a

[11] Cf. W. Reese, "Philosophic Realism: A Study in the Modality of Being," *Studies*, Wiener and Young, p. 225. One such qualification which scholastics would certainly make is a distinction between cause and sufficient reason.

mere uniformity. The dice might happen fortuitously to turn
up sixes a thousand times running. But that would not
afford the slightest security for a prediction that they
would turn up sixes the next time. (1.26)

The case of the pair of dice is not at all the same as the case of a stone
in my hand of which I predict that it will fall if I let it go. In that case,
says Peirce, I *know* that it will act according to the law of gravitation
(5.96). What affords us a safe basis for prediction must be the fact
that the future events conform to a general rule.

"Oh," but say the nominalists, "this general rule is nothing
but a mere word or couple of words!" I reply, "Nobody
ever dreamed of denying that what is general is of the
nature of a general sign; but the question is whether future
events will conform to it or not. If they will, your
adjective 'mere' seems to be ill-placed." (1.26)

A rule to which future events show a decided tendency to conform is
an important element in the happening of those events.

. . . the fact that I *know* that this stone will fall to the
floor when I let it go, as you all must confess, if you are not
blinded by theory, that I *do* know . . . is the proof that
the formula, or uniformity, as furnishing a safe basis for
prediction, is, or if you like it better, *corresponds to*, a
reality. (5.96)

Peirce also offers a number of negative arguments in support of
realism, that is, he reduces certain nominalistic positions to absurdity
or exposes certain errors to which they lead. Thus, for example, he
shows the absurd inconsistency of the following nominalistic positions:
that qualities are not real except insofar as they are actually perceived
(1.422); that percepts are not subject to certain general laws (2.149);
that possibles are not real but only a function of our ignorance as to
whether a given supposition can be made (6.367–368); that there are
no real connections between individual things (5.48–49). Again, by
way of example, Peirce argues that nominalism is responsible for that
widespread misunderstanding of inductive argumentation which
makes it impossible to justify, and ought to lead to an outright denial

of its validity (6.99–100).[12] A nominalistic view gave rise to the mechanistic error (6.93, 6.274) and continues to set up roadblocks in the path of inquiry (6.273). Peirce could hardly have been more severe in his condemnation of what he considered to be the source of just about every philosophical mistake ever made. There is no doubt but that he was convinced that any sound philosophy must adopt metaphysical realism, and indeed of an extreme type.[13]

If Peirce made synechism the metaphysical basis for pragmaticism, he also made realism the basis for synechism. Synechism assured that his metaphysics must be monistic; extreme metaphysical realism assured that it must be idealistic; epistemological realism assured that it must be objective. There is still a fourth element to be explored, tychism, which assures that it must be evolutionist. But now we must consider in a more systematic way precisely what Peirce understood by "law."

[12] Peirce is criticizing John Stuart Mill's claim (*System of Logic*) that the validity of induction depends upon "uniformity." According to Peirce, Mill uses the word in order to avoid talking about "law" which would imply the reality of a general. Mill could not admit this, Peirce says, because of his strong nominalistic prejudice. The substitution of "uniformity" for "law," therefore, implies "that the facts are, in themselves, entirely disconnected, and that it is the mind alone which unites them" (6.99). In Peirce's view this position raises insuperable obstacles to showing the validity of inductive reasoning. Mill seems to have recognized the difficulty and so had recourse to the notion of "uniformity of nature" which he says means that if all the circumstances attending two phenomena are the same, they will be alike. Peirce argues that this statement taken literally is meaningless "since no two phenomena ever can happen in circumstances precisely alike, nor are two phenomena precisely alike" (6.100). If the statement is modified to give it some meaning, then (1) either it becomes grossly false, (2) or a purely gratuitous assertion, (3) or "a quasi subjective truth, not lending any colour of validity to induction proper." Peirce goes on to develop each of these alternatives. Finally, in 6.101 Peirce lists several senses in which nature may reasonably be said to be uniform and outlines his own position.

[13] See 8.145 ff., for a strong criticism of Karl Pearson's *Grammar of Science*.

2. Law as Thirdness

By now, the reader ought not be surprised to learn that Peirce's theory of "law" is intimately connected with his universal categories. It has already become clear that he situates law in the category of Thirdness and that Thirdness involves generality or continuity. We propose to examine in detail the characteristics of this category as Peirce applied them to "real laws of nature." Again, however, we must realize that we can hardly expect to find absolute consistency in the formulations employed over so many years in such prolific writing for such varied occasions. At best, we can hope to find a clear and firm line of thought—a uniform direction in which Peirce's whole philosophic thinking is developing. With these cautions in mind let us begin by examining the chief characteristics ascribed to Thirdness and hence to law in order to see how they are interrelated.

Fundamentally Thirdness is mediation. It is a *medium* between Firstness and Secondness. In terms of Peirce's modes of being, then, law mediates between pure possibility and actual fact. But in order so to mediate it must be general; it must be neither of the extremes and yet partake of aspects of both. Finally, because of its generality Thirdness must essentially refer to the future.

First, Thirdness is mediation.[1] Consider Peirce's homely but apt illustration of the cook who desires to make an apple pie for her master. The apple pie she desires is no particular one, but only one of a certain kind, of a certain general description. She has an idea of the sort of pie she desires and this idea taken in itself, independently of the deliberate decision to take the necessary steps to produce a concrete singular instance of that type of pie, is a pure possible—the airy object of a dream. Between the dream and the finished product is the efficacious desire. Again, to make the pie she has to pick out some

---

[1] "By the third, I mean the medium or connecting bond between the absolute first and last. . . . Continuity represents Thirdness almost to perfection" (1.337 from a fragment, "Third," *ca.* 1875). Peirce came to this notion early in his career.

apples. Any good apples will do although she cannot pick out "any apple" but this one or that. It is her desire to select apples of a certain type which mediates between the given quality and the concrete case.

> What she desires is something of a given quality; what she has to take is this or that particular apple. From the nature of things, she cannot take the quality but must take the particular thing. Sensation and volition being affairs of action and reaction relate to particular things. She has seen only particular apples. But the desire has nothing to do with particulars; it relates to qualities. Desire is not a reaction with reference to a particular thing; it is an idea about an idea, namely, the idea of how delightful it would be for me, the cook's master, to eat an apple pie. (1.341)

The object of the desire is not an unattached quality.

> She [the cook] has no particular apple pie she particularly prefers to serve; but she does desire and intend to serve an apple pie to a particular person. . . . Throughout her whole proceedings she pursues an idea or dream without any particular thisness or thatness—or, as we say, *hecceity* —to it, but this dream she wishes to realize in connection with an object of experience, which as such, does possess hecceity; and since she has to act, and action only relates to this and that, she has to be perpetually making random selections, that is, taking whatever comes handiest. (1.341)

Peirce explicitly spells out the moral of the story.

> The dream itself has no prominent thirdness; it is, on the contrary, utterly irresponsible; it is whatever it pleases. The object of experience as a reality is a second. But the desire in seeking to attach the one to the other is a third, or medium. (1.342)

It illustrates what Peirce understands by mediation and why mediation always involves a Third. Yet it must not be taken as a rigorous analysis, because it turns out that, more strictly speaking, representation and not desire is the prime analogue of mediation.[2] All that interests us for the moment is Peirce's generalization of the principle involved and its direct application to laws of nature.

> So it is with any law of nature. Were it but a mere idea
> unrealized—and it is of the nature of an idea—it would be
> a pure first. The cases to which it applies, are seconds.
> (1.342)

But that condition is contrary to fact. Precisely because it applies to Seconds, a law of nature is not a pure First. It is then a Third or medium, and consequently belongs to the category of Thirdness since "Thirdness is nothing but the character of an object which embodies Betweenness or Mediation in its simplest and most rudimentary form . . ." (5.104).

Second, mediation supposes generality. In the illustration of the cook and the pie we have seen that generality is involved in her desire. She desired to make some particular instance of a general kind. Furthermore all her actions in the actual process of baking, for example selecting the apples, were governed by general rules of conduct. But let us see if we can go a little deeper into the reason why mediation necessarily involves generality. Just what is required that anything at all be a *medium*? It must be distinct from what it mediates, although not necessarily separable. It is a Third, not a First nor a Second. Yet it must partake of the natures of what it brings together. It must be like a First and like a Second, that is, it must be both a First and not a First, and both a Second and not a Second.[3] In other words, a

---

[2] See Appendix II concerning the final logical interpretant.

[3] For Peirce vagueness and generality are two kinds of indeterminacy. The former is the antithetical analogue of the latter. A sign is objectively general, if it leaves it to the *interpreter* to supply further determinations. A sign is objectively *vague*, if it reserves for *some other possible sign* and not for the interpreter, the function of completing the determination. Thus, in the sentence "Man is mortal" the term "man" is objectively general because the answer to the question "What man?" is "Any one at all whom you may choose." But in the sentence, "This month a great event will happen," the term "a great event" is objectively vague because the answer to the question "What event?" is not "Any one you like," but rather "Let us wait and see." Thus it is that the principle of excluded middle does not apply to the

medium is essentially indeterminate (5.447–449, 5.505). It is both vague and general, although not in the same respect (5.506). It is vague because in one sense the principle of contradiction does not apply to it and it is general because in another sense the principle of excluded middle does not apply to it (5.505).[4] Thus the cook's desire is indeterminate with respect to her dream on the one hand and the product of her industry on the other. In terms of logic her desire is of the nature of a sign. Indeed Peirce sometimes says that mediation "reaches its fullness in Representation" (5.104), or that law is a matter of thought or meaning in things (1.343), or that law is of the nature of a general sign (1.27, 1.27 n. 1, 1.26, 5.107). In terms of mathematics, the essential indeterminateness of a medium, its vagueness and generality, is nothing but continuity. Hence he tells us that "true generality is . . . nothing but a rudimentary form of true continuity" (6.172). A point on a line, for example, could not connect the portions of that line if it were truly discrete and atomic. In that case it would be a break in the line. It can be thought of as joining the parts of the line only if it is continuous with its immediate predecessor and im-

general, while the principle of contradiction does not apply to the vague (5.505). No sign can be both vague and general at one and the same time and in one and the same respect, "since insofar as the right of determination is not distinctly extended to the interpreter it remains the right of the utterer" (5.506). The only way a sign can escape being either general or vague is by not being indeterminate, that is, by being both singular and definite. While a general predicate renders the singular subject of which it is predicated determinate with respect to itself, it leaves that subject indeterminate with regard to other predicates and remains itself indeterminate with regard to other subjects. A vague predicate does not determine its singular subject with regard to itself and *a fortiori* is not itself determined to that subject. A vague predicate remains indefinite with respect to the subject. For Peirce, no communication between persons can be entirely definite. Wherever degree or any other possible continuous variation subsists no absolute precision is possible. And since no man's experience is exactly the same as another's, his interpretation of a word must be to some degree imprecise (5.506).

[4] Cf. M. Thompson, *op. cit.*, pp. 213–218, for discussion of Peirce's analysis of vagueness. In two unpublished papers (1903 and 1909 respectively) Peirce explains that the principle of contradiction does not apply to "may-be's" or possibility and that the principle of excluded middle does not apply to "would-be's" or laws (Peirce Papers, #641, pp. 24 4/5–24 5/6; #642, pp. 20–22).

mediate successor. This is the idea one tries to express by saying that a point has no length or breadth but only position. Or again, colors in a spectrum are continuous. There are no sharp gaps. The borderlines are assigned arbitrarily because in themselves the colors gradually blend one into the other so that at places on the scale it is impossible to say objectively whether the color is orange or red; perhaps it is both or neither.

Mediation, then, implies on Peirce's analysis both vagueness and generality. The continuous involves both these sorts of indeterminateness. Therefore, by applying the ultrarealistic principle that all logical distinctions are also metaphysical, it follows that real mediation implies real vagueness and real generality. Continuity is ingredient in reality.

Third, and finally, generality necessarily refers to the future. To understand what this assertion means we will have to consider in some detail the kind of generality Peirce ascribes to quality and the kind he ascribes to law. At first sight it may seem strange that Peirce should ascribe any generality at all to quality since he usually puts quality in the first category and not in the third. Indeed, it might be argued that here Peirce collapses Firstness into Thirdness. We think, however, that such an objection is based on a misunderstanding of the interdependence of Peirce's categories and a failure to distinguish between at least two ways in which he uses the term "quality."

Peirce does ascribe a certain generality to quality as well as to law. Thus in the "Logic of Mathematics" (*ca.* 1896) he says that qualities "merge into one another" (1.418) and thus exhibit a certain continuity. Again he says that qualities are somewhat vague and potential in contrast to occurrences which are perfectly individual. And that is why qualities do not make up facts although they are "concerned in" them (1.419). Or again, explaining what a general fact might be, he attributes its generality to its connection with the potential world of quality (1.420). The thing to note here is that quality is a "mere abstract potentiality" or possibility (1.422). Some have taken the position that Peirce is talking about *logical* possibility instead of real *power.*[5] This is certainly a mistake. In the text Peirce criticizes those

---

[5] E.g. Thomas A. Goudge, "The Views of Charles Peirce on the Given in Experience," *Journal of Philosophy,* XXXII (1935), 533–544. Cf. John Dewey's refutation, "Peirce's Theory of Quality," *ibid.,* 701–708, reprinted in

who claim that a thing does not have the quality of red in the dark, or that a piece of iron is not hard except when actually resisting pressure. Of course the quality of hardness or of redness is actualized only when the thing that has it interacts with something else, but before that interaction the thing really has that quality potentially, as a real power and not just as a logical possibility. Peirce describes quality as what "might happen" given the suitable conditions. It is a *way of* behaving and consequently it is understandable why Peirce sees it as general. It would be a nominalistic error to deny that things really have ways of behaving, that is, to deny that they have real potentialities. Yet this is the position to which one is forced who would make qualities merely logical possibilities.

Now the question is whether Peirce thought that quality, in the sense of potentiality, fits the category of Firstness. The answer is no. We have already cited in the previous section the text which makes this conclusion inescapable. It will be well to repeat it here.

> A Firstness is exemplified in every quality of a total feeling. It is perfectly simple and without parts; and everything has its quality. Thus the tragedy of King Lear has its Firstness, its flavor *sui generis*. That wherein all such qualities agree is universal Firstness, the very being of Firstness. The word *possibility* fits it, except that possibility implies a relation to what exists, while universal Firstness is the mode of being of itself. That is why a new word was required for it. Otherwise, "possibility" would have answered the purpose. (1.531)

Possibility or potentiality, therefore, *almost* fits Firstness as such, but not quite. Consequently quality considered as potentiality does not quite fit Firstness either, because as potentiality quality implies a relation to Secondness or existence. Still, it is clear that Peirce does use quality to exemplify Firstness. Firstness is the "sheer totality and pervading unity of quality in everything experienced, whether it be odor, the drama of King Lear, or philosophic or scientific systems."[6] Peirce,

R. Bernstein's *John Dewey on Experience, Nature and Freedom* (New York: Liberal Arts Press, 1960), pp. 199–210. I am much indebted to Dewey's article for this section.

[6] Dewey, *art. cit.*, p. 200, in Bernstein's edition.

however, uses the term "quality" in two senses: as it is in itself, sheer totality and pervading unity, and in its relation to other aspects of a phenomenon, and in particular, to Secondness or existence. In this second sense, quality is not pure Firstness, precisely because it involves a relation to Secondness. More exactly, quality here is the Firstness of Secondness, and the co-presence of these two categories yields the generality necessary for potentiality or Thirdness. Quality *per se*, that is, in the first sense distinguished above, is pure Firstness, but as such is neither general nor individual. It is something like the scholastic *natura communis*, an abstract nature which is neither formally universal nor individuated. Or again it is like the comprehension of a term taken without any reference to its extension. In this sense, then, quality does not signify potentiality or possibility and there is some question in Peirce's mind whether quality *per se* can be conceived at all. He seems to say, as we shall see in the next paragraph, that it can only be pointed to by an indexical sign. Secondness *per se* is not general either. It is individual and even antigeneral (7.132)[7] in that it resists generalization to the point where it would lose its character as Secondness if it were generalized. In this, Secondness *per se* differs from quality *per se* or pure Firstness. Quality *per se* does not resist generalization. In fact, it is what makes generality possible at all. Hence, strictly speaking, Secondnesses taken in themselves have no common quality (1.532). Each Secondness is unique. Nevertheless Secondnesses as we experience them do have common qualities precisely because, as we experience them, they are inseparably bound up with Firstnesses. It follows, too, of course, that we can never experience pure Firstnesses or qualities *per se* either. We can experience them only in relation to Secondnesses, that is to say, only as real potentialities. Our human experience always involves this Thirdness, mediation, lawfulness. Indeed, Peirce defines Thirdness as

> . . . that mode of being which *consists,* mind my word if
> you please, the mode of being which *consists* in the fact that
> future facts of Secondness will take on a determinate
> general character [Firstness]. (1.26)

[7] By "anti-general" is meant that Secondness cannot be generalized after the manner of a law without losing its character of Secondness. Firstness may be so generalized without destruction of its character.

It is no wonder, then, that Peirce finds no difficulty in assimilating qualities considered as potentialities to law expressible in conditionals.

The point to remember here is that Peirce's categories are never *experienced* in their purity. And we saw in our discussion of the categories in connection with the normative sciences, Firstness, Secondness, and Thirdness are distinguished as elements in every experience by precisive abstraction. Certainly, they are irreducible elements into which an experience must be analysed, but they are nonetheless inseparable. Thus, it will be recalled, Peirce warned us that it is very difficult so to distinguish them as to hold them each in their purity and yet in their full meaning (1.353). In the same paragraph he says that the categories are so intangible that they are tints or tones upon conceptions rather than conceptions. In yet another place, Peirce points out that the categories, "being enormously large, very promiscuous, and known but in small part, cannot be satisfactorily defined, and therefore can only be denoted by Indices" (4.544). The categorial structure which Peirce uses is therefore highly subtle and complex, admitting of various combinations. The more familiar terms which Peirce applies to his categories, therefore, must be approached with caution. They do not always fit exactly (e.g. "quality" and "possibility" for Firstness).[8] Indeed no term describing our *experience* could exactly capture just one of the categories since our experience will always involve all three categories. At least this will be true of any experience which we are consciously examining. By examining it, we are knowing it. By knowing it we are judging and interpreting it. Whatever is known, insofar as it is known, has a share of Thirdness. But Thirdness is logically dependent upon Firstness and Secondness.

Thus Peirce himself distinguishes qualities in themselves and qualities as reflected upon.

> When we say that qualities are general, are partial
> determinations, are mere potentialities, etc., all that is true

---

[8] Peirce distinguished the matter of phenomena from the forms of experience. The categories of the former are quality, fact, and law, while the categories of the latter are the monad, the dyad, and the polyad. Both sets of categories are under Firstness, Secondness, and Thirdness as universal categories (see 1.452).

of qualities reflected upon; but these things do not belong
to the quality-element of experience. (1.425)

A quality reflected upon is one asserted of a subject in a judgment. It
is referred to some other aspect of a phenomenon and so takes on
generality. But in itself, taken in abstraction, "the quality is what
presents itself in the *monadic* aspect" of experience (1.424).

> The phenomenon may be ever so complex and
> heterogeneous. That circumstance will make no particular
> difference in the quality. It will make it more general.
> But one quality is in itself, in its monadic aspect, no more
> general than another. The resultant effect has no parts. The
> quality in itself is indecomposable and *sui generis*. (1.425)

Notice that the monadic aspect of experience is not itself experienced.
It is gotten from experience through precisive abstraction. This is the
"quality-element" of experience.

In a later fragment (*ca.* 1904) Peirce characterized these qualities
in themselves as mere "may-be's" which are not necessarily realized.
Their being consists in the fact that there *might be* such a peculiar,
positive, suchness in a "phaneron." And to emphasize that these qualities in themselves do not imply any relation to Secondness or existence,
he adds that they are merely a question of what one can imagine (e.g.
a being whose whole life "should consist in nothing at all but a violet
color or a stink of cabbage") and not of what psychological laws permit. This very fact

> . . . shows that such a feeling is not *general,* in the sense in
> which the law of gravitation is general. For nobody can
> imagine that law to have any being of any kind if it were
> impossible that there should exist two masses of matter, or
> if there were no such thing as motion. *A true general*
> *cannot have any being unless there is to be some prospect*
> *of its sometime having occasion to be embodied in a fact,*
> which is itself not a law or anything like a law. A quality
> of feeling can be imagined to be without any occurrence,
> as it seems to me. Its mere may-being gets along without
> any realization at all. (1.304, emphasis added)

Potentiality, or quality as reflected upon, and law, therefore, are "true generals" in Peirce's sense. Now since the very notion of potentiality refers to the future (what *can* or *could* be) and since only something which is or involves potentiality is a true general, we have established the proposition that generality necessarily refers to the future.

And yet we are not quite finished. It remains to discuss the relation between potentiality and law, for Peirce explicitly distinguishes the sort of "true generality" proper to each. In the *Logic of Mathematics,* explaining what must be excluded from the category of fact or Secondness, Peirce writes,

> This is the general, and with it the permanent or eternal
> (for permanence is a species of generality), and the
> conditional (which equally involves generality). Generality
> is either of that negative sort which belongs to the merely
> potential, as such, and this is peculiar to the category
> of quality; or it is of that positive kind which belongs to
> conditional necessity, and this is peculiar to the category of
> law. (1.427)

Peirce never explains in so many words what he means by negative and positive generality. He only gives us hints and leaves us to puzzle it out. The clue he gives us is a set of contrasts: (1) the permanent or eternal as opposed to the conditional, (2) the potential in contrast to the conditionally necessary, (3) quality compared with law. Presumably, then, negative generality is that generality which characterizes quality as potentiality, and potentiality has something permanent or eternal about it. The permanent or eternal is what is time-independent. It holds good always, under any circumstances. It would seem, therefore, to be an *a priori* condition or formal law. Did we not just say, however, that the potential necessarily refers to the future? Is it not, therefore, time-dependent and mutable? The way out of this dilemma can be found by examining more closely how we express potentiality. Consider Peirce's own famous example of "hardness." The test of a material's hardness is scratching. But no one would want to say that the testing *constituted* the hardness. The material was hard antecedent to the test (even though perhaps we did not know it until the test was made). Furthermore, a different specimen of the same sort of material would still be judged hard even if no test were ever made upon it. Therefore, we express real potentiality in terms of subjunctive conditionals: "If such and such *were* rubbed with this material, it *would* resist marking." This conditional might be a contrary-to-fact, yet it would still be true. In one sense then it is permanent, eternal, time-independent. The conditional does not specify any particular time or time-interval *t*. And yet the conditional does in a general way refer to the future. It says that *would* happen, if a certain set of conditions were fulfilled. This sort of conditional proposition does not assert the antecedent or the consequent (neither as contingent nor as necessary); it asserts the connection between them or the *consequence* as necessary. The Universe of this sort of proposition is that of possibility. It is therefore independent of the actual time-order, but not independent of a possible time-order.[9] It should be clear, however, that what the subjunctive conditional asserts as true gives no direct information concerning how one knows that it is true, nor does the assertion *qua* assertion need to furnish the evidence for its truth. The point is that while the assertion of real potentiality concerns the Universe of Possibility, the evidence for the truth of that assertion must be obtained in and through the Universe of Actuality by means of induction.[10]

Thus potentiality is in a sense permanent or eternal in that it expresses a necessary relationship. The necessity, however, is not unconditional. Unconditional necessity would attach to the antecedent or to the consequ*ent* either as brute fact which happened once and for all in the irretrievable past, or as *brute* force—force without law or reason (1.427). The necessity is conditional or relational, and has permanence or eternality as a *relationship*. Of course, if the conditions of the relation are altered one has another and different relation. The former does not *ipso facto* cease to be a real possibility (at the very

[9] In "Prolegomena to an Apology for Pragmaticism" (*Monist*, 16 [1906]), Peirce identifies the modes of being (actuality, possibility, destiny) with the universes, *not with his categories*. "On the contrary," he says, "the succession of Predicates of Predicates is different in the different Modes of Being" (4.549). Each of the three universes must be divided into "realms" for the different predicaments or categories. Potentiality then would turn out to be the Thirdness of the universe of possibility.

[10] For Peirce, what distinguishes a "true law" from mere "regularities" or summations of past experience is the way in which they are discovered (7.84).

least a *logical* possibility). We see no objection to nor inconsistency in Peirce's regarding potentiality as a kind of law.

Still Peirce distinguished the sort of generality proper to law, positive generality, from that proper to potentiality, negative generality. Consequently, he does not simply identify "law" and "potentiality." Indeed, Peirce's usual formulation of what a law is, is not in terms of the "would-be" of potentiality but in those of the "will-be" of actuality. To be sure, law in this more usual sense is expressed in a conditional, but that conditional is usually in the indicative mood. It takes the form of a prediction. "If such and such material *is* rubbed, it *will* resist marking."

> A law of nature, then, will be regarded as having a sort of *esse in futuro*. That is to say they will have a present reality which consists in the fact that events *will* happen according to the formulation of those laws. (5.48)

Again, enumerating the three modes of being, Peirce describes the being of law as that which "will govern facts in the future" (1.23). In another place, he writes:

> When an experimentalist speaks of *phenomenon* . . . he does not mean any particular event that did happen to somebody in the dead past, but what *surely will* happen to everybody in the living future who shall fulfill certain conditions. (5.425)

In yet another context, Peirce describes law as "how an endless future must continue to be" (1.534), stressing the necessity, albeit conditional, of a true law.

In the light of these clear statements it is perhaps fair to say that the distinction between negative and positive generality is the same (or almost the same) as that which exists between "would-be" and "will-be," between the subjunctive and the indicative. The difference which the speaker intends to convey by his choice of mood is one of emphasis. The mood signals a point of view or point of interest to be taken into consideration in determining the sentence's meaning. It signals what we called before a Universe.[11] Peirce's Universes are

---

[11] A shift in the modal auxiliary indicates another change of emphasis, namely, a change of category. For example, a shift to "may-be" and "might-

those which correspond to what he takes to be the basic modes of being. Both "would-be" and "will-be" are forms employed in *future* conditional sentences. The "would-be" emphasizes the necessary connection or the *consequence*, leaving out of consideration the factual status of antecedent and consequent. It stresses the relationship between kinds of antecedents and consequents, and only implies a relation to actual instances (as the basis for the generalization, let us say, in past experience). The "will-be" formulation, while including the necessary connection or consequence of the "would-be" as the very basis for the prediction, emphasizes the factual status of antecedent and consequent as about to be realized, probably to be realized, surely to be realized in the long run, etc. While it deals with kinds of facts and their relations, it adds an explicit reference to the actual instances in the order of our actual experience.

1) If X were rubbed with Z, X would resist marking by Z.
2) If X is rubbed with Z, X will resist marking by Z.

For Peirce, Sentence 2 is a confident prediction as to the actual occurrence of an actual fact in our experience on the condition that another actual occurrence of an actual fact be realized. The confidence of this prediction is based on the necessary connection or consequence expressed in Sentence 1, even though Sentence 1 gives no indication, expectation, or hope that Z will ever, as a matter of fact, touch X. We suggest, therefore, that the distinction between negative and positive generality has to do with the absence or the presence in the formulation of explicit reference to the actual world of our experience. Potentiality, expressed in would-be's, the foundation of and necessary condition for law, expressed in will-be's (and, therefore, capable of being called a "law" by analogy), is only negatively general for Peirce because it consciously refrains from explicit reference to the factual status of its antecedent and consequent, while law is positively general because it consciously makes such a reference. From one point of view, then, "would-be" conditionals are stronger claims than "will-be's" since they are the basis for the prediction in the first place. Yet from another point of view they *say* less because they prescind from the actual occurrences in our world of experiences.

be" seems to indicate in Peirce a shift to Firstness as such, to quality in itself (1.304).

We have indeed gone far afield in attempting to understand why Peirce conceived generality as necessarily implying a reference to the future. Whether we understand generality as negative or as positive our discussion has clearly shown that both indeed do so refer. Both potentiality and conditional necessity by definition imply such a reference, and so both are characterized by Thirdness.[12] There are several other problems which must be explored (e.g. the distinction between formal and material laws, and the notion of destiny), but at this point a summary of what we have seen may be useful. So far in searching for an understanding of Peirce's use of the term "law," we have found that as essentially Thirdness or thought (1) it mediates between qualities in themselves (Firstnesses) and facts or actualities (Secondnesses), (2) it is therefore indeterminate, that is, vague and general, and so is a special case of continuity, and finally (3) its

---

[12] "We may say that the bulk of what is actually done consists of Secondness—or better, Secondness is the predominant character of what *has been* done. The immediate present, could we seize it, would have no character but its Firstness. Nor that I mean to say that immediate consciousness (a pure fiction, by the way), would be Firstness, but that the *quality* of what we are immediately conscious of, which is no fiction, is Firstness. . . . [W]hat is to be, according to our conception of it, can never be wholly past. . . . I call this element of the phenomenon or object of thought the element of Thirdness. It is that which is what it is by virtue of imparting a quality to reactions in the future" (1.343).

Past as past is over and done with. It can never be retrieved. It is frozen as it were with all the singularity and concreteness of its happening. To this extent, then, Secondness is its specific characteristic. Still, this does not mean that there is nothing of Firstness and Thirdness in past events. Since everything and every event is what it is, past events have Firstness about them—but not insofar as they are past. Again, since we can and do generalize about past events and since every concrete, singular event is also an instance of a type, past events have Thirdness about them, but not *qua* past. Similarly, the present as present, the indivisible *nunc*, is only what it is with no reference to anything else. Its specific character is Firstness. Yet it manifests Secondness and Thirdness: secondness because any quality to be experienced must be embodied in an actual event; Thirdness because the present is embedded in a continuum. The future *qua* future is characterized by Thirdness, because it is indeterminate. It has reality only as potentiality really in actual things capable of future determination. But of course, future events will manifest Firstness and Secondness insofar as they are events, not insofar as they are future.

specific sort of generality ("true generality") refers to the future. In short, law is founded in real potentiality in things, and can be best formulated in a conditional proposition. Here are some of the ways in which Peirce describes law. (Bracketed words have been inserted to indicate the presence of the three elements just enumerated.)

> A law of nature, then, will be regarded . . . as having a sort of *esse in futuro.* That is to say they will have a present reality [real potentiality] which consists in the fact that events [Secondnesses] *will* happen according to the formulation [a symbolic representation to which Firstnesses are essential] of those laws. (5.48)

In another place, and perhaps more clearly, he says:

> [Thirdness is that mode of being] which *consists,* mind my word if you please, the mode of being which *consists* in the fact that future facts of Secondness will take on a determinate general character [Firstness]. . . . (1.26)

Or again,

> My view is that there are three modes of being. I hold that we can directly observe them in elements of whatever is at any time before the mind in any way. They are the being of positive qualitative possibility, the being of actual fact, and the being of law that will govern [hence mediate] facts [of a certain positive quality] in the future. (1.23)

In another place, Peirce underlines the conditional element in law.

> When an experimentalist speaks of *phenomenon* . . . he does not mean any particular event that did happen to somebody in the dead past [Secondness], but what *surely will* happen to every body in the living future who shall fulfill certain conditions. (5.425)

Again, in answering the objection that one cannot consistently hold both that to be and to be represented are not identical and that the nature of *real* law is to be represented (if the laws are real, they are not of the nature of representation; if they are of the nature of representation, they are not real), he writes,

> My answer to this would be that it rests upon an ambiguity.
> When I say that the general proposition as to what will
> happen, whenever a certain condition may be fulfilled, is of
> the nature of a representation, I mean that it refers to
> experiences *in futuro,* which I do not know are all of them
> experienced and never can know have been all experienced.
> But when I say that really to be is different from being
> represented, I mean that what really is, ultimately consists
> in what shall be forced upon us in experience, that there is
> an element of brute compulsion in fact, and that fact is not
> a mere question of reasonableness. (5.97)

It is this reference to the future which distinguishes lawfulness from mere uniformity exhibited in past events. Rolling six straight passes with honest dice is a mere uniformity serving no basis for prediction concerning the seventh throw. Thus in a review of Herbert Nichol's *A Treatise on Cosmology* (*ca.* 1904) he criticizes John Stuart Mill for not having seen precisely this difference.

> We all know that John Mill banished the word 'law' and
> substituted 'uniformity' for it, as more precisely expressing
> what it meant. But pragmatism discovers a serious error
> here. For while uniformity is a character which might be
> realized, in all its fulness, in a short series of past events,
> law, on the other hand, is essentially a character of an
> indefinite future; and while uniformity involves a regularity
> exact and exceptionless, law only requires an approach to
> uniformity in a decided majority of cases. (8.192)

Peirce explains that law could reasonably affect human conduct only through the knowledge of such a law creating and warranting anticipations of future experience. And what this requires is

> ... that the law should be a truth expressible as a conditional
> proposition whose antecedent and consequent express
> experiences *in a future tense,* and further, that, as long as
> the law retains the character of a law, there should be

possible occasions in an indefinite future when events of the kind described in the antecedent may come to pass. (8.192)

Such, then, Peirce declares, *ought* to be our conception of law.

In a very early paper (*ca.* 1866) Peirce discussed the question whether in a world of chance all law would be abrogated. His opinion was that they would not, because there are two kinds of law, formal and material.

Suppose that in throwing the die other numbers had turned up from those which actually turned up, so that the row of numbers would have been somewhat different; still the laws would have held; they would hold with one set of numbers as well as with another. Whereas if we were to give a whale legs or a woman wings, the laws of the animal kingdom would be interfered with. So that there are two kinds of laws, those which in a different state of things would continue to hold good and those which in a different state of things would not hold good. The former we call *formal* laws, the latter *material* laws. (7.137)

Peirce gives the principle of induction as an example of a formal law, namely, as is the sample so is the whole and the sameness of a number of characters manifests identity of objects (7.137, cf. 7.131).

But so long as there are any laws whatsoever, *these* laws . . . must exist. . . . Now all law may, in one sense, be contingent. But that there should be knowledge without the existence of law, that there should be intelligence without anything being intelligible, all admit to be impossible. These laws therefore cannot be abrogated without abrogating knowledge; and thus are the formal conditions of all knowledge. (7.138)

The laws of logic, therefore, including the laws of probability, are universal laws that do not depend for their validity upon the peculiarities of the world in which we happen to live. They would hold good in any world whatsoever that was knowable. Even a world of pure chance, if it were at all knowable, would be subject to these laws of reason. This notion of formal law, law of reason, plays an important role in Peirce's theory of tychism. The world in which we live is not a world of pure chance nor is it a world of absolute determinism. As a matter of fact the material laws of our world admit of variation, exception, and growth, which can be accounted for only by admitting that chance is a real principle in its constitution. Nevertheless, in a world of chance and of law Peirce will hold that there is a destiny—something to be fulfilled: the growth of concrete reasonableness. This growth requires formal laws of reason which give it direction and stability amid the variation and vagaries of particular material laws.

Forty years later, Peirce described the third mode of reality as that which was destined or sure to come true (4.547), and he explained that "destined" meant that which is sure to come "although there is no necessitating reason for it" (4.547, n. 1). The example he uses is that if a pair of dice are thrown often enough, they will be sure to turn up sixes some time, although there is no necessity that they should. What assures us that they will surely turn up sixes sometime or other is the law of probability. Indeed, the probability that they will so behave in the long run is one. And yet there is no necessitating cause that they should. The throw of the dice follow the *formal* law of probability, although there is no given set of circumstances which determine just when the sixes will appear. Still as a matter of fact there are no formal laws really at work except in some sort of universe with its material laws. Indeed we believe that Peirce held that it is the formal laws that not only allow us to discover the material laws of our universe at any particular time but also make those laws to be laws. It is the formal laws of reason that create in the world regularities, potentialities, habits of uniform activity (subject, of course, to modification and growth through the operation of chance variations which may tend to establish new regularities).[13] There is evidence for such an interpretation in the following portion of the paragraph under consideration.

I do not see by what confusion of thought anybody can

---

[13] Hence Peirce's remark to Calderoni that classification of the elements of thought and consciousness according to their *formal* structure is what is important. This he tried to do in his categories (8.213).

persuade himself that he does not believe that tomorrow is destined to come. The point is that it is today really true that tomorrow the sun will rise; or that, even if it does not, the clocks or *something*, will go on. For if it be not real it can only be fiction: a Proposition is either True or False. But we are too apt to confound destiny with the impossibility of the opposite. I see no impossibility in the sudden stoppage of everything. In order to show the difference, I remind you that "impossibility" is that which, for example, describes the mode of falsity of the idea that there should be a collection of objects so multitudinous that there would not be characters enough in the universe of characters to distinguish all those things from one another. Is there anything of that sort about the stoppage of all motion? There is, perhaps, a *law of nature* against it; but that is all. (4.547)

Clearly Peirce is trying to distinguish "destiny" from "the impossibility of the opposite." He asks us to consider two cases: (1) the sudden stoppage of all motion, and (2) a greatest multitude of actual objects. These cases cannot be called "impossible" in precisely the same sense. Case 2 is *logically* impossible because it involves a *contradiction*.[14] In other words, it is strictly unthinkable because it violates a formal law of intelligibility. Case 1 may be *physically* impossible given the structure of our world, that is, there may be a "law of nature" against it, but it is not strictly unthinkable since it does not seem to involve any contradiction in terms.

[14] At least this is how we interpret that rather obscure sentence, "In order to show the difference . . . ." From the context it seems certain that he is talking about logical "impossibility" because he is referring to a mode of falsity. But something is logically impossible only if it violates the principle of contradiction. The obscurity arises from the example which Peirce proposes. It has to do with the thorny issue of whether there can be a greatest multitude. Is the notion contradictory? As Murphey points out, the term "multitude" is used ambiguously for both series and collection (*op. cit.*, p. 274). It is clear, however, that, regardless of whether Peirce's proof of his paradox is correct or not, he meant to show a contradiction and hence an example of the strictly "impossible." See *ibid.*, 238–288, for an excellent discussion of the issue involved.

Now, Peirce wants to say that the indefinite continuation of motion may be *destined* even though its opposite does not involve a contradiction. Neither the continuation of motion indefinitely, nor the sudden stoppage of everything is unthinkable. Either might serve as an hypothesis which must be supported by observation and analysis of experience. Neither can be ruled out *a priori*. On the other hand, we can infer that a "greatest multitude" of actual objects *could not be destined* since it is contradictory. Whatever be the constitution of our world, *a priori* knowledge indicates at least one characteristic it could not have.

Regardless of how apt one might judge Peirce's examples to be, the point he is making is clear enough and bears out our discussion concerning formal and material laws. To summarize what can be deduced from this passage: (1) for Peirce the "impossibility of the opposite" means "what involves a contradiction;" (2) since the principle of contradiction is a logical law, the sort of possibility Peirce here has in mind is "logical" (logical possibility is a necessary, but not sufficient, condition for real potentiality); (3) the formal or logical law of contradiction does not afford us any positive evidence of what the real potentialities of our world are, but rather sets a negative boundary to them; (4) therefore, the laws of nature or material laws must be discovered by inductive inference; (5) these alone are the basis for our beliefs about future occurrences; (6) the logical possibility of these laws being contravened does not alter the fact that the evidence on hand that they will not be so contravened may give us a probability of one. The formal laws of logic therefore are the unchanging conditions necessary for our knowledge of changeable material laws. But since, as has been shown, Peirce's synechism requires that the laws of logic also be laws of being, the formal laws of thought are not simply laws of "our mind," but laws of the intelligibility of things. They furnish, therefore, the formal principle of regularity to the world of changing fact. At any given moment our knowledge of the laws of nature (material laws) is a union of the known facts and the laws of scientific inference governing the facts. The facts might change and so the material laws, but not the laws of rationality. The change in the facts, if and when it occurs, is to be set down to real chance. Peirce's tychism will put it this way: no material law is exact, not merely because we have imperfect knowledge of it, but also because of the very nature of our world. Destiny, therefore, is the inevitable working out in the world of the laws of reason without absolute determination of the facts. Destiny seems to be for Peirce something like an objectified probability theory.[15] Thus the *summum bonum* is the growth of concrete reasonableness—the continual process of the embodiment of laws of reason in fact.[16]

We have remarked that Peirce frequently likens law to a general sign. Indeed, Thirdness or mediation, he says, "reaches its fullness in Representation" (5.104). Perhaps this lead will throw more light on our inquiry into the nature of law as Thirdness.

In a paper entitled, "The Regenerated Logic," published in the *Monist* (1896) Peirce analyses what is involved in making an assertion. Every assertion supposes a sign-maker who delivers it and some interpreter or other who will receive it. Some of the signs employed are supposed to excite in the mind of the receiver familiar images ("we might almost say, *dreams*"), that is, "reminiscences of sights, sounds, feelings, tastes, smells, or other sensations, *now quite detached* from the original circumstances of their first occurrence, so that they are free to be attached to new occasions" (3.433, emphasis added). These images themselves are signs—signs by resemblance, or *icons*—of the *real quality* (Firstness) of the thing referred to. This is the assertion's *predicate* (3.433). But the assertion which the deliverer seeks to convey to the receiver relates to some object or objects forced on his attention in the course of experience, and if he is to communicate he must also succeed in forcing those same objects on the receiver's attention. The icon, however, cannot do the job because it does not relate to any particular thing. Some sign like "this" or "that" or "hullo" must be used. This sort of sign is called an

---

[15] ". . . thought, controlled by a rational experimental logic, tends to the fixation of certain opinions, equally destined, the nature of which will be the same in the end, however the perversity of thought of whole generations may cause the postponement of the ultimate fixation" (5.430).

[16] Since "generals" are not only real, but active forces in the world, Peirce could write: "Accordingly, the pragmaticist . . . makes it [the *summum bonum*] to consist in that process of evolution whereby the existent comes more and more to embody those generals which were just now said to be *destined*, which is what we strive to express in calling them *reasonable*" (5.433).

index. An index does not describe the quality of its object; it merely points to it (Secondness, or "hecceity"). This is the assertion's *subject(s)* (3.434). But Peirce observed, "Neither the predicate, nor the subjects, nor both together, can make an assertion" (3.435). The assertion represents a compulsion which experience brings upon the deliverer or sign-maker to attach the predicate to the subjects in a particular way. Once this compulsion is felt, it attains a certain permanence.

> This compulsion strikes him at a certain instant; and he remains under it forever after. It is, therefore, different from the temporary force which the hecceities exert upon his attention. This new compulsion may pass out of mind for the time being; but it continues just the same, and will act whenever the occasion arises, that is, whenever those particular hecceities and that first intention are called to mind together. (3.435)

As Peirce observes, this is merely the description of a permanent conditional force, or *law*. Therefore, to make an assertion the deliverer requires a new kind of sign distinct from the icon and the index which shall signify a law to the effect that "to objects of indices an icon appertains as a sign of them in a given way." That sort of sign is a *symbol*, and is the *copula* of the assertion (Thirdness).[17]

The following year (1897) in the same journal Peirce expounded the same ideas in "The Logic of Relatives." Arguing that class names should be dispensed with in favor of verbs, he writes:

> A verb by itself signifies a mere dream, an imagination unattached to any particular occasion. It calls up in the mind an *icon*. A *relative* is just that, an icon, or image, without attachments to experience, without "a local habitation and a name," but with indications of the need of such attachments. (3.459)

This, of course, is unattached quality or Firstness.

> An indexical word, such as a proper noun or demonstrative or selective pronoun, has force to draw the attention of the

---

[17] Cf. also 2.249 ff., 2.293.

listener to some hecceity common to the experience of the speaker and listener. (3.460)

This is the concrete individual or Secondness to which the quality is attached or in which it is embodied in experience.

Contrast this [the "hecceity"] with the signification of the verb, which is sometimes in my thought, sometimes in yours, and which has no other identity than the agreement between its several manifestations. That is what we call an abstraction or idea. (3.460)

This is what the nominalist would call a *mere* name and what the platonizing realist would say *is* real. According to Peirce the correct opinion requires that we strike out the nominalist's "mere" and replace the Platonist's "is" by "may be." The force of the "may-be" is this: An idea *is* or *exists*

provided experience and reason shall, as their final upshot, uphold the truth of the particular predicate, *and the natural existence of the law it expresses*, and this is likewise true. (3.460, emphasis added)

In other words, to go from "may be" to "is" requires the mediation of some law or conditional necessity. It is only real law which allows one to *assert* that such and such an *icon* belongs to such and such an index—or, if one prefers, that such and such a quality is embodied in such and such a "hecceity." It is the sentence or proposition which makes the assertion. It signifies or expresses a law.

The proposition, or sentence, signifies that an eternal fitness, or truth, a permanent conditional force, or law, attaches certain hecceities to certain parts of an idea. (3.461)

Ideas or abstractions, therefore, escape from being "lifeless things" by being embodied in concrete instances through real laws of nature (4.447–448).

3. Law as Living Power

IT WOULD NOT BE INAPPROPRIATE to say that for Peirce the notion of thought as a living force in the world sums up his notion of law, and that thought as living force in the world is nothing other than real potentiality or power, the ground for laws of nature. In more than one place he explicitly says just that. For example, in working out a detailed classification of the sciences (*ca.* 1902), he argues that "the idea of right and wrong is" (like Truth) the "greatest power on earth, to which every knee must sooner or later bow or be broken down" (1.217). Nor do these master ideas get their life and power from powerful men who are disposed to make them so, rather "it is the idea which will create its defenders and render them powerful" (1.217).[1] In yet another place, he says:

> Whatever one's theory may be as to the invalidity of human reason, there are certain cases where the force of conviction practically cannot be resisted; and one of these is the experience that one opinion is so far from being as strong as another in the long run, though it receives equally warm support, that on the contrary, ideas utterly despised and frowned upon have an inherent power of working their way to the governance of the world, at last. True, they cannot do this without machinery, without supporters, without facts; but the ideas somehow manage to grow their machinery, and their supporters, and their facts, and to render the machinery, the supporters, and the facts strong. As intellectual development proceeds, we all come to believe this more or less. Most of us, such is the depravity of the human heart, look askance at the notion that ideas have any power; although that some power they have we cannot but admit. (2.149)

[1] See letter to James, June 12, 1902, in R. B. Perry's *The Thought and Character of William James*, vol. II (Boston: Little, Brown and Co., 1935), pp. 424–425.

Peirce argues that even if one does not accept this opinion, one must see that it is perfectly intelligible (1.217). Not only does he himself subscribe to this belief (1.219), but is willing to defend "the extreme position that every general idea has more or less power of working itself out into fact . . ." (2.149). Whether or not he be correct in this "extreme position"

> . . . it must at any rate be admitted by every candid man that he does believe firmly and without doubt that to some extent phenomena are regular, that is, are governed by general ideas; and so far as they are so, they are capable of prediction by reasoning. (2.149)

Ideas, then, have "generative life" (1.219); they are real laws governing events.

That something like this is so, Peirce maintains, is a matter of experiential fact. But it is not the sort of factual claim that can be verified "by producing a microscope or telescope or any recondite observations of any kind" (1.219). Its evidence, he says, stares us all in the face every hour of our lives. It is, then, the type of factual question with which philosophy, not physical science, deals. The fact is there in front of us, but we must open our eyes to see it and then try to understand it.

> If one does not see it, it is for the same reason that some men have not a sense of sin; and there is nothing for it but to be born again and become as a little child. If you do not see it, you have to look upon the world with new eyes. (1.219)

Indeed, if anyone were to deny that ideas have power to work out physical and psychical results, it would be a sufficient refutation to point out that the denial involves a belief in that very same proposition. After all, any controversy, or more generally any communication, involves an interchange of ideas and these ideas produce effects on the parties, in their thinking or acting.

> Words then do produce physical effects. It is madness to deny it. The very denial of it involves a belief in it; and nobody can consistently fail to acknowledge it until he sinks to a complete mental paresis. (5.106)

The fact is beyond any doubt; the question to be answered is "how?" Peirce will offer his own "guess" (5.106).

Peirce felt obliged to explain in detail his unusual and controversial position. The main question to be answered was the nature of thought's efficacy or power to work itself out in the world and thus "transform the face of the earth" (1.217). In more traditional terms, the question was what sort of causality do ideas exercise. Peirce turns to tradition for the answer—to Aristotle's distinction between final and efficient causation (cf. 1.211 ff.). Peirce had been arguing that a "natural" or "real" class (an efficacious idea or law) is one "the existence of whose members is due to a common and peculiar final cause" (1.211). Ideas have their power by exercising final causality. Now the term "final cause" must not be limited to purpose. Rather, purpose is but one type of final cause—more familiar in our human experience because human purpose is conscious and controlled. But an idea—a thought as opposed to thinking—is not necessarily confined to a consciousness, to a brain, to a soul (1.216, cf. 1.211). Final causation, therefore, means simply

> ... that mode of bringing facts about according to which a general description of result is made to come about, quite irrespective of any compulsion for it to come about in this or that particular way; although the means may be adapted to the end. The general result may be brought about at one time in one way, and at another in another way. Final causation does not determine in what particular way it is to be brought about, but only that the result shall have a certain general character. (1.211)

In scholastic terminology, the final cause specifies the effect an agent or efficient cause produces, that is, determines it to be of a certain kind.[2] Again, since the means must be adapted to the end, the end specifies what means are appropriate in a general, not necessarily in a particular, way. Efficient causation, on the other hand,

> ... is a compulsion determined by the particular condition of things, and is a compulsion acting to make that situation

[2] See e.g. *Summa Theologica* I–II, q. 1, a. 2; *Summa Contra Gentiles*, III, 2, Item 2.

begin to change in a perfectly determinate way; and what
the general character of the result may be in no way concerns
the efficient causation. (1.212)

The efficient cause, then, is what produces the effect by its own activity
or action, *hic et nunc*, in these particular and determinate circumstances. The efficiency as such has nothing general about it. It is brute
force, or compulsion. Thus in terms of Peirce's categories, what characterizes final causation is Thirdness and what characterizes efficient
causation is Secondness.

To say that efficient and final causation are distinct and indeed
irreducible is not to say that they are separable.[3] Peirce tells us
explicitly:

Final causality cannot be imagined without efficient
causality; but no whit the less on that account are their modes
of action polar contraries. (1.213)

We are beginning to get some insight into what Peirce means when
he continually insists that there can be no law without cases under the
law—there can be no true generals without instances, and so on. His
favorite illustration of the intimate connection between final and
efficient causality, between law and force, between Thirdness and
Secondness generally, is the relation between the court and the sheriff.

Law, without force to carry it out, would be a court without
a sheriff; and all its dicta would be vaporings. (1.212)

The court cannot be imagined without a sheriff. . . . The
sheriff would still have his fist, even if there were no court;
but an efficient cause, detached from a final cause in the form
of a law, would not even possess efficiency: it might exert
itself, and something might follow *post hoc*, but not *propter
hoc*; for *propter* implies potential regularity. (1.213)

. . . a law of nature left to itself would be quite analogous to
a court without a sheriff. A court in that predicament might
probably be able to induce some citizen to act as sheriff;
but until it had so provided itself with an officer who, unlike
itself, could not discourse authoritatively but who could put

[3] See the discussion of Peirce's theory of distinctions in Part I.

forth the strong arm, its law might be the perfection of
human reason but would remain mere fireworks, *brutum
fulmen.* (5.48)

A reaction cannot be generalized without entirely losing its
character as a reaction. A generalized reaction is a law. But
a law, by itself without the addition of a living reaction
to carry it out on each separate occasion, is as impotent as a
judge without a sheriff. It is an idle formula entirely different
from a reaction. A reaction may be ever so conformable to
law or reason, that is, it may occur when law or reason calls
for it. But in itself, as reaction it is arbitrary, blind, and
brute exertion of force. (7.532)

Generally speaking genuine secondness consists in one thing
acting upon another,—brute action. I say brute, because so
far as the idea of any *law* or *reason* comes in, Thirdness
comes in. When a stone falls to the ground, the law of
gravitation does not act to make it fall. The law of gravitation
is the judge upon the bench who may pronounce the law
until doomsday, but unless the strong arm of the law, the
brutal sheriff, gives effect to the law, it amounts to nothing.
True, the judge can create a sheriff if need be; but he must
have one. The stone's falling is purely the affair of the
stone and the earth at the time. (8.330)

The Court takes authoritative decisions; the sheriff carries them out.
The Court guides and directs; the sheriff does and acts. Together they
achieve order and maintain the peace; separated, the one is impotent,
the other brutal. Indeed neither Court nor sheriff are imaginable except in reference one to another and yet they and their activity ever
remain clearly distinct. So it is with efficient and final causation (cf.
1.213).[4]

---

[4] Every analogy limps. So does this one and Peirce of course knew it.
The weak point is this: a court must make practical judgments of conscience with the theoretical judgments of rationality. "Conscience is like our
Supreme Court, which intends to frame its decisions according to the principles of law. But when it has decided a point, its decision becomes law,
whether the wisest counsels would have maintained it or not. For the actual
law consists in that which the court's officers will sustain. But according to

To put the relation between final and efficient causality in another way, we might say that

Efficient causation is that kind of causation whereby the parts compose the whole; final causation is that kind of causation whereby the whole calls out its parts. (1.220)

Peirce gives this illustration. If you took a corpse and dissected it very carefully, separated all the various systems of the anatomy and hung them in a cabinet, one superimposed over the other, so that each appeared to be in its proper place, this would be a very instructive specimen, but nobody would dream of calling it a man (1.220). What is missing is the final causation, the unity of parts, "which is what characterizes the *definitum*" (1.220). Final causation is what organizes the parts in a particular way, what gives them life and direction. Final causation is more than the mere sum of the parts—merely putting back all the dissected members of the corpse does not yield the man, (nor the corpse for that matter!). Thus, while final causation without efficient causation is helpless,

Efficient causation without final causation . . . is worse than helpless, by far; it is mere chaos; and chaos is not even so much as chaos, without final causation; it is blank nothing. (1.220)

Thus an idea (a natural class) is a *vera causa,* a power conferring existence upon its instances, not in the sense that it creates new matter (for "blind force is an element of experience distinct from rationality, or logical force" 1.220) but in the sense that it confers upon the instances a direction, an intelligibility, a power of working out results in the world, an organic existence, life (1.220).

the English logicians it is otherwise with rationality" (2.153). For Peirce, then, making a practical decision has an element of the arbitrary about it which is out of place in theoretical inquiry. There is a "fiat" involved which enters into the legislation itself. Thus conscience must decide how we are to act here and now, granted all the limitations here and now of our knowledge of principle and of fact. It must say "yes" or "no"; it must decide and that decision is final. This sense of "law," the decision of conscience, is characterized chiefly by Secondness. This is not the same as "law of nature" since nature's laws do not depend upon our fiat; we discover them and submit to them; we do not make them. Cf. 1.55.

The doctrine that natural or "real" classes are constituted by their members all having the same final cause is closely connected with Peirce's conception of pragmatism. We saw that the pragmatic maxim is in the first instance a logical or semantical maxim. It tells us how to make our ideas clear. It is a way to get at meaning. But meaning is an idea's "intellectual purport" and intellectual purport has to do with "purpose," "intention," final cause. Thus the pragmatic maxim has to do with the normative—with what our ideas ought to mean (or perhaps more accurately, with how we ought to determine what they do mean). In this connection it is important to point out the connection Peirce sees between definition and the discovery of natural classes. The question is whether it is the definition which determines what the class shall be or whether something else (final cause) determines what the definition shall be. The first alternative is that taken by nominalists; according to it any one class is as "natural" or "real" as another, because every class has a defining character, and of course every member of that class must have that character. Furthermore, any collection of objects whatsoever has some characteristic in common, and so any collection of objects, no matter how heterogeneous, could be made members of a natural or real class. This position is the denial of real or natural classes altogether, since absolutely every class would be real or natural. Peirce adopts the second alternative: find the natural classes first through an investigation into their respective common final causes and *then* define them. The pragmatic maxim will aid in this sort of investigation by directing our attention to the sort of consequences that might conceivably result from an idea, and those *results* reveal its finality. Strictly speaking the maxim does not yield an abstract definition but "intellectual *purport.*"

> So then, a natural class being a family whose members are
> the sole offspring and vehicles of one idea, from which they
> derive their peculiar faculty, to classify by abstract definitions
> is simply a sure means of avoiding a natural classification.
> I am not decrying definitions. . . . I only say that it should
> not be by means of definitions that one should seek to find
> natural classes. When the classes have been found, then
> it is proper to try to define them; and one may even, with
> great caution and reserve, allow the definitions to lead us to

turn back and see whether our classes ought not to have
their boundaries differently drawn. After all, boundary lines
in some cases can only be artificial, although the classes were
natural. . . . When one can lay one's finger upon the purpose
to which a class owes its origin, then indeed abstract
definition may formulate that purpose. But when one cannot
do that, but one can trace the genesis of a class and ascertain
how several have been derived by different lines of descent
from one less specialized form, this is the best route toward
an understanding of what the natural classes are. This is
true even in biology; it is much more clearly so when the
objects generated are, like sciences, themselves of the
nature of ideas. (1.222)

Commentators[5] have pointed out that the pragmatic maxim so
understood is very similar to the scholastic maxim, *agere sequitur
esse*. This principle was understood to have a double thrust. As a
maxim of investigation it meant that the way to know what a thing is,
how it is structured, is to observe how it acts. The real potentialities
of a thing are manifested in its activity. On the basis of this principle
the scholastics, too, specified "real" or "natural" classes or "natures."
As an ontological theorem it meant that a thing can act only in accordance with its structure or nature. Its being specifies its activity.
Peirce's only objection to this principle is that the scholastics, due to
their limited logic, thought of the dispositional structure of a being in
terms of substantial forms instead of in terms of relations.[6]

The type of causation, therefore, exercised by laws as opposed to
"forces," is final and not efficient. But final causation is logical causation, the causation of mind (1.250).

Mind has its universal mode of action, namely, by final
causation. The microscopist looks to see whether the motions
of a little creature show any purpose. If so, there is mind
there. Passing from the little to the large, natural selection is
the theory of how forms come to be adaptive, that is, to
be governed by a *quasi* purpose. It suggests a machinery of

[5] E.g. Boler, *op. cit.*, p. 102.
[6] Cf. Gallie, *op. cit.*, pp. 124 ff.

efficiency to bring about the end—a machinery inadequate
perhaps—yet which must contribute some help toward
the result. But the being governed by a purpose or other final
cause is the very essence of the psychical phenomenon,
in general. (1.269)

Thus in the concluding paragraph of an undated fragment in which
Peirce was striving to classify ends, he writes:

... there have been three grand classes of rationalistic
moralists who have differed from one another upon the much
more important question of the mode of being of the end.
Namely, there have been those who have made the end
purely subjective, a feeling of pleasure; there have been those
who have made the end purely objective and material, the
multiplication of the race; and finally there have been *those
who have attributed to the end the same kind of being
that a law of nature has,* making it lie in the rationalization
of the universe. (1.590, emphasis added)

Peirce, of course, identifies himself with the last group, but what is of
immediate interest is that he identifies the nature of law with the
nature of end or final cause. Therefore, wherever there is law, regularity, real potentiality, there is mind, reason, rationality. And once
again, for Peirce, mind, reason, rationality, do not necessarily suppose
consciousness. So he can say that logic need not suppose that there is
consciousness (2.66). All it is obliged to suppose is that there is knowledge embodied in some form (a thought thought) and inference, in
the sense that one embodiment of knowledge affects another (2.66).
Under these conditions all its rules hold good. Thus

the essence of rationality lies in the fact that the rational
being *will* act so as to attain certain ends. Prevent his doing
so in one way, and he will act in some utterly different way
which will produce the same result. Rationality is being
governed by final causes. (2.66)

Indeed, for Peirce, since consciousness is in itself only a quality of
feeling, it has no room for rationality. And the notion that logic is in

any way concerned with it "is a fallacy closely allied to hedonism in ethics."[7]

True laws of nature, we have seen, belong to the category of Thirdness and as such are manifestations of the presence of mind or reason in the world of our experience. Laws are living ideas which have force and power to work themselves out in the cosmos. It is this conviction which as a matter of fact motivates men of science in their arduous research.[8] Peirce has explained that the type of causation proper to reason and law is final—that of a type or form or ideal— which, of course, to be effective needs some mechanism of efficient causation, and therefore the very being of law is to govern actual

[7] See the discussion of hedonism in Part I. The point of the comparison is this: just as it is a mistake to think that the feeling of pleasure or pain which accompanies some moral act constitutes that act's rightness or wrongness, so too it is a mistake to think that the awareness we have of an argument's validity or invalidity constitutes that validity or invalidity. The point is directed against those logicians who would make logic rest upon a feeling or instinct for what is sound and what is unsound reasoning. Of course, in another sense of "reasoning" Peirce will admit that control is an essential ingredient and that consciousness is required for such control. Cf. 2.148, 2.169 ff., 2.179 ff. for discussion of "expectation" in reasoning. Thus man is the "reasoner" *par excellence* since his power of critical review and of self-control is more highly developed than in any other animal we know. Cf. 5.85–87.

[8] "The man of science has received a deep impression of the majesty of truth, as that to which, sooner or later, every knee must bow. He has further found that his own mind is sufficiently akin to that truth, to enable him, on condition of submissive observation, to interpret it in some measure. As he gradually becomes better and better acquainted with the character of cosmical truth, and learns that human reason is its issue and can be brought step by step into accord with it, he conceives a passion for its fuller revelation. He is keenly aware of his own ignorance, and knows that personally he can make but small steps in discovery. Yet, small as they are, he deems them precious; and he hopes that by conscientiously pursuing the method of science he may erect a foundation upon which his successors may climb higher. This, for him, is what makes life worth living and what makes the human race worth perpetuation. The very being of law, general truth, reason—call it what you will—consists in its expressing itself in a cosmos and in intellects which reflect it, and in doing this progressively; and that which makes progressive creation worth doing—so the researcher comes to feel—is precisely the reason, the law, the general truth for the sake of which it takes place" (8.136).

events. The question now arises: just how, in detail, does this final causation work; how does it govern actual cases; how is it ingredient in events? Peirce faced this question in a brilliant essay, "Ideals of Conduct," read as part of the 1903 Lowell Lectures.

Directly, this paper examines only deliberate human action or conduct and so only analyzes one kind of final cause, the one "most familiar in our experience," human purpose. In particular, then, the question is how human purpose enters into human activity in such a way as to make it controlled or reasoned action. In virtue of the doctrine of continuity, however, Peirce will try to extend the results of his analysis to other levels of reality where mind or reason is embodied in other forms. Peirce was aware that this sort of analysis is open to the criticism of being anthropomorphic. He knew that objectors would allege that he was reading things into the data which are proper only to his own experience as a man. Peirce considers this objection explicitly in several places. He says that to say an hypothesis is unscientific because it is "anthropomorphic" is an objection "of a very shallow kind, that arises from prejudices based upon much too narrow considerations" (5.47). In fact, he maintains, almost all human conceptions are at bottom anthropomorphic. What else would we or could we expect them to be? All man's knowledge is based upon his experience. How else could he elaborate a theory or an hypothesis except in those terms? There is no way for man to peek outside of his own experiencing-apparatus to get a look at "things-in-themselves."

> I hold . . . that man is so completely hemmed in by the
> bounds of his possible practical experience, his mind is so
> restricted to being the instrument of his needs, that he
> cannot, in the least, *mean* anything that transcends those
> limits. (5.536)

The limits of his possible practical experience insure that all his conceptions will be "anthropomorphic" in some sense. As he says, one might just as well pass a law forbidding man to jump over the moon. Such a law, however, would not prevent him from jumping as high as he could. So too man cannot have an idea of any cause or agency so stupendous that there would be any more adequate way of conceiving it than as vaguely like a man. Furthermore, Peirce recalls that the only satisfactory explanation of man's ability to form any hypothesis and so make any scientific discovery is man's affinity to the universe.

> And in regard to any preference for one kind of theory over another, it is well to remember that every single truth of science is due to the affinity of the human soul to the soul of the universe, imperfect as that affinity no doubt is. To say, therefore, that a conception is one natural to man, which comes to just about the same thing as to say that it is anthropomorphic, is as high a recommendation as one could give to it in the eyes of an Exact Logician. (5.47)

Let us, then, begin with what might be called the prime analogue of mind's embodiments, conscious human reason, governing, controlling, and guiding conduct.

Peirce begins his analysis with the matter-of-fact claim that all men have some idea about the sort of conduct which befits a rational animal in his particular circumstances. Men have some vague notion at least of "what most accords with his total nature and relations" (1.591). *Natura humana complete spectata,* as the scholastics following Aristotle would say, is for Peirce too in some sense the material norm of human conduct. Again, by inductive generalization, Peirce remarks that the ideals of conduct culled from this sort of reflection upon one's nature and condition usually and rightly recommend themselves in three ways: (1) they have a certain esthetic quality about them, a certain fittingness and proportion, which makes us judge them "fine"; (2) they must be consistent with each other; and (3) they must be seen to lead to consequences which, if fully carried out, are desirable (1.591). Ideals of conduct, then, must submit to a triple criterion: esthetic, logical, and pragmatic. Failure to live up to any of them indicates that the ideals do not in fact conform to man's total nature and relations.

These ideals, final causes, laws of conduct, however, are not innate ideas[9] nor intuitions nor even, in the beginning anyway, conclusions based on experience. In the beginning they are learned from parents

---

[9] They are not innate in respect to their particular content, although, as we shall see, there are innate cognitive powers or potentialities which must be informed and developed by habits acquired through experience. In other words, what is innate is a structure or natural disposition to take habits and, in conscious beings, to control those taken. Cf. 5.504.

or guardians. As the child develops his own personality, through grow-ing awareness of himself and his environment, he gradually begins to interiorize these ideals, to make them his own and to shape them to his own situation. In other words, he begins to reflect upon the ideals he has learned and to *intend* to conform his conduct to at least part of them. He makes this intention articulate and explicit by formulating *rules of conduct*. Since his reflection is not external to himself but rather the exercise of his natural powers and dispositions, that activity has in turn an effect upon his dispositions. They are modified and moulded by the ideals upon which he reflects. In the course of these reflections he will consider possible future situations in which he will have to act and in which he ought to act in accordance with the dis-position such as it has been formed in him through his reflections. Thus he gathers his inner forces and *resolves* so to act when the occa-sion arises. He makes his plan. Still, resolve, in this sense of a plan, is not enough in itself to assure that he will as a matter of fact act upon it. He has to work the resolve into his muscles, as it were. He has to convert it *into determination* or real efficient agency "such that if one knows what its special character is, one can forecast the man's conduct on the special occasion" (1.592). Thus the ideal of conduct through reflection is made into a real power or potentiality which could be the ground for prediction. It has become the "would-be" which is the basis for a "will-be." The ideal has become a law of con-duct. And we readily recognize Peirce's psychological description as that of what we ordinarily call a *habit*.

Peirce admits that we do not know with certitude what the ma-chinery is which converts resolution into determination (1.593). It is "something hidden in the depths of our nature." Peirce is interested for the moment only in a phenomenological analysis of what does happen. He adds that while we are conscious of forming our habits, later we are not necessarily aware of them. One of the ways in which we ordinarily recognize them on the appropriate occasion is by a feel-ing of need or desire. Peirce offers the following case as illustrative of the process he has been describing. Upon reflection I decide that I should talk to a certain person in a certain way. I plan or resolve to do so when I meet him. And to be sure that I will not be carried away in the heat of conversation I impress the resolution upon my mind so that when I do get into animated conversation with this person, although my mind is completely occupied with the topic of conversation and I never advert to my resolution, still it influences my conduct (1.594). After I have left my friend, I begin reviewing what transpired and ask myself whether I lived up to my resolution. If the answer is affirmative, I am in the very formulation of the answer aware of a feeling of satisfaction (1.596).

In his illustration Peirce introduces the notion of *critical review* of conduct. It is this review which allows for control of conduct in the future in terms of ideals. Conformity produces satisfaction and consequently a pleasurable feeling; disconformity produces dissatisfaction and a painful feeling which indicates that our resolve is not yet fully a determination and this may lead us to resolve again, thus strengthening the determination.

This sort of process, Peirce proceeds to say, can be brought to bear on the question of whether my conduct conforms to my *general* as well as to my particular intentions. It can be applied still further to the question of the conformity of my conduct to the most general ideal of conduct befitting a man like me.

> In any and all these ways a man may criticize his own
> conduct; and it is essential to remark that it is not mere idle
> praise or blame such as writers who are not of the wisest
> often distribute among the personages of history. No indeed!
> It is approval or disapproval of the only respectable kind,
> that which will bear fruit in the future. Whether the man
> is satisfied with himself or dissatisfied, his nature will absorb
> the lesson like a sponge; and the next time he will tend
> to do better than he did before. (1.598)

A man must frequently review his ideals; he must criticize them; he must control them. The job is never done once and for all time, because experience is continually contributing more cases, more situations, which throw more or less light on those ideals. According to Peirce the new data of experience are first digested in the depths of man's reasonable being and then brought to consciousness. "But meditation seems to agitate a mass of tendencies and allow them more quickly to settle down so as to be really more conformed to what is fit for the man" (1.599).

All these cases are practical. They deal with a man's review of his conduct and ideals with a view to improvement. Peirce now points out that critical reflection can also be brought to bear on the theoretical question concerning in what the *fitness* of an ideal of conduct consists, and from that deduce what conduct ought to be. His concern is to remark once more that such theoretical inquiry is quite distinct from the practical business of forming conduct, while at the same time he admits that if one does not lose sight of the difference, such theoretical study "is more or less favorable to right living" (1.600).[10] Peirce, then, admits a certain interplay between practical affairs and theoretical reasoning, but he is careful to offer a warning based on theoretical grounds and advice based on practical experience: do not rashly and precipitously abandon practical maxims and rules of conduct gleaned from ages of experience because some theoretical consideration or speculation casts a shadow of a doubt thereon, precisely because reason is notoriously fallible and so very slow to accept new principles as indubitable (2.177). Patience and prudence are the watchwords in translating the theoretical opinions into everyday rules of thumb. The theoretical search for truth must ever be pressed forward if man is to be true to his nature, but experience and nature are the final teachers

[10] See Part I of this book for a discussion of theoretical and practical science. Peirce was forever pointing out the advisability of following instinct and traditional *mores* in practical issues of moral conduct. He thought of reasoning—theoretical reasoning—as very unreliable in these matters and instinct as practically infallible. And he thought that there was theoretical evidence for this position. His thoughts come through in a striking way in the ironic and satirical papers, "Detached Ideas on Vitally Important Topics." He told his Harvard audience that if by vitally important topics they understood matters of everyday moral decisions, how to succeed in business, or practical matters in general, they would be better off not to get involved in logic and philosophy. They just had to follow common sense and the accumulated wisdom of the ages. But these "vitally important topics" are not for Peirce so "vitally important." The most important, because specifically human, enterprise is the search for truth. And this can only be accomplished by reasoning and by engaging in theoretical investigation. To be sure, progress is halting and conclusions are fallible, but success is assured if men as a community persevere. Being a part of the community of researchers is what sets man off from the beast and what makes life worth living. That is why in another essay he could say that we are *fortunate* not to be tied to the infallible instincts of the animal kingdom. (See 2.178.)

and correctors of theory. Gamaliel once told the Sanhedrin that if this work was not of God it would pass away, while if it was, nothing they could do would destroy it (Acts 5, 34–37). This is much like Peirce's attitude toward practical principles of action. If they are true, theory will not change them; if they are false, experience will sooner or later destroy them. Man's search for truth according to the canons of right reason and in the spirit of humility can be, and indeed is, one of Nature's most powerful means of making the truth appear because right reason requires respect for facts of experience and at the same time is itself a fact of experience which must be taken into account.

Thus Peirce has described what he takes to be the phenomenon of controlled action. He has found in man at least five grades of self-control which he listed in another place as follows: (1) inhibitions and coordinations that entirely escape consciousness; (2) instinctive modes of self-control; (3) self-control which results from training; (4) the power to control self-control (as when one becomes his own training master) in terms of some moral rule; (5) the power to control one's control of control, that is, when one undertakes to improve his rules of conduct through a study of the normative sciences (5.533). Peirce, then, has tried to show how human purposes are both normative and capable of modification by critical review. Human purpose, the archetype of final causes, involves habits acquired and/or modified by reflection on experience. It is this capacity for critical review and control of actions and of habits of action which for Peirce defines reason. It is this capacity which defines man as a rational animal and therefore, while it supposes freedom on man's part, freedom of choice, man is not free to accept or reject his nature and its freedom. Man is a rational animal whether he likes it or not; he has a final cause which even his perversity cannot completely frustrate; he is compelled to make his life more reasonable and in this lies his true dignity and liberty (1.602).

Thus Peirce discovers that man himself belongs to a natural or real class quite independent of his own doing or willing or wishing. While specific human purposes are subject to man's control and so to his will, the purpose of his purposes, the final cause or end of man, is found not to be subject to control in the same sense. Man cannot completely vote himself out of the human race, because even the most drastic step of suicide would be a deliberate choice and so paradoxically reaffirm that man is man unto the end. The only sort of control to which man's end is subjected in the hands of man himself is the extent to which it is fulfilled and developed in individual cases. Thus while human purposes are the "most familiar in our experience" and therefore the most easily analyzed, they are not the most basic final causes even for man. Even though man is in a process of evolution, rather *because* man is in a process of evolution, he cannot abandon the deep-seated drive toward more and more rational behavior. That would be to turn back the clock; it would be the end of his evolution or growth; it would be devolution or decay. Man's destiny in this process of growth is to contribute more and more by his own decisions and choices to the process itself.

Out of these considerations we are able to draw a distinction between acquired habit and natural disposition often overlooked by the commentators and yet one which throws considerable light on Peirce's doctrine. It is true that Peirce sometimes uses the word "habit" to cover both what is congenital and what is acquired (5.367, 2.711), but when he does so it is with full knowledge that strictly speaking habits are only acquired (5.538). Furthermore, at least once he explicitly warns his reader that he is about to use habit in a loose sense to cover any sort of disposition at all. What is important to notice is that for Peirce, while a given individual man can and does control his acquired habits he cannot control his natural disposition (his "nature," what he came into the world with, what he is), at least not in the same sense.[11] It may be indeed that his nature is a habit or bundle of habits of something else—Nature, matter, mind or what have you—and Peirce sometimes talks this way (1.416). As we shall have occasion to see, his evolutionary theory of the emergence of conscious human mind from nature is in terms of habit-taking and grouping of habits.

Man, then, finds himself in the world with the power to reason, and the power to reason is none other than the power to submit actions, purposes, and ideals to critical review and control. Reasoning, then, is a type of moral or ethical conduct. If it is not subjected to any check or control, it is not deliberately approved and so is not reasoning. All deliberate conduct is conduct according to a rule, norm, or

[11] Is Peirce here groping toward a notion of "substance," a principle of unity for the "habits"? See Boler, *op. cit.*, pp. 160–165, for a criticism of Peirce for holding a realism without substance.

general pattern of what is appropriate under the circumstances. These rules, norms or general patterns are habits, that is, acquired dispositions to act in a certain way rather than in another. These habits are themselves capable of critical review and control. This type of examination is what is undertaken in the normative sciences. Thus, if we ask in what does right reasoning consist, what habits of reasoning ought we to follow and to develop, the answer is that right reasoning consists in such reasoning as is conducive to our ultimate aim. What is or ought to be our ultimate aim? It cannot be something narrow or selfish. It must be the highest, broadest and most general possible aim; it must be something admirable in itself (1.611). We recognize the hierarchy of logic, ethics, and esthetics—sciences which investigate, respectively, what habits of thought, of conduct, and of feeling man ought to deliberately cultivate in order to fulfill himself.[12]

Laws of nature, therefore, are in Peirce's view founded upon real active powers or potentialities in things. The type of causality proper to "would-be's" is final, that is, specifying *kinds* of activity, specifying *kinds* of objects by imparting such a unity to the whole that the whole

[12] In the following paragraphs (1.612–1.614) Peirce is careful to reject any semblance of hedonism. In Peirce's hierarchical arrangement of the normative sciences, aesthetics turns out to be what commands the rest and what is least satisfactorily developed. Not only is Peirce's elaboration slight, but also appears to be confused and inconsistent. On the one hand, he seems to assimilate aesthetics to questions of taste, to feeling, to the subjective. And on the other hand, he rejects mere qualities of feeling as admirable in themselves without any reason and at least once talks of an intellectual side to aesthetic appreciation. The difficulties can be met satisfactorily, we believe, if we keep in mind that (1) Peirce's final opinion about aesthetics was that it dealt with the formation of right *habits* of feeling and not with qualities of feeling, and (2) Peirce's categories can never be separated or found in their isolated purity anywhere in experience. The *summum bonum* itself, therefore, could not be just a pure Firstness, at least not insofar as it is operative in our world of experience. Again a habit of feeling is a Thirdness while a quality of feeling, in itself and unreflected upon, is a Firstness. The error of the hedonist is to confound the admirable in itself with the perfectly self-satisfied, the stationary, the self-contained. Peirce, in other words, challenges the contention that the admirable in itself must be pure Firstness. His counterproposal is to make it consist in the concrete growth of reasonableness—an evolutionary process of growth which needs all the categories to be understood but which is identified absolutely with no one of them (1.615).

calls out its parts. Final causality is the causality of norms, rules, or general patterns in terms of which deviations are recognized and thought to be not only exceptions but also in some sense aberrations. The most familiar and therefore most readily analyzed sort of final causality is that exercised by human beings in their purposive, deliberate conduct. Upon analysis it becomes clear that human purposes are, or at least ultimately involve, developed habits—developed within the context of man's natural dispositions or nature—which allow man to criticize and control his activity and which themselves are subject to review and modification in terms of other habits and of experience. The critical review and control of habits is the object studied by the normative sciences. When, therefore, man is called a rational animal, it means that he is capable of consciously taking habits, and this itself is a habit (not precisely *of* man, since rather it defines him, but of *nature* in whatever that may be found ultimately to consist).

The similarity between the role which habit plays in Peirce's scheme and the role of form in Aristotle's is too striking to go unmentioned (cf. 6.347, for Peirce's study of "matter" and "form" in Aristotle and in Kant). Of course for Aristotle form has a variety of meanings. It can be the sensible shape (*morphé*) of a material object, the intelligible structure (*eidos*) of a thing expressed in a definition, or the final cause. The latter two meanings will concern us here. In effect Aristotle took Plato's transcendent forms and made them completely immanent. The Aristotelian form functions like the Platonic in that it accounts for the intelligibility of the object informed, arms it with power to act, and guides that activity along certain lines rather than along others. Thus for Aristotle a thing's nature is the norm for its activity. Form puts finality into the object and allows that finality to be truly active. A final cause which remained in every sense extrinsic to an object could not produce any effect at all on the object. At best it might be a *terminus de facto* reached. Briefly, for Aristotle formal and final cause in natural objects tend to become identified. But this formal-final cause is also evident in the principle by which an agent acts as an efficient cause since it is what sets the agent to work and is the source of its activity. It is what the scholastics called *causa causae*.[13] Peirce's "habit" plays just the same roles. He undoubtedly

13 *An. Post.* 71 b9–12, 94 a20; *Phys.* 184 a10–14; *De Coelo*, 311

preferred "habit" to "form" because the latter was too static a notion. Habit was much more flexible and allowed for changes, modifications, growth and development, and at the same time preserved the important Aristotelian insight into real potencies or powers in things.

In order to generalize the results of his analysis of human conduct, Peirce must show that consciousness does not always entail the power of self-control. Although Peirce holds that there can be no self-control without consciousness he is not committed to the proposition that all consciousnesses exercise self-control. To appreciate this point a scholastic distinction may help, namely, that between *conscientia directa* and *conscientia reflexiva*. For self-control, reflexive consciousness is *required*, and of course that sort of consciousness supposes direct consciousness. The distinction between first and second intentions is based on this distinction of types of consciousness. The exercise of self-control supposes some sort of reflexive consciousness over and above direct consciousness.

We have seen that Peirce's analysis of man revealed that there are some elements of his mind over which he has control and others over which he has none, but which are nevertheless necessary for the control which he does exercise.

> Our logically controlled thoughts compose a small part of the mind, the mere blossom of a vast complexus, which we may call the instinctive mind, in which this man will not say that he has *faith*, because that implies the conceivability of distrust, but upon which he builds as the very fact to which it is the whole business of his logic to be true. (5.212)

One of the mind's elements over which man has no control is the perceptual judgment, and yet it is through such judgment that he has experience of and contact with his environment. It is through the perceptual judgment that he has data to think about. One of Peirce's most imaginative formulations of the pragmatic maxim incorporates this very idea:

> The elements of every concept enter into logical thought at the gate of perception and make their exit at the gate of

a1–6; i.e. *Meta.*, Book Z, *passim*. Cf. D. Ross, *Aristotle* (New York: Barnes & Noble, University Paperbacks, 1964), pp. 71–75; 172–173.

purposive action; and whatever cannot show its passports
at both those two gates is to be arrested as unauthorized
by reason. (5.212)[14]

This "instinctive mind" through which every concept enters into logical thought Peirce elsewhere calls "Insight . . . into the Thirdnesses,
the general elements, of Nature." Again he refers to it as a "faculty"
which man must have because otherwise there would be no accounting for his undeniable ability to guess right among the millions of
possible hypotheses which might explain a fact often enough to allow
him to make genuine discoveries (5.171 ff.). Man, in other words,
manifests an affinity to nature—he is in it, is part of it, and finally it
is this affinity which gives him "il lume naturale" for choosing appropriate hypotheses at all (cf. e.g. 1.80, 2.750, 5.47, 5.603–604, 6.10).
Instinctive mind, then, is part of the natural disposition with which
man comes into the world, and must ultimately be constituted of "in
posse innate cognitive habits, which is all that anybody but John
Locke ever meant by innate ideas" (5.504).

Peirce finds that the gamut of self-control in man (from control
of one's control of control down to no control) is reflected in the
higher forms of animal life lower than man, with the exception, of
course, of that highest type of control which distinguishes man from
the brute.

The brutes are certainly capable of more than one grade
of control; but it seems to me that our superiority to them is
more due to our greater number of grades of self-control
than it is to our versatility. (5.533)

The brutes, for example, use some sort of language (a phenomenon
of self-control) and seem to exercise some little control over it (5.534).
They are, of course, conscious beings, and the grade of their consciousness is judged precisely by the sort of self-control they manifest.
For Peirce, what sets man apart from even the highest brute is the
power to criticize his thought logically—the power to think about

---

[14] When Peirce claimed that pragmatism is only a step in synechism
(5.4), he was thinking of the latter as a generalization of the elements of
mind or reason discovered in the analysis of reasoning which yielded his
famous maxim.

thought. One form of this distinctive feature of man's consciousness is the power of hypostatic abstraction. The brutes do not show any tendency toward activities which require this sort of reflection (for example, they are not engaged in mathematical research or in the logic of mathematics) (5.534). The same sort of reasoning which led to the affirmation of uncontrolled elements in the human mind would lead to the same conclusion in the case of the mind of brutes.

Clearly for Peirce man is directly aware of at least some of those uncontrolled elements. For example, man is directly aware of his perceptual judgments, even though he is not conscious of the psychological and physiological processes involved. In so far as the brute too must have some kind of perceptual judgment (*vis aestimativa,* in scholastic terminology), the same holds for him. This consciousness of elements over which no control can be exercised is direct, not reflexive. Besides, Peirce argues for three degrees of consciousness: (1) consciousness of feeling, (2) consciousness of an interruption of consciousness, and (3) consciousness of learning (1.377–382). The first two degrees are certainly beyond the control of those beings which have them. Even the third type, consciousness of learning, might be in certain cases simply the result of random reinforcement of reflex responses to external stimuli, and be, therefore, only direct and not reflexive consciousness. Indeed Peirce proposes as an hypothesis that the physiological basis of any sort of consciousness is tied up with the activity of nerve cells discharging over different possible paths at random and slowly taking on an habitual response, that is, manifesting a tendency to reinforce that response which removed the stimulus (1.390 and 6.259 ff.). In the case of a frog whose brain has been removed and yet whose leg muscles respond to stimulation (say, by a drop of acid), there is some feeling or awareness of the stimulus, and so some sort of consciousness present. But the random kicking and rubbing of the leg does not show control over the movements, but rather that the movements are controlled by the stimulus. The "learning" that takes place is merely a conditioning of the reflex response by "reward" (removal of stimulation). Peirce goes even further and proposes that these properties of the nervous system (to feel, to discharge, to "learn") are rooted in the very stuff out of which all living tissue is made, protoplasm. He suggests that all the properties of protoplasm can be grouped under the headings sensibility, motion, and growth (again corresponding to his three categories) and that this "life-slime" is in some sense "aware" of its environment and that it acquires habits (e.g., in regard to its feeding) (1.393 ff., and 6.246 ff., 6.278 ff.).

Not every conscious being, therefore, is capable of self-control, although every being which is capable of self-control is necessarily conscious.[15] Indeed, in terms of a doctrine of continuity and evolution Peirce must say that self-control developed out of a more rudimentary form of consciousness in which the power of self-control was present only *virtually*. And now that Peirce has succeeded in generalizing the role of habit in giving direction to all living beings from man to cells, he proceeds to extend the notion still further to include what the man in the street calls "nonliving" beings. Again, Peirce's commitment to continuity does not allow him to admit a sharp line of demarcation between "living" and "nonliving," between "mind" and "matter." The fact that Peirce thought of his system as an objective idealism indicates what direction his analysis must take. Perhaps his remarks about the classification of the sciences will help us to see the point. Peirce classified the special sciences under two general headings, physical and psychical, the former dealing with the workings of efficient causation, the latter with the working of final causation (1.242). Just as efficient and final causation cannot be separated, so physical and psychical sciences are interdependent to some slight degree at least (1.252 ff.) and both are dependent upon philosophy (1.249–250). Philosophy, however, cannot be divided into an efficient and final wing. "For . . . to philosophy must fall the task of comparing the

---

[15] Peirce tells us in one place that man lives in two worlds, an inner and an outer, and that these worlds are bridged by his acquired habits and his natural dispositions (5.487). He defines consciousness in general as a congeries of nonrelative predicates (feelings), symptomatic of the interaction of the outer world and of the inner world, and amenable to direct effort of various kinds with feeble reactions. The outer world seems to act directly on the inner, while the inner only indirectly, through habits, on the outer. Thus consciousness is necessary for self-control since without it or at least without that of which it is symptomatic, "the resolves and exercises of the inner world could not affect the real determinations and habits of the outer world" (5.493). Peirce's "inner" and "outer" worlds bear a remarkable similarity to Teilhard de Chardin's "within" and "without."

two stems of causation and of exhuming their common root" (1.273). Given a choice between Cartesian dualism and some variety of monism, philosophy must adopt the latter. Peirce sees three possible directions in which monism can be developed: (1) *neutralism*, which would take physical and psychical laws as independent of each other and stemming from some third *Urstoff*, (2) *materialism*, which would take the psychical laws as derived from the physical, and (3) *idealism*, which would take the physical laws as derived from the psychical. Peirce disposes of neutralism by Ockham's razor and of materialism by the first principle of scientific logic, that is, do not resort to the ultimate and inexplicable as an explanation (6.24). Objective idealism is the only rational alternative: matter is effete mind.

Leaving aside for the moment Peirce's objections to materialistic monism which he identifies with the absolute determinism of mechanistic philosophies, let us consider the strategy of argumentation dictated by the espousal of objective idealism. If matter is effete mind, and if physical laws are derived from psychical, the great law of the universe is that of mind. What is the law of mind?

> Logical analysis applied to mental phenomena [for example, the analysis in "Ideals of Conduct"] shows that there is but one law of mind, namely, that ideas tend to spread continuously and to affect certain others which stand to them in a peculiar relation of affectability. In this spreading they lose intensity, and especially the power of affecting others, but gain generality and become welded with other ideas. (6.104)[16]

This is recognizable as the tendency to generalize and to form associations (6.21). This tendency is nothing other than the tendency to form habits, itself a habit (6.612). Yet a habit, as a tendency to generalize, cannot become wooden and fixed without ceasing to be a habit. The generalizing of habit only makes it more likely that something will react in one way rather than in another because it has already so reacted (6.148, 13.90 ff., 1.409). As Peirce remarks, did habits establish an absolute necessity,

16 See 6.102–163 for a lengthy development of the law of mind.

> . . . habits would become wooden and ineradicable and, no
> room being left for the formation of new habits, intellectual
> life would come to a speedy close. (6.148)

In other words, the law of mind would destroy itself. The uncertainty of its action, therefore, is no defect in this law but rather its very essence. Mind is not subject to law in the absolute sense of the determinists, nor indeed is matter. Mind only experiences "gentle forces" which make it more likely to act one way rather than in another. And now we come to the key sentence: "There always remains a certain amount of arbitrary *spontaneity* in its action, *without which it would be dead*" (6.148, emphasis added). The action of mind, then, requires spontaneity, and spontaneity is characteristic of life.

The relationship between law, evolution, and chance[17] in Peirce's cosmology is beginning to take definite shape. We will discuss this in detail later on, but for the moment we want to see how these considerations enter into Peirce's extension of habit down to the world of physics and chemistry, down to the world of "physical laws." The strategy of the move is clear enough. Peirce must claim that even atoms manifest a certain spontaneity in their activity and are not, therefore, contrary to the unsophisticated judgment of the man in the street, completely dead. To accomplish that, Peirce must show that no laws of nature whatsoever are completely exact and unvariable, not merely in the sense that our expression of those laws is inexact nor merely that there are errors in observation, but that the observed objects themselves do not conform precisely to the general ideal governing them. In turn, this will require an analysis of the laws of conservative and nonconservative action.

Peirce is explicit in siding with the ancient atomists who made the atoms swerve as they whirled in the void (6.36, 6.201). Atoms are not completely dead. By swerving they manifest a certain spontaneity, "immanent action" in scholastic terms, and in so doing reveal themselves as conscious in some rudimentary way.[18] Consciousness, for

---

[17] See 6.201, "chance" is a mathematical term for "spontaneity."

[18] Peirce seems to imply that any activity subject to any law of reason whatsoever, even only the law of statistics in the case of the chance swerving of atoms, is really a sort of *conduct*, and so ultimately subject to control. To the control of what or whom? Who or What is the Objective Mind? In

Peirce, is, we have seen, in the category of Firstness. So is spontaneity. Peirce feels he can conclude, therefore, that

> . . . whatever is First is *ipso facto* sentient. If I make atoms swerve—as I do—I make them swerve but very very little, because I conceive they are not absolutely dead. And by that I do not mean exactly that I hold them to be physically such as the materialists hold them to be, only with a small dose of sentiency superadded. For that, I grant, would be feeble enough. But what I mean is, that all that there is, is First, Feelings; Second, Efforts; Third, Habits—all of which are more familiar to us on their psychical side than on their physical side; and that dead matter would be merely the final result of the complete induration of habit reducing the free play of feeling and the brute irrationality of effort to complete death. (6.201)

Thus by introducing spontaneity, chance, rudimentary consciousness into the physical world, Peirce feels that he can break the vise-like grip of mechanism which not only does not explain any of the phenomena but so chokes the life out of everything that any movement at all, even purely "mechanical" would be impossible. What Peirce is getting at is that there is no such thing as purely mechanical movement. All movement requires some degree of spontaneity, and indeed, paradoxically, so does the observed regularity of the movement. As Peirce himself puts it,

> I make use of chance chiefly to make room for a principle of generalization, or tendency to form habits, which I hold has produced all regularities. The mechanical philosopher leaves the whole specification of the world utterly unaccounted for, which is pretty nearly as bad as to baldly attribute it to chance. I attribute it altogether to chance, it is true, but to chance in the form of spontaneity which is in some degree regular. [That is, governed by laws of probability.] (6.63)[19]

places, Peirce seems to tend toward identifying it with God and in other places seems to consider the question unnecessary.

[19] ". . . the *existence* of absolute chance, as well as many of its charac-

To put it in another way, for Peirce there is no physical without the psychical, just as there is no pure efficient causation without final. While spontaneity, chance, or rudimentary consciousness is not identical with mind or reason and its fundamental law of habit-taking, it breaks the bonds of pure efficient causation and allows Mind and its law entrance, making the physical intelligible.[20]

Peirce centers his analysis of physical laws on the question of causation. He is considering the relation between efficient and final cause, which we discussed above, from another side. There are, he tells us, many examples of "empirical laws" in books on physics which, although they are satisfied by observation of the facts under limited circumstances, do not "go down to the roots of existence" exhibiting the general form of all phenomena (7.468). The law of centrifugal force is a good example. It applies to the force exerted on railroad tracks by the wheels of a train negotiating a curve. The force is real and it even leaves its mark on the tracks and on the wheels. But what happens when the formula for centrifugal force is extended to cases where the motion in question is not restrained and guided by something rigid like railroad tracks? What happens when it is applied to the revolution of the planets?

In this case, centrifugal force is a mere formula,—a formula

---

ters, are not themselves absolute chances, or sporadic events, unsubject to general law. On the contrary, these things *are* general laws. Everybody is familiar with the fact that chance has laws, and that statistical results follow therefrom. Very well: I do not propose to explain anything as due to the action of chance, that is, as being lawless. I do not countenance the idea that Bible stories, for instance, show that nature's laws were violated; though they may help to show that nature's laws are not so mechanical as we are accustomed to think. But I only propose to explain the regularities of nature as consequences of the only uniformity, or general fact, there was in the chaos, namely, the general absence of any determinate law. In fact, after the first step is taken, I only use *chance* to give room for the development of law by means of the law of habits" (6.606, rejoinder to Dr. Carus).

[20] As has been pointed out elsewhere, in virtue of the general doctrine of the categories, consciousness and habit are distinct as Firstness and Thirdness. In many passages Peirce makes the point even more explicitly: a general idea is the *mark* of a habit (7.498); consciousness of a habit constitutes a general idea (6.21); habits themselves are unconscious, but feelings are symptomatic of their presence (5.492); etc.

which is undoubtedly quite correct as far as the effect
goes, while yet the centrifugal force is a merely formal
affair with nothing at all corresponding to it in nature. (7.468)

Peirce likens this sort of extension to a bookkeeping fiction.[21]

It is very much as if between two men, A and B, there had
been a single transaction consisting in A lending B $5. Now
if B were to keep his books in such a manner that the state
of the account as entered on those books made A owe
him $100 with $105 on the opposite side of the account, the
entries would in effect be correct; but yet that hundred
dollars would be a fiction of book-keeping. In like manner
the centrifugal force of a planet is a fiction due to using
polar coordinates in place of rectangular coordinates. (7.468)

Certainly, if the sun's gravitation were suddenly destroyed, "there
would be at the first instant an acceleration of the plant away from
the circular orbit equal to the centrifugal force," but, Peirce argues,
this acceleration away from the circular orbit is simply the entry we
have to make on one side of our accounts to balance the first fictitious
entry we virtually made on the other side by taking the planet's circular motion as the standard from which to reckon accelerations
(7.468).[22] The question Peirce wishes to raise, therefore, is whether

[21] The technique of "balancing the books" is now called by physicists
"renormalization." It consists in certain adjustments that must be made
between theoretical computation and observation. Fermi used precisely the
analogy of bookkeeping.

[22] The concept of centrifugal force comes from such phenomena as
wheels following a curved track or the motion of a sling whirled in the air.
Once we generalize the idea in such a way that we remove the string which
keeps the object in a circular path or the rigid track forcing the wheels to
turn, we have a mathematical formula only, useful perhaps for explaining
the phenomena but no longer a "real force" or real entity. Peirce was not
alone in realizing this. Indeed, as Max Jammer has shown, physicists were
already well on their way to making the notion of force as applied to gravitation operational, and were inclined to jettison the notion that force is some
sort of entity in its own right. See Concepts of Force (New York: Harper
Torchbooks, 1962), Ch. 10 and 11, pp. 188–240. Peirce would be willing
to go along with this interpretation within physics, but would not be willing
to admit there are no forces at work in the cosmos with which philosophy

or not there is any way to tell that any "empirical law" is not just a bookkeeping fiction but a "real and a living action in nature" (7.469). Peirce realizes that nominalistic logicians will not admit any such distinction in virtue of their "preconceived metaphysical opinions" and that "of absolute knowledge there can be no question" (7.469). What he is after is the hypothesis sanctioned by synechism—the hypothesis which does not block the road to inquiry.

Peirce immediately formulates his hypothesis, and it is not hard to recognize the notion of habit therein implied.

> But if we see that as soon as circumstances are somewhat varied, the form of the law is lost, the inference would seem to be that it is not a universal or living mode of action. If on the other hand, we find that as soon as the form is prevented from manifestation in one shape it immediately reappears in another shape, and especially if it shows a power of spreading and of reproducing itself, these phenomena may be considered as evidence of genuine vitality and fundamental reality in the form of the law. (7.469)[23]

What he intends to prove is that causation, as distinct from the action of conservative force, "is a real, fundamental, and vital element both in the outer and in the inner world" (7.469). In another place Peirce

must reckon. One of his main theses is precisely that potentialities are real and living forces in nature.

[23] Here Peirce seems to be groping toward a formulation of the second basic principle of special relativity theory: the covariance of basic physical laws. (See A. Einstein and L. Infeld, *The Evolution of Physics* [New York: Simon and Schuster, 1961], pp. 177–178.) Of course, he never put it quite that way since he was not dealing with exactly the same sort of problems as Einstein. This is not surprising when we remember that relativity was in the air about this time. Physicists were beginning to run into problems which Newtonian space, time and laws of motion could not handle satisfactorily. The time was fast becoming ripe for a fresh look at the whole structure of that science. As early as 1904 Poincaré formulated a theory of relativity very much like Einstein's. (See Sir Edmund Whittake, *A History of the Theories of Aether and Electricity* [New York: Harper Torchbooks, 1960], pp. 30 ff.) Peirce knew of these developments and could not have been surprised when, in 1905, Einstein's paper amplifying and modifying the relativity theory of Poincaré and Lorentz appeared.

examines just what is meant by the principle of causation and finds that it means many different things to different people at different times (6.66). For the sake of the argument, however, he assumes that the principle involves three propositions to which most thinkers of his day would subscribe, namely, (1) that the state of things at any one instant is completely and exactly determined by the state of things at *one* other instant; (2) the cause, or determining state of things, precedes the effect or determined state of things in time; and (3) no fact determines a fact preceding it in time in the same sense in which it determines a fact following it in time (6.68). Although Peirce himself does not admit the absolute determinism implied in this formulation, it will serve his purposes, namely, to show that all three of these propositions are in flat contradiction to the laws of mechanics, and that causation is not reducible to any such law even though it has its origin in the very same thing as those laws. If the laws of dynamics contradict the principle of causation in its most deterministic form, it follows that a determinist cannot appeal to those laws to support his metaphysical position. If, on the other hand, causation in some sense of the term can be shown to be different from conservative force and irreducible to it, there is then room for end-directed activity even in the physical world.[24] If, finally, both conservative action and nonconservative action (causation) can be shown to arise from a common root, it follows that neither alone provides a satisfactory understanding of the universe.

There is no point in examining the details of how Peirce shows that the laws of dynamics contradict the three propositions belonging to the mechanistic version of the principle of causation cited above (cf. 6.68–69). Let us simply point out that since, in terms of the laws of dynamics, the future determines the past in exactly the same way in which the past determines the future, he can define the essential characteristic of conservative action as *reversibility*. The classic example of reversibility is a ball falling and striking a perfectly elastic horizontal surface. Its velocities before and after striking the surface will be exactly the same except in reverse order, and the reason ob-

---

[24] Peirce remarks that if the word "teleological" is too strong, then we might invent the word "finious" to describe the end-directed nature of nonconservative action (7.471). Modern biologists have invented another word for the same idea, "teleonomic."

viously is because velocity is a function of the *square* of the time. Since even powers admit both positive and negative values without affecting the result, every law of dynamics in which an even power appears is conservative. As we would expect, then, nonconservative action is characterized by irreversibility of phenomena and a tendency toward a final state (finiosity) (7.472). While it is clear that psychical phenomena show nonconservative action, what is more interesting is that even phenomena in the physical world which are of psychical interest seem at least to be under the governance of the same kind of action. For example, birth, growth, life, friction, viscosity, combustion, conduction of heat, capillarity, diffusion of liquids, to mention but a few, all seem to be nonconservative.

Physicists generally explain those actions which seem to violate the law of the conservation of energy (nonconservative actions) in terms of the action of chance. Thus, for example, the phenomenon of gas escaping through a hole in a cylinder can be analyzed into the change of movement of millions of molecules. Again, friction can be looked on as the chance interlacing and rupturing of molecules forming the surfaces in contact (7.472). Peirce is in complete accord with this sort of explanation (cf. 7.470, 6.73).

> As to those explanations which the physicists propose for irreversible phenomena by means of the doctrine of chances as applied to trillions of molecules, I accept them fully as one of the finest achievements of science. . . . This explanation demonstrates that the agency of energy is disseminated through every department of physical phenomena. But in one thing it fails; namely, it fails to show the absence of a very different kind of agency; and it not only fails to show its absence, but even supplies the means of proving its presence. (7.470)

The agency to which Peirce refers is spontaneity or rudimentary consciousness.[25]

[25] When Peirce comes to work out his evolutionary hypothesis, he will refer to this rudimentary consciousness as quale-consciousness. Strictly speaking it is the first emergence from the "Nothing of boundless freedom" and is not a *waking* consciousness. It is a potential consciousness (6.219–221, 6.198).

We will not attempt to go into the mathematico-logical analysis of chance and probability worked out so carefully by Peirce. It is sufficient for an understanding of what he is up to simply to remark that he does not put chance down to our ignorance.

> Surely, I need not waste breath in refuting that feeblest of attempts at analysis which makes chance to consist in our ignorance. For that has already been sufficiently done in the *Logic of Chance* of John Venn. . . . It is the operation of chance which produces the retardation of the upper layer of air [an example of friction which Peirce had just considered] . . . ; but surely it is no ignorance of ours that has that effect. Chance, then, as an objective phenomenon, is a property of a *distribution*. (6.74)

In one place, Peirce tells us clearly that chance *is* "that diversity and variety of things and events which law does not prevent" (6.612). This is the real chance upon which kinetic theory, for example, depends. It can be shown, Peirce declares, that this chance must be absolute, that is, not derivable from law, by the very logic of explanation (cf. Part III, Chapter 1) and at the same time it is not totally lawless since it exhibits at least the uniformity of the absence of any determinate law (6.606). This is the only sort of regularity chaos could manifest, but because of it chaos can be reasoned about statistically and could allow for the development of determinate law by means of the law of habit (6.606). And if it be objected that Peirce does not escape making law absolute, since the tendency to take habits is itself a law, the reply is that while the word "law" is convenient to describe that tendency, it is not used in the sense of inviolable, mechanical law but in the sense of mental law the violation of which is so included in its essence that unless it were violated it would cease to exist (6.612).

If chance is a property of a distribution, a distribution is a property of a collection. Since, however, there are different kinds of collections, the sorts of distribution of which each is capable are different and so each must be considered in turn to determine whether or not it can have a chance or fortuitous distribution. Peirce examines in turn denumeral, enumerable, and more than denumeral (continuous) collections (6.75–78). His conclusion is that chance is governed by the laws of probabilities, formal laws of mind or reason, present in any world that is knowable. They are not themselves material laws of nature, but are the very condition for there being any such laws since these formal laws permit the gradual formation of material laws through habit.

A fortuitous distribution of, let us say, colored and white objects, is the highest pitch of irregularity. Any departure from this irregularity, that is to say, any regularity, may tend in either of two directions: (1) the colored things and the white things may become more perfectly and uniformly mixed as when they would become arranged alternately, or (2) the colored things and the white things may tend to become grouped together. Both these tendencies may be called a process of sifting (6.80). Can a conservative force bring about sifting? Peirce answers, yes and quite inevitably (6.80). He gives the example of a ray of white light striking a prism. The different wave lengths of light, fortuitously distributed in that ray, are sifted out to form the spectrum. Another might be the case of gas escaping from one container into a larger. Because the pressure is lowered, the molecules' state of equilibrium in container A is disturbed and so the particles rush out into container B, but they will re-establish a state of equilibrium again in the new container.

Conservative action, however, is characterized by its reversibility. Consequently, if each wave of light diffracted by the prism, and each molecule of escaping gas, were to strike a perfectly elastic surface at right angles to its path, it would reverse its direction and the original state of the system would be restored—white light and gas in container A. Peirce points out that this does not happen, except perhaps in a laboratory, and then only imperfectly, due to the elaborate contrivance of the experimenter (6.80).

> Conservative force, left to itself, can produce no such result, because it depends on the *purposeful* exact adjustment of each pencil of light. Now one of the first things that the mechanical philosophy discovered was that there are no final causes in pure mechanical action. (6.80)

Still, it is true to say that the experimenter could not intervene in this purposeful way unless he were dealing with a conservative force. He could not so intervene, for example, in the process of organic growth.

Can conservative forces bring about a fortuitous distribution? Peirce answers in the negative. The reason is that a fortuitous distribution in a phenomenon can only be brought about by another fortuitous distribution in the conditions of the phenomenon. Take a jar containing some hot nitrogen and then add some cold oxygen. At first the nitrogen molecules will be moving with various *vires vivae* fortuitously distributed, and so will the oxygen molecules. On the average, however, the oxygen molecules will be moving more slowly than the nitrogen molecules. In this state of things the distribution of the *vires vivae* of nitrogen and oxygen molecules taken as one collection will *not* be fortuitious. Now in the course of time there will be continual fortuitous encounters of the two sorts of molecules and consequently there will be a continual interchange of *vis viva* with the result that gradually there will be an approximation to one fortuitous distribution of *vis viva* among all the molecules.

> That which happens, happens entirely under the governance
> of conservative forces; but the character of fortuitous
> distribution toward which there is a tendency is entirely due
> to the various fortuitous distributions existing in the different
> initial conditions of the motion, with which conservatve
> forces never have anything to do. (6.81)

This is more remarkable, Peirce observes, because although the initial distribution of *vires vivae* tends gradually to die out, the subsequent fortuitous distributions dependent upon the initial conditions not only hold their ground, but mark their effect wherever the conservative forces act. "Hence, it is that we find ourselves forced to speak of the 'action of chance'" (6.81).

So far, then, Peirce has shown that from a fortuitous distribution of objects acting under conservative forces can arise a *uniform* distribution (state of equilibrium). Now this is very much like one of the characteristics of nonconservative force, namely, *finiosity*. He also maintains that this phenomenon cannot be reversed except by the purposeful intervention of an experimenter, either by introducing new energy into the system to disturb the equilibrium or by introducing perfectly elastic reflectors to make the molecules reverse their direction. Perhaps such intervention could happen by the chance interference of one dynamical system by another, but the point is that the conservative forces within a system, left to themselves, cannot bring about such a reversal. Thus, the tendency of an inertial system to move from a completely fortuitous distribution to a uniform distribution manifests the other characteristic of nonconservative force, *irreversibility*. Now Peirce draws attention to two other important facts about uniform distributions: (1) not all of them seem to be the result of fortuitous distributions, and (2) even those which are, also involve some regularity in the conditions. Chemical reaction and electricity, for example, seem to involve a uniformity not due to fortuitous interaction, but to a definite relationship between the particles interacting— a fixed relation of attraction and repulsion in one case, fixed valences in the other. In the case of Boyle's law (illustrating fact 2 above), the density of a gas varies directly as the pressure, because more molecules confined to a smaller space will strike the walls of the container per unit time. But Peirce observes that this is not due to the fortuitous distributions of the molecules alone; it also requires that the paths of the molecules be *all* nearly rectilinear. But what is true of all the molecules is a regularity (7.519). Boyle's law, therefore, is due to fortuitous distribution *plus* a regularity. Peirce concludes that regularity in a phenomenon supposes some regularity in its initial conditions; irregularity supposes a fortuitous distribution in these conditions.

It would seem, therefore, that Peirce has effectively done away with monism altogether. He appears to have painted himself into a corner, hemmed in by two ultimate principles: law and chance (7.521). If it were only a question of some *formal* law at the base of every uniform distribution, there would be some hope of a *rational* explanation (7.511).[26] But it is not merely that, because in many cases *constants* are involved.

> The explanation of the laws of nature must be of such a
> nature that it shall explain why these quantities should have
> the particular values they have. But these particular values
> have nothing rational about them. They are mere arbitrary

[26] Peirce means by "rational" in this context "rationalistic" or "*a priori*." In his day a number of physicists, influenced by Kant, were trying to deduce all the laws of dynamics *a priori*. For example, Heinrich Hertz's *The Principles of Mechanics* (1894) brings in the role of experience in a single paragraph. See Dover edition, 1956, p. 145.

Secondnesses. The explanation cannot then be a purely
rational one. (7.511)

The way out of the difficulty, then, is to look for an explanation which
is not "purely rational," that is not purely rationalistic. In other words,
Peirce does not give up immediately in face of a serious difficulty. To
do so would be to violate his fundamental law of scientific logic: do
not block the road to inquiry. The fact that on extreme rationalistic
principles he would have to admit law and chance as two ultimates,
two inexplicables, as the explanation of the cosmos is an argument
against the adequacy of those principles. Deductive logic is not the
only kind of logic, nor is deduction the only kind of valid argumentation, nor is necessary reasoning the only kind of reasoning. There are
also probable reasoning, abductive inference, and evolutionary logic
in Peirce's "weapons-system." Indeed as soon as he stated this difficulty he added:

> Or if we are to escape this duality at all, urged to do so by
> the principle of retroduction, according to which we ought
> to begin by pressing the hypothesis of unity as far as we
> can, the only possible way of doing so is to suppose that the
> first germ of law was an *entity*, which itself arose by chance,
> that is as a First. (7.521)

Chance, then, after all, can explain law if it is integrated into a process
of evolution (7.512 ff.). This process, however, must proceed according to some principle, itself of the nature of a law, but such a law as
is capable of developing itself, not perhaps such that if it were entirely
absent it would create itself, but such that, when present, would
strengthen itself. Thus we are led to the hypothesis of a universal tendency in all things toward generalization and habit-taking (7.515).

Peirce, then, believed that he had driven life, spontaneity, chance,
and rudimentary consciousness, all the way down to the atomic world,
and thus had loosened the bonds of mechanistic determinism to allow
the entrance of mind into the world. He also thought that this kind of
reasoning would allow him to pivot and so to explain the development
of higher grades of consciousness through a philosophical theory of
evolution or emergence. The logical principles of pragmatism, he was
convinced, would permit no other sort of explanation, for the alterna-

tive, absolute determinism, would block the road of further inquiry in science and in philosophy, leaving an increasing number of questions unanswered supposedly because they were unanswerable. Logic requires that any meaningful question have an answer and that before one too hastily declares a question meaningless because it is yet to be answered, he explore as many alternative hypotheses as he can or as there are.

Peirce always insisted that his tychism was merely a corollary to his synechism.[27] He objected to having his philosophy as a whole called tychism because that would be to misrepresent and to distort his views. Synechism is the very heart of Peirce's thought. Fidelity to the pragmatic maxim, he considered to be a step leading to that view. Tychism enters into the picture only because synechism requires it. Synechism requires it because there is no other way to account for the world except in terms of an evolutionary hypothesis, and without spontaneity there could be no growth or development of any kind. It is no wonder, then, that the synechistic theory of law which we have been analyzing makes law to be founded in living potentiality manifesting itself in the tendency toward habit-taking and generalization.

> This habit is a generalizing tendency, and as such a
> generalization, and as such a general, and as such a
> continuum or continuity. It must have its origin in the original
> continuity which is inherent in potentiality. Continuity, as
> generality, is inherent in potentiality, which is essentially
> general. (6.204)

It only remains for us now to examine in some closer detail Peirce's philosophical theory of evolution. But before leaving this section on synechism, it might be helpful to reproduce here Peirce's own summary which appeared as the conclusion to his paper "The Law of Mind." Although he was very dissatisfied with this article as a whole, its conclusion does make clear those elements Peirce meant synechism to include.

> I have thus developed as well as I could in a little space
> the *synechistic* philosophy, as applied to mind. I think that

[27] Cf. e.g. letters to James, March 13, and December 26, 1897; Perry, *op. cit.*, p. 222 and 419.

I have succeeded in making it clear that this doctrine gives room for explanations of many facts which without it are absolutely and hopelessly inexplicable; and further that it carries along with it the following doctrines: first, a logical realism of the most pronounced type; second, objective idealism; third, tychism, with its consequent thoroughgoing evolutionism. We also notice that the doctrine presents no hindrances to spiritual influences, such as some philosophies are felt to do. (6.163)

III

Tychism & Evolution

Introduction

In one of his lectures on pragmatism at Harvard, Peirce recounted this anecdote about himself and Chauncey Wright. When Darwin's great book appeared in 1859, Peirce, engaged in surveying in the "wilds of Louisiana," knew of the sensation it caused only through letters. Upon his return to Cambridge, Peirce heard that Wright was very enthusiastic about Darwin's theory, and decided to sound him out on the subject. In the course of the conversation Peirce remarked that Darwin's ideas must inevitably kill mechanical philosophy. Although Wright, of course, did not agree, he was perplexed enough by the statement to inquire why Peirce thought so. Peirce answered that Darwin's theory, nourished by positive observation, must be deadly to a merely "metaphysical" opinion (5.64).

The story sums up the views Peirce was to develop over the next forty years and indicates succinctly the general intellectual climate in which he would have to air them. Wright was a devotee of Mill's positivism and thoroughly convinced of mechanical determinism.[1] Yet he was one of the staunchest defenders of evolutionism and of Darwinism in particular. Peirce contended that mechanical determinism and evolutionism are basically incompatible. Mechanical philosophy, an *a priori* ("metaphysical") position, is not only unsupported by observational evidence such as Darwin's but positively contradicted by it. Wright's inability to see that mechanical determinism precluded the possibility of growth and development was typical of the intellectual condition of most of Peirce's contemporaries.

The preceding section has shown Peirce's insistence upon the reality of law and regularity in the universe and has indicated in passing that he could not admit that laws of nature were absolutely rigid. That line of thought must be pursued farther. A synechistic theory of

[1] See E. H. Madden, *Chauncey Wright and the Foundations of Pragmatism* (Seattle: University of Washington Press, 1963), Ch. 1 and Ch. 4. See also P. P. Wiener, *Evolution and the Founders of Pragmatism* (Cambridge: Harvard University Press, 1949), Ch. III.

law requires that chance be operative in the universe, for otherwise there would be no room for mind. To admit tychism is to admit growth and development as fundamental to the entire cosmos. Conversely, to hold a thoroughgoing and consistent evolutionary account of the universe, one must admit real chance.

1. Tychism versus Determinism

ALTHOUGH PEIRCE SOMETIMES calls his philosophical position "Critical Common-sensism," he knew that not all "common-sense" opinions are helpful in the task of finding out the truth. Hence he uses the word "critical." Sound philosophy must take "common-sense" convictions seriously, but must not be led down the garden path by a naive trust in what seems obvious. Those common-sense positions which can stand up under scrutiny are philosophy's pure gold; those which cannot are its dross. The dross not only contributes nothing positive to the enterprise but can seriously hinder any further progress by blocking the road to inquiry. One such uncritical common-sense opinion prevalent in Peirce's day was the conviction "which makes the real things in this world blind unconscious objects working by mechanical laws together with consciousness as idle spectator" (7.559). This position takes for granted, even as self-evident, "that every event is *precisely* determined by general laws" (1.132, emphasis added). Peirce proposed to submit this "necessitarian" dogma to the test of criticism.

Necessitarianism has taken many forms throughout the history of philosophy and it would be well to state more exactly what brand Peirce's attack was aimed at. It is what he calls "mechanical philosophy" or materialism.

> Whoever holds that every act of the will as well as every idea of the mind is under the rigid governance of a necessity coordinated with that of the physical world will logically be carried to the proposition that minds are part of the physical world in such a sense that the laws of mechanics determine anything that happens according to immutable attractions and repulsions. (6.38)

Peirce calls this "the usual and most logical form of necessitarianism."[1]

---

[1] Alternate forms of necessitarianism, less usual in Peirce's day because they involve so many logical difficulties, are the numerous versions of Descartes' dualism.

Peirce claims that the necessitarian viewpoint arose in the first place because so many of the great metaphysicians had been mathematicians, and so, understandably enough, made mathematics the model of metaphysics. The Ionians, Pythagoreans, and Platonists, in early times, the Cartesians and Newtonians, in modern times, all explicitly looked to the ideal of rigid demonstration from first principles as normative in any and every scientific undertaking, physical and philosophical (1.130, 1.400). Since the discovery of non-Euclidean geometry, however, the status of mathematic's first principles has been somewhat revised, namely, from what was self-evidently true to postulates of a logical system. It had always been recognized, of course, that mathematical first principles were never strictly and exactly confirmed by observation (1.30, 1.400 ff.) but that had been put down simply to faulty measurement. If, however, the first principles of Euclidean geometry are only postulates of a system, and if different assumptions will yield different but equally valid geometries, there is no *a priori* reason to expect that first principles are true of the world at all, much less exactly true of it. That is a question to be decided by observation, and all experimental evidence points to the conclusion that all such mathematical principles are only approximated in the physical world, not simply because methods of measurement are crude but because the world itself does not quite fit the mathematical mold.[2] The more refined the means of measurement become, the more evident it becomes that there will always be some inexactitude because what is being measured is continuous while exact measurement supposes discrete units (cf. 1.130, 1.400, 6.45).

Peirce argues, therefore, that since exactitude is despaired of even by mathematicians, it can no longer be hoped for in metaphysics. That is to say, no metaphysical first principle can be expected to be more than an approximation of how things are in the world. Consequently, common sense has no longer any right to assume that every

---

[2] In a rejoinder to Dr. Paul Carus' defense of necessitarianism, Peirce distinguishes between mathematics' ideal constructions and physical laws. The former are exact only insofar as they are analytic; the latter, because they come from experience through ampliative inference, can only be approximative. If, and insofar as, ideal mathematical constructions can be interpreted in a physical system, their application to the real world can only be approximate (6.595).

event is precisely determined by law. Rather, common sense ought to expect just the opposite. A critical examination into the arguments usually given by philosophers in support of the necessitarian thesis must be undertaken.

Peirce classifies the arguments under three general headings: (1) absolute determinism is a postulate of scientific reasoning; (2) it is supported by observational evidence; and (3) it is supported by various *a priori* reasons. The first class of arguments is based upon a faulty analysis of the logic of scientific reasoning; the second is simply gratuitously asserted; and the third does not take into account various theories of chance forcefully argued from Aristotle down to Peirce.

What are we to think of the contention that absolute determinism is a postulate of scientific reasoning?[3] In the first place, even if it were a postulate of scientific reasoning that would not make it true, nor would it afford any solid reason for thinking that it may be true. It would merely be the expression of a hope that it may be the case (6.39). In practical matters, of course, in cases where a decision to act must be taken, it is legitimate to assume certain things to be true, because if they are not true there would be no reason to act in one way rather than in another. But, Peirce contends, in these cases what is assumed as true is always some *individual fact*, never an absolutely universal principle:

> . . . it is manifest that no universal principle can in its
> universality be comprised in a special case or can be
> requisite for the validity of any ordinary inference. (6.39)

In other words, what is at issue here is the justification of valid induction and a judgment as to what can be expected of such argumentation. On the one hand, Peirce seems to be saying, no particular instance of a general ever exhausts that general nor contains in it the general's generality. How, then, from a limited sample could one ever hope to draw an absolutely exact general principle? An approximation, yes, but that is not what is at stake. On the other hand, if some postulate were required for the most simple and ordinary type of inference, how would we be able to begin reasoning in the first place?

[3] See 3.632–635 for Peirce's discussion of the terms "postulate" and "presupposition" which appeared in Baldwin's *Dictionary of Philosophy and Psychology*.

Would we have to wait until someone supplied us with the latent major premise?[4] Is that premise innately known? Is it unknown but operative in our reasoning anyway? But then in what sense could it be said to be reasoning at all, since reasoning supposes control over the process and hence awareness of the premises? Or perhaps what is meant by the defenders of the postulate theory is that the postulate is not strictly speaking a hidden premise of our reasoning but a condition for our reasoning discovered when we make a reflexive analysis of reasoning (*logica utens*). This last possibility makes sense, but then the question is reduced to what is the correct analysis of scientific reasoning.

Peirce thinks of inference as divided into two major types, explicative and ampliative, a distinction inspired by Kant's synthetic-analytic dichotomy. Deduction is explicative, that is, it does not extend our knowledge of the world but rather enriches our knowledge of the relations among ideas. Induction, hypothesis, and analogy do extend our knowledge of the world. This difference is so fundamental that it dooms to failure any attempt to make induction (and other forms of ampliative reasoning) merely a special kind of deduction.[5] No doubt the influence of the mathematical model of reasoning is back of this faulty analysis of induction. For Peirce, all nondeductive or ampliative reasoning is based on the same principle and procedure, namely, sampling (6.40). The example he gives is this: from samples of a shipment of wheat (mixed and stirred up with great thoroughness) we find that $\frac{4}{5}$ of the sample contains quality A wheat; therefore, we infer *experientially* and *provisionally*, that about $\frac{4}{5}$ of all the grain in the shipment is of the same quality.

> By saying that we infer it *experientially*, I mean that our
> conclusion makes no pretension to knowledge of wheat-in-
> itself, our *aletheia*, as the derivation of the word implies, has
> nothing to do with *latent* wheat. We are dealing only with
> the matter of possible experience—experience in the full

[4] This is the position which those who would reduce induction to a form of deduction must hold.

[5] Mill's theory of induction takes "uniformity of nature" as the hidden major premise. See 2.761–767 for Peirce's criticism of Mill.

acceptation of the term as something not merely affecting the senses but also as the subject of thought. (6.40)

In other words, Peirce is saying that our argument is based only on what we have experienced or can experience of the wheat in future samplings. It excludes from consideration: (a) wheat hidden on the ship that will never turn up, (b) wheat half-hidden in such a way that it may turn up but is less likely to do so than the rest (this situation would alter the randomness of the sampling since it would be false that any grain of wheat has as much chance as any other of turning up in the sample), (c) wheat which can affect our senses or pockets but which cannot be reasoned about (is unknown and unknowable).[6] Because our reasoning about the wheat is so conditioned by our actual and possible experience of it, our conclusion concerning the true proportion of quality A is drawn only *provisionally*.

> By saying that we draw the inference *provisionally*, I mean that we do not hold that we have reached any assigned degree of approximation as yet, but only hold that if our experience be indefinitely extended, and if every fact of whatever nature, as fast as it presents itself, be duly applied, according to the inductive method, in correcting the inferred ratio, then our approximation will become indefinitely close in the long run . . . . (6.40)[7]

At any given time, then, the inferred ratio is only an approximation of what we will find in future experiences of sampling. That ratio becomes an hypothesis to be verified and/or modified by experience. If experience fluctuates irregularly so that the ratio cannot be assigned any definite value, we can find out approximately within what limits

[6] In another paper written a year or so later (1893) Peirce attributed the errors of mechanical philosophy to the "incautious assumption" that there is a difference between "to look red" and "to see red," the assumption of a *Ding an sich* (7.561).

[7] Goudge points out that there is a certain ambiguity in Peirce's use of the term "probable deduction." It sometimes seems to mean necessary reasoning about probabilities; sometimes it seems to mean that the conclusion drawn is only probable, that is, approximately true. *Op. cit.*, p. 172 ff.

it fluctuates. If experience changes from one definite ratio to another, we will be able to find that out and modify our approximation.

> . . . and in short, whatever may be the variations of this ratio in experience, experience indefinitely extended will enable us to detect them, so as to predict rightly, at last, what its ultimate value may be, if it have any ultimate value, or what the ultimate law of succession of values may be, if there be any such ultimate law, or that it fluctuates irregularly within certain limits, if it does so ultimately fluctuate. (6.40)

Peirce's contention, therefore, is that what ultimately justifies ampliative reasoning is its self-corrective power (cf. 2.769, 5.575 ff.),[8] and that for this reason the inference, claiming to be no more than experiential and provisional, involves no postulate whatever.[9]

On Peirce's analysis every postulate of scientific reasoning is cut off either by the provisionality or by the experientiality of such inference. Any fact which might be supposed postulated, must either be

---

[8] Cf. Goudge, op. cit., pp. 189–190; J. W. Lenz, "Induction as Self-Corrective," Studies, Moore and Robin, pp. 151–162.

[9] See Goudge, op. cit., pp. 191–193 for a lengthy discussion of whether or not Peirce's account of induction does not presuppose something like Mill's uniformity of nature after all. He rightly concludes that it does not, and makes a good distinction between Mill's positive assumption about uniformity and Peirce's negative assumption about the intervention of "supernal powers." Undoubtedly it is true that any existential subject matter must be ordered in some way, and no doubt Peirce held this view. Again it is undoubtedly the case that Peirce was convinced that random sampling will find out that order. But would it be accurate to say that the validity of induction depends upon those assumptions, no matter how analytic one would make them? Would it not be enough to say that if there is any order, random sampling will find that out in the long run, and alternately, if there is no definite order, sampling will find that out too? Peirce makes a great deal of the fact that for an induction to be valid the character for which we sample must be predesignated. This means, it seems to us, that we first form an hypothesis as to what regularity we are likely to find or are interested in verifying, and the induction merely confirms or disconfirms it in some ratio. The induction does not suppose antecedently that there is necessarily the order we have assumed in the subject matter. The induction is precisely the method of finding out whether or not the order is there at all and to what degree.

such that it would ultimately present itself in experience, or would not (6.41). If it will show up in experience, there is no need to postulate it; if it will not show up in experience, it is irrelevant to the validity of our conclusion since the only pretension that conclusion makes is to say what is valid as far as possible experience goes. By linking induction to experience in such a way that experience is allowed to modify the ratio provisionally assigned, induction becomes self-corrective and dependent upon no postulate whatsoever, but only upon future experience.

Peirce sees one important objection to his position, namely, that it does not give induction the full force that it in fact does have. For, on his view, no matter how thoroughly the mixing had been, the examination of a sample would not give any insurance that the next sample would not greatly modify the value of the ratio under inquiry (6.43). Yet as a matter of fact the assurance is very high that the error is not great. Peirce admits that ideally the assurance would be high, but that in most cases we fall somewhat short of perfect conditions. The ideal induction requires that the sampling had been truly random and that the character sampled for had been determined before the sample was examined. These ideals should always be striven for, but when they cannot be perfectly satisfied, provided the induction is carried out honestly, the inference still has some value. Peirce's account was meant to show what that minimum value is, namely, that the process is self-corrective and so will lead to the truth of the matter if persevered in.

Now what about the observational evidence in support of necessitarianism (cf. 6.609)? Peirce does not see how anyone acquainted with scientific research on the inside could take any such claim seriously. Every scientist knows that no observation determines the value of a continuous quantity with a probable error of zero (6.45). But it is objected that this is true only of continuous quantities. What about those continuous quantities that are discontinuous at one or at two limits? Take a line, for instance. We know that it cannot have a length less than zero. Peirce proposes a case where it is a question of determining the length of a line that a certain person had drawn from a marked point on a piece of paper. If we can see no line at all, the observed length is zero;

> . . . and the only conclusion this observation warrants is that
> the length of the line is less than the smallest length visible
> with the optical power employed. (6.45)

To conclude that probably no line had been drawn at all the experimenter would need to have recourse to some indirect evidence such
as that the person in question was never near enough to the paper to
draw any such line. The general point that Peirce wants to make is
that to conclude that some quantity or other is absent from a certain
subject matter there must be some experiential evidence, direct or re-
mote, to that effect. It is not enough simply to say that we are unable
to detect it. All that we can do in strictest logic in cases where there
is no such evidence available is to abstain from any opinion as to the
presence of the substance in question (6.45).

Consequently, in Peirce's opinion, not only is there no observational evidence to support the necessitarian view, but all the observational evidence on hand is directly contrary to it. All that the evidence
shows is that there is some regularity in nature, a regularity indeed
which is anything but exact.

> Try to verify any law of nature, and you will find that the
> more precise your observations, the more certain they will be
> to show irregular departures from the law. (6.46)

Heisenberg did not enunciate his indeterminacy principle until more
than a quarter of a century later (1927), but Peirce would not have
been surprised if he had lived to see science so conclude. He certainly
would have sided with those who have interpreted the principle to
mean that atoms are endowed with a certain spontaneity in their
movement against others who attribute the apparent indeterminacy
to the intrinsic limitations of measurement techniques.

What most clearly characterizes the universe around us is its
enormous variety and diversity (1.159 ff.). But the regularity of law
cannot produce irregularity of itself (1.161, 1.174 ff.). Even a rather
gross, common-sense sort of observation, therefore, supports the thesis
that the universe is not the mere mechanical result of blind law
(1.162). Only the truly scientific attitude of humble fallibilism allows
one to see that this is the case. Synechism is nothing more than fallibilism objectified (1.171 ff.); in other words, a correct logical analy-

sis will lead one inevitably to a doctrine of continuity and a doctrine of continuity precludes the possibility of law ever being absolutely precise and exact.

The defenders of rigid determinism, therefore, are driven to *a priori* reasons to support their case (6.48). They usually argue either that the human mind cannot help thinking that everything is precisely determined by law (6.49), or that this is a natural belief and natural beliefs usually are borne out by experience (6.50), or that absolute chance is inconceivable (6.51), or that, although it may be conceivable, it is unintelligible in the sense that it does not explain the how or why of things, the only justification for any hypothesis (6.52). Peirce does not consider arguments from conceivability or inconceivability to be serious enough to warrant any great attention. The history of ideas and of science has shown all too vividly how precarious a position that is. He thinks that an appeal to "natural belief" is somewhat stronger but still not convincing since the obvious rejoinder is that natural beliefs must be purged through criticism of natural illusions. The genuine natural belief at the bottom of necessitarianism is that there is some regularity in nature. The natural illusion is to think that this regularity is absolutely universal and absolutely exact. The only argument, then, that deserves a closer look is the one which claims absolute chance is not an explanation. The issue to be settled is what is an explanation and when is one required.[10]

Now the paragraphs we have been considering here come from one of a series of five articles which Peirce published in the *Monist* between 1891 and 1892. This article, entitled "The Doctrine of Necessity Examined," was in fact the second of that series. In the very first article, called "The Architecture of Theories," Peirce briefly took up the question of what required an explanation and concluded:

[10] "One of the architectonic—and, therefore, I suppose, by Dr. Carus considered as highly reprehensible—features of my theory, is that, instead of saying off-hand what elements strike me as requiring explanation and what as not doing so, which seems to be his way, I have devoted a long time to the study of the whole logical doctrine of explanation, and of the history of explanations, and have based upon the general principles so ascertained my conclusions as to what things do and what do not require to be explained" (6.612).

Uniformities are precisely the sort of facts that need to be accounted for. That a pitched coin should sometimes turn up heads and sometimes tails calls for no particular explanation; but if it shows heads every time, we wish to know how this result has been brought about. Law is *par excellence* the thing that wants a reason. (6.12)

In his detailed reply to Dr. Carus' criticism of Peirce's refutation of necessitarianism, Peirce chides the *Monist*'s editor for saying "off-hand" what requires an explanation rather than carefully studying the logical problems involved. If he had, Peirce says, he would not have claimed that absolute chance requires an explanation in terms of law (6.611–612).

First, then, let us see how Peirce defines "explanation" and second, how he arrived at that definition. Something can be called an "explanation" in a strict or in a loose sense. In the loose sense an "explanation" is a "reason." Restricting the term "explanation" to the strict sense, Peirce defines it as

... the replacement of a complex predicate, or one which seems improbable or extraordinary, by a simple predicate from which the complex predicate follows on known principles. (6.612)

A reason, or "explanation" in the loose sense, he defines as

... the replacement of a multiple subject of an observational proposition by a general subject, which by the very conditions of the special experience is predicable of the multiple subject. (6.612)[11]

If these definitions are justified, it follows immediately that only co-

---

[11] Dr. Carus defined "explanation" as a description of a special process of nature in such a way that the process is recognized as a transformation (6.612). To this, Peirce has four major objections: (1) it is not true that special processes of nature are the only things to be explained; (2) an explanation cannot simply be a description of the fact to be explained; (3) not every recognition of a transformation is an explanation, but may indeed itself call for an explanation; and (4) not every explanation as a matter of fact involves the recognition of a transformation, e.g. in certain astronomical explanations.

incidences or regularities need an explanation and hence law is the thing, *par excellence,* to be explained.

The analysis which led Peirce to these definitions will be taken from a paper he wrote a few years later (*ca.* 1901) concerning the logic of history, because it is worked out there in some detail. To begin, he asks what is the psychological sign that an explanation is needed. What spurs us to ask further questions? It is surprise, the emotion we experience when we run into the unexpected (7.189). Is it regularity or irregularity which causes us surprise?

> Nobody is surprised that the trees in a forest do not form a regular pattern, or asks for any explanation of such a fact. So, irregularity does not prompt us to ask for an explanation. Nor can it be said that it is because the explanation is obvious; for there is, on the contrary, no explanation to be given, except that there is no particular reason why there should be a regular pattern .... (7.189)

On the other hand, if we were to meet some equally unexpected regularity during our forest stroll, we would start wondering about the explanation. Perhaps this forest is a government conservation project and the trees were planted deliberately in a certain order. The reason for the difference in our reaction to equally unexpected regularity and irregularity is simply this: we are surprised at the regularity because irregularity is "the overwhelming preponderant rule of experience" (7.189). Nature's most obvious characteristic is variety and almost infinite diversity (1.159). Irregularity, then, is not surprising. But, Peirce continues, a breach of an existing regularity does call for explanation. Notice, it is not enough merely to have expected antecedently to investigation some regularity and then to have found only irregularity. In this case we do not demand an explanation of the irregularity which we found but rather revise our reasons for having expected regularity in the first place (7.191).

Let us look at the matter in another way. The whole purpose of science is to find out truth about phenomena, to work out their rationale. The acid test of whether a scientific proposition is true or approaches the truth about phenomena is verification of prediction. Scientific method then looks to making predictions, thus letting us know more or less what to expect. A scientific explanation of a phenomenon supplies a proposition which, if it had been known before the phenomenon presented itself, would have made it predictable. In other words, a scientific explanation makes the phenomenon a logical consequence, necessary or probable, and so renders it rational. Suppose a die is thrown and it turns up six. Does this fact call for any particular explanation? Not unless there is reason to believe that there are peculiar and pertinent features about that particular throw in which the six turned up. The reason is simply because antecedently to any trial we knew that over the long run it will turn up six about once in six throws (7.192). The case would be very different, however, if a certain die continually turned up six despite the law of probability. We would immediately suspect that it was loaded. In other words, we would immediately seek an explanation because the unexpected had happened. Or again, suppose that on the day of the Lisbon earthquake a new star appeared in the heavens. Does this require a special explanation? The answer again is no. Although it is possible that there is some explanation of the coincidence, it would be foolish to adopt this as a working hypothesis since there is no evidence that there is any connection, this is, antecedently to the event there was no more reason to expect it than not to expect it (7.193). Peirce's conclusion, therefore, is that the only case in which an explanation is called for is when the phenomenon, without some special explanation, would be expected *not* to present itself (7.194).

In summary, according to Peirce's analysis the following cases require no explanation: (1) sheer irregularity, because it engenders no expectation as to what is likely to turn up, and (2) purely formal regularities (e.g., law of probability), according to which a certain phenomenon is bound to turn up sometime or other in the chance medley of things because these are simply part of the *a priori* conditions of our knowing randomness at all. The following cases do require an explanation: (1) empirically observed regularities in nature, because they are the exception to the preponderance of experience, (2) breaches in empirically observed regularities, since the regularity has led one to expect certain phenomena to happen and when they do not come to pass, questions must be asked, and (3) failure to discover empirical confirmation of a postulated regularity, and in this case the explanation sought is not precisely why there was no observed regularity but why we were led to postulate it. Explanation, then, has to do with the rationality of things and so is in the category of Thirdness. Sheer Firstness and brutal Secondness as such require no explanations because in themselves they are not reasonable. Only when Firstness and Secondness are brought together through the mediation of Thirdness or law are we forced to reason, to ask questions, to inquire, to seek explanations.

The general conclusion to be drawn in the context of Peirce's criticism of necessitarianism is this: law and law alone requires an explanation; consequently, it cannot be posited as the ultimate explanation of the cosmos. Such a position leads to this rather curious sort of reasoning: on the one hand, since law and regularity cannot explain irregularity and growing diversity, the latter are to be set down as inexplicable; on the other hand, since he holds that laws cannot have evolved out of irregularity because they are immutable and ultimate facts, no explanation can be given of them. In short both the regularity and the irregularity of the world are inexplicable (6.60). This is hardly a doctrine sound logic would sanction since it blocks the road to inquiry. The rejection of the hypothesis of absolute chance as a real factor in the universe for *a priori* reasons leads to a blind alley (see also 1.405 ff.).

Necessitarianism, then, stands on no firm ground. It is not a postulate of scientific reason, is not supported by observational data, and leads to a hopeless logical position on *a priori* arguments. All that remains is for Peirce to give positive reasons for adopting his position. Briefly, they are four: (1) the general prevalence of growth which seems to be opposed to the conservation of energy, (2) the immense variety of the universe, which *is* chance, and needs no explanation, (3) law, which since it requires an explanation must be explained in terms of something else, namely, chance, and (4) the reality of feeling and consciousness, for which there is no room in a mechanical universe (6.58–61, 6.613).

In regard to the first argument, Peirce simply invites the reader to examine any science which deals with the course of time: history, geology, paleontology, astronomy. All testify to growth and increasing complexity.[12] Death and corruption are merely secondary and accidental phenomena.

[12] This is one of the major points made by Teilhard de Chardin in *The Phenomenon of Man.*

From these broad and ubiquitous facts we may fairly infer, by the most unexceptionable logic, that there is probably in nature some agency by which the complexity and diversity of things can be increased; and that consequently the rule of mechanical necessity meets in some way with interference. (6.58)

Peirce tells Dr. Carus that a real understanding of the force of this argument requires a thorough familiarity with the way in which physicists explain nonconservative action in terms of conservative action.[13] We have already seen how they take refuge in the laws of probability "as preventive of the velocities ever getting reversed" (6.613). Consider again the example of white light refracted through a prism. It is possible for the colored light to be reversed through the prism so as to reconstitute the original white light. But as a matter of fact, without special intervention on the part of the experimenter, this rarely happens because the probabilities are so overwhelmingly against just the right combinations of circumstances being present to bring about the effect. The nonconservative effect of friction and viscosity are similarly explained in terms of probabilities. Peirce's point is that the physicists are calling upon the action of chance to explain these phenomena.

I do no more, then, than follow the usual method of the physicists, in calling in chance to explain the apparent violation of the law of energy which is presented by the phenomena of growth: only instead of chance, as they understand it, I call in absolute chance. (6.613)

The difference between Peirce's interpretation of chance and the usual one of the physicist is that Peirce's makes chance something in nature and not merely a function of our ignorance of an extremely complex causal system. The general principle behind this view is that

. . . in a broad view of the universe a simulation of a given elementary mode of action can hardly be explained except by supposing the genuine mode of action somewhere has place. (6.613)

[13] See the treatment in Part II, Ch. 3.

Of course, there is no question of strict and absolute proof but merely of which hypothesis is better warranted by logic. The pragmatic maxim and the synechistic rule of logic, based as they are on realism, indicate that we should assume that a simulated violation of the law of energy has a real violation of the same law as its ultimate explanation (6.613).

> Now, growth *appears* to violate the law of energy. To explain
> it, we must, at least, suppose a simulated, or *quasi,* chance,
> such as Darwin calls in to produce his fortuitous variations
> from strict heredity. (6.613)

Even if it be argued that there is no real violation of the law and no real chance in the immediate phenomenon, must not the conditions upon which the phenomenon depends require real chance? Or it might be argued that the law of conservation of energy is not strictly accurate while the other laws of dynamics are and that therefore there is no absolute chance. But Peirce thinks that physicists would not allow such a distinction and that if the exactitude of the law of energy were called into question all the other laws' exactitude would be questioned too. In that case, mechanical philosophy would have yielded its position.[14] Add to this the fact that most psychologists

[14] Peirce thinks of the laws of dynamics as formal laws or regulative principles used to account for phenomena governed by real forces or material laws. The formal laws are ways of thinking about the phenomena but do not exhaust their reality, and hence the formal laws are never exactly verified. They are really mathematical constructions giving us a way of interpreting observed regularities. These formal laws are not laws of the phenomena, nor do they make the real regularities or material laws any the less real and objective. Thus writing in 1905, Peirce declares: "As to the common aversion to recognizing *thought* as an active factor in the real world, some of its causes are easily traced. In the first place, people are persuaded that everything that happens in the material universe is a motion completely determined by inviolable laws of dynamics; and that, they think, leaves no room for any other influence. But the laws of dynamics stand on quite a different footing from the laws of gravitation, elasticity, electricity, and the like. The laws of dynamics are very much like logical principles, if they are not precisely that. They say only how bodies will move after you have said what the forces are. They permit any forces, and therefore any motions. . . . Setting dynamical laws to one side, then, as hardly being positive laws, but rather mere formal principles, we have only the laws of gravitation, elasticity,

will admit the intimate connection between the law of growth and the law of habit, which would be destroyed if it were rigidly obeyed, the phenomenon of growth surely seems to indicate a positive violation of energy's law (6.613).

Peirce invites us next to consider the third argument since it fortifies the first. We have already seen how and why the logic of explanation requires that law or regularity be explained. What Peirce wants to consider here is that among the physical laws which appear to be so different there are analogies which also have to be explained. He gives as examples gravitation, electricity, and radiation, all of which, despite the differences in the forces involved, obey an inverse square law. This calls for an explanation and as we have seen, if the laws are fundamentally original and absolute, there can be no explanation. The only way out is to suppose that law is not so absolute and that there is real absolute chance (6.613).

As regards the second argument, variety in the universe, insofar as it consists in the unlikenesses between things, calls for no explanation. Still variety is a *general* characteristic of the world, and its generality needs some explanation. Peirce sees this as the question to be answered:

> . . . whether this manifold specificalness was put into the
> universe at the outset, whether God created the universe in
> the infinitely distant past and has left it to its own machinery
> ever since, or whether there is an incessant influx of
> specificalness. (6.613)

Peirce sees two alternatives: one can argue that the phenomenon of growth in the universe is limited to certain intervals and to certain parts of the universe, but that the universe as a whole is not growing; or one can argue that the pervasiveness of growth through the cosmos as far as science can tell seems to argue that the whole is constantly growing and constantly has new diversity and variety introduced. This is the position of the evolutionist and, for Peirce, the hypothesis recommended by all sound logic (6.613). The reason is always the

electricity, and chemistry. Now who will deliberately say that our knowledge of these laws is sufficient to make us reasonably confident that they are absolutely eternal and immutable, and that they escape the great law of evolution?" (1.348).

same: the anti-evolutionist hypothesis renders phenomena ultimately inexplicable and so blocks the road to inquiry.

> . . . to say no process of diversification takes place in nature leaves the infinite diversity of nature unaccounted for; while to say the diversity is the result of a general tendency to diversification is a perfectly logical probable inference. (6.613)

Sound logic prescribes that we may not legitimately conclude to what goes beyond what we observe, except insofar as it explains or accounts for what we observe. The evolutionistic hypothesis does just that. It is no explanation to say that there is diversity in the world because God made it so. This is simply to state the fact that there is diversity in the world, not to give an explanation of how it got there, whether all at once in the beginning or continually throughout time by an evolution.[15]

As to the fourth argument, Peirce contends that necessitarians are embarrassed by the fact of consciousness and must do their best to make up accounts with a reality which by all rights according to their theory should not be real at all. Indeed, they do try to reduce it to some sort of illusion, an illusion of a material system. Colors are

---

[15] Peirce goes on to remark that we do not know God's secret counsels. We only know what He *does* do, and nothing more. Then he says, "For the same reason one cannot logically infer the existence of God; one can only know Him by direct perception" (6.613). It seems that what Peirce is rejecting is "God as hypothesis" or "the God of the gaps." We agree that one may not call upon the existence of God as a substitute for scientific explanation, but we would have some reservations as to the illegitimacy of inferring the existence of God as ground and goal of phenomena as such. Might not one argue that God is the necessary condition of possibility for there being anything at all? At least we do not see that it is *logically* impossible. Even Peirce admits that we can legitimately conclude to something beyond what we have observed if it accounts for or explains what we have observed. This would not be necessarily simply to fall back into the "God-of-the-gaps" trap, because the sort of question it seeks to answer is different. It is not a scientific question and so does not require a scientific explanation. It is properly philosophical and addresses itself not merely to the question of understanding a given structure, but to the question of why and how there should be anything at all, even bits of matter swirling at random through space.

reduced to rates of vibrations; brain matter is nothing more than protoplasm, itself merely an arrangement of mechanical particles, of a certain degree of complexity. All feeling is reduced to some "inward aspect" of matter, to a phantom. Peirce's hypothesis is not so encumbered by observed psychical facts, as empirical as any physical facts, as to be forced to explain them away.

> On the other hand, by supposing the rigid exactitude of causation to yield, I care not how little—be it but by a strictly infinitesimal amount—we gain room to insert mind into our scheme, and to put it into the place where it is needed, into the position which, as the sole self-intelligible thing, it is entitled to occupy, that of the fountain of existence; and in so doing we resolve the problem of the connection of soul and body. (6.61)

Now that Peirce has attacked the great redoubt blocking the road to further progress in science and in philosophy, he must sketch in some detail the position he proposes to erect in its place, a position which will help traffic move smoothly and continuously over the road to be travelled by inquirers after the truth. We must, therefore, now follow Peirce in working out his philosophical account of the cosmos as it arises out of absolute chance.

2. Evolutionary Love

PEIRCE ONCE REMARKED that in philosophy one must have a thoroughgoing evolutionism or none at all (6.14). In our day perhaps it would seem very odd for a thoroughgoing evolutionist to have reservations about Darwin's theory of natural selection. And yet Peirce had them. He was never very enthusiastic about the *Origin of Species* and to appreciate his own "thoroughgoing" evolutionism we must try to understand why. Peirce's reluctance to endorse Darwin wholeheartedly might simply have been due to the theory's novelty and lack of sufficient confirmation. No doubt, this is part of the reason, but it certainly is not the whole.

In reading what Peirce has to say about Darwinism we note that one thing stands out: Peirce was abashed that the new theory should receive such widespread, enthusiastic, and comparatively uncritical acceptance among scientists and philosophers. It was not that Peirce did not recognize in Darwin's work a truly great and significant scientific advance. He did and said so in many places. He could not understand, nor approve, the sweeping generalizations in fields as far removed from biology as political economy, ethics, and religion which followed almost immediately Darwin's book (published late in the year 1859). No sober mind, guided in its speculations by sound logic, could honestly and in good conscience indulge in such irresponsible declarations. Even from a purely scientific viewpoint, Darwin's work was not beyond criticism. Peirce was genuinely disturbed at these developments.

On the other hand, there were reactions, equally violent, in the opposite direction, which must have equally disturbed Peirce. There were philosophers and religious leaders who vigorously condemned Darwin's hypothesis on various *a priori* grounds. But evolution was not a new idea with Darwin. Why, then, did his account of it make such a sensation? Why was it that men could hardly discuss it dispassionately?[1]

[1] Lamarck's theory was formulated between the years 1801 and 1809.

To understand Peirce's position, it will be helpful to keep in mind the distinction between evolution as a scientific hypothesis aimed at explaining the development of organic species and evolution as a philosophical hypothesis aimed at explaining the entire cosmos. Though Peirce was primarily interested in the latter, he always modeled it on the former. He realized that philosophical adaptation of scientific theories is always a risky business and so he insisted that it be based upon a sound and sane logic which would enable one to judge accurately exactly what science had established (and to what degree of probability) and what it had not. Only sound logical method enables one to see clearly where science ends and philosophical speculation begins, and so to avoid confusing the claims of each. The mistake of philosophers and scientists who thought that science confirms necessitarianism is of this kind—faulty analysis of the logical weight of the evidence. Peirce's reservations about Darwinism are both scientific and philosophical.

Why, then, was Darwin's theory so enthusiastically received by most of the scientific world even though it was far from being proved? Darwin himself in the *Origin of Species* accepted the inheritance of acquired characteristics as playing a role in evolution. It was only after Weismann's work that Lamarck's principle was seriously challenged and controversy split the biologist's camp. Furthermore, evolutionism had always been a part of western thought since the Ionians. Anaximander, Empedocles and Anaxagoras proposed versions of natural selection and the survival of the fittest on observational and philosophic grounds. The Stoics advocated a theory of *"logoi spermatikoi"* for philosophical reasons. St. Augustine adapted the Stoic cosmology for theological reasons. His followers throughout the Middle Ages saw no conflict between *"rationes seminales"* and the Christian doctrine of creation. Indeed Augustine's theological reason for proposing a version of that Stoic doctrine was to reconcile certain passages in Scripture concerning creation (cf. *De. Gen. ad litt.* 6, 5, 8; *De Trinit.* 3, 8, 13). It was the influence of Aristotle which inclined most medieval thinkers to hold to fixity of species, and so to interpret creation in that light. It might be that the opposition to Darwinism among nineteenth century philosophers was due to the influence of *a prioristic* dogmatism prevalent in many German Schools, and the reaction among religious leaders was due to a loss of contact with a part of the Christian tradition and to fundamentalism. On the other hand, the over-enthusiastic reception of Darwinism might be due to smouldering rebellion against both *a prioristic* metaphysics and fundamentalist religion which needed only the slightest fanning from science to burst into new flames.

Peirce finds the answer in the intellectual climate of the scientific world at the time, dominated as it was by mechanical philosophy and the "statistical method." Addressing himself to this very question, Peirce briefly surveyed the state of science from 1846 to 1859. He called this period *the* most productive period of equal length in the entire history of science (6.297). The big breakthrough came with the realization that chance begets order. According to Peirce it was put into its clearest light in 1847 by Quetelet's paper on the application of probability theory to moral and political sciences. In the same year, Herapath, an English chemist, outlined kinetic theory and Helmholtz formulated the conservation of energy principle. In 1850 Clausius and Rankine, independently, worked out the mechanical theory of heat. Buckle's *History of Civilization* (1857) met with great success because he had made use of Quetelet's suggestion. In the very summer preceding Darwin's publication of the *Origin of Species* Maxwell read the most important paper to date on the dynamical theory of gases before the British Association. Peirce observes:

> The consequence was that the idea that fortuitous events
> may result in a physical law, and further that this is the way
> in which those laws which appear to conflict with the
> principle of the conservation of energy are to be explained,
> had taken a strong hold upon the minds of all those who
> were abreast of the leaders of thought. (6.297)

It was inevitable that Darwin's work should be welcomed by minds thinking along these lines. The *Origin of Species* was simply the application of the same principle to another "nonconservative" action, organic development. They looked on Darwinism as another confirmation of mechanical philosophy, a very special and a most welcome one, since it applied to life and growth, the two phenomena which fitted in least well with their philosophical view of the world. In other words, Peirce maintains that philosophical prejudice more than the intrinsic scientific worth (great though that was) of Darwin's theory insured its warm and uncritical acceptance by a large part of the scientific community.

Nor was mechanism the only intellectual prejudice of the nineteenth century which provided a favorable environment in which Darwinism could rapidly take root in popular as well as in scientific thought. The dominant ethical theory of the day was utilitarianism. The strong family resemblance is unmistakable. The greatest good for the greatest number was merely the ethical counterpart of the survival of the fittest.

> All this time, utilitarianism—that improved substitute for the Gospel—was in its fullest feather; and was a natural ally of an individualistic theory. Dean Mansell's injudicious advocacy had led to mutiny among the bondsmen of Sir William Hamilton, and the nominalism of Mill had profited accordingly; and although the real science that Darwin was leading men to was sure some day to give a death blow to the sham-science of Mill, yet there were several elements of the Darwinian theory which were sure to charm the followers of Mill. (6.297)

Add to the various interpretations of utilitarian ethics, the economic theory and policy which dominated the nineteenth century, *laissez-faire*, and the picture is complete. All the sciences, physical and social, were using probability theory. Darwinism fitted right in.

Peirce's explanation of why the *Origin of Species* was an immediate success in certain quarters also tells us why he was opposed to it as a philosophical account of the development of the universe. He had both theoretical and practical reasons against it. For him, Darwinism generalized into a philosophical thesis was nothing more than another form of mechanism and so labored under all the same theoretical difficulties which beset mechanical philosophy in general. Besides, if it is only a faulty logical analysis of chance (viz. merely ignorance of the causes at work) which led some philosophers to conclude that reduction of nonconservative physical forces to probability curves finally vindicated absolute determinism, it is the very same error to think that Darwinism added any force to that position. Statistical analysis as applied in kinetic theory or in natural selection, when properly analyzed, does not support philosophical mechanism. As we have seen, Peirce contends that just the opposite is the case. These scientific theories have a place in our understanding of the world, but they are not in themselves answers to philosophical questions about the nature of the cosmos. They may serve as data for philosophical speculation but that speculation is only as good as its logic. It is simply a mistake, a very naive one at that, to appeal to a scientific theory as the justification of a philosophical theory designed to explain the scientific one. Mechanical philosophy is designed to explain scientific laws and laws of nature. No scientific theory will or can justify that doctrine. Peirce's theory of tychism is a philosophical theory designed to explain scientific laws and laws of nature. The laws of nature cannot establish that theory.[2]

It must be thoroughly understood that Peirce is not criticizing the use of probabilities in scientific method. On the contrary, he advocates it wholeheartedly. Peirce is not saying that kinetic theory is a poor physical theory, nor even that Darwinism is scientifically unacceptable. The point he is making has to do with philosophical interpretations given those theories and the implications they are supposed to support.

The practical motive for Peirce's opposition to a generalized Darwinism is that it encourages a basically unsound and immoral social order. The nineteenth century, according to Peirce, was the "Economical Century" in which political economy had been reduced to "a philosophy of greed" (6.290). Of course Peirce did not think for a minute that this was a legitimate conclusion of political economy, any more than he thought necessitarianism was a legitimate

[2] Cf. R. Wells, "The True Nature of Peirce's Evolutionism," *Studies*, Moore and Robin, pp. 304–322. Wells is very hard on Peirce. Peirce's whole undertaking, he feels, is so misguided that it cannot be repaired, only replaced. The basic reason is that the scientific ideal of testability is incompatible with the metaphysical ideal of all-comprehensiveness (p. 305). Any attempt to write them into a "scientific metaphysics" is doomed from the start. All that Peirce achieves in metaphysics, it seems, is to make some analytical statements which are true but irrelevant (p. 322). We disagree with this position, but, of course, we cannot enter into details here. We think, perhaps, there is some misunderstanding as to what Peirce means by "scientific metaphysics." It does not mean substituting scientific hypotheses for philosophical ones. Indeed, according to us, Peirce condemns "Social Darwinists" for doing just that. It seems to us to be a different thing to use scientific theories as models or guides for specifically philosophical explanations. To distinguish natural science from metaphysics is not necessarily to "drive them apart"; it may be that one distinguishes in order to unite. This, of course, makes no sense if one is already committed to the proposition that natural science is the only source of knowledge about the world.

conclusion of physics. The injustice and exploitation which the greed philosophy not only condoned but raised to the rank of virtue could not, in Peirce's view, produce anything but the direst consequences.

> Soon a flash and quick peal will shake economists quite out of their complacency, too late. The twentieth century, in its latter half, shall surely see the deluge-tempest burst upon the social order—to clear upon a world as deep in ruin as that greed-philosophy has long plunged it into guilt. (6.292)

The only inaccuracy about this apocalyptic prediction is that the deluge twice engulfed the world in the first half of the twentieth century. And it is not over yet by any means. By raising Darwin's limited scientific hypothesis to the status of a philosophical and moral dogma, Peirce saw aid and comfort going to mankind's mortal enemy. According to the crudest version of the pragmatic maxim, this sort of philosophy meant disaster and it could not be accepted as true without absolutely compelling evidence.[3] Peirce did not think, however, nor did he mean to imply, that Darwin's researches were motivated particularly by any political or ethical considerations, least of all by any conscious desire to further greed-philosophy. The only point is that as a matter of fact it played right into the hands of those who did desire to justify such a philosophy (6.297).[4]

[3] "*The Origin of Species* . . . merely extends politico-economical views of progress to the entire realm of animal and vegetable life. The vast majority of our contemporary naturalists hold the opinion that the true cause of those exquisite and marvelous adaptations of nature . . . is that creatures are so crowded together that those of them that happen to have the slightest advantage force those less pushing into situations unfavorable to multiplication or even kill them before they reach the age of reproduction. Among animals, the mere mechanical individualism is vastly reenforced as a power making for good by the animal's ruthless greed. As Darwin puts it on his title-page, it is the struggle for existence; and he should have added for his motto: Every individual for himself, and the Devil take the hindmost!" (6.293). In an unpublished fragment Peirce speculates whether Darwin was influenced by Malthus and political economy. This fragment also contains a summary of his evolutionary theory. (Peirce Papers, #954)

[4] Karl Pearson in *Grammar of Science*, Chap. I, argued that in accordance with Darwinian theory the *summum bonum* is social happiness, and social stability. Peirce argues that this does not follow from Darwinism.

There is no need to enter into details concerning Peirce's reservation about Darwinism as a strictly scientific hypothesis designed to explain the origin and development of organic species. At the time, the hypothesis was simply not sufficiently confirmed to warrant making it the sole factor in evolution. Peirce remarks that it had not been proved by the evidence as Darwin first presented it and that more than twenty years after the publication of the *Origin of Species* a sober mind must judge the case even less likely of ever being established (6.297). Peirce thought, however, that Darwin showed beyond serious doubt that natural selection played some role in the process but just how great was not yet clear. When we remember that Lamarckism was still biologically respectable, Peirce's doubts about Darwinism are not hard to understand. Indeed, further developments in genetics have shown Peirce's logic to be correct in that Darwinism has had to be revised. This scientific prudence and sobriety was merely an application of "humble fallibilism": do not be "cocksure" of anything in science (cf. 1.366 n. 1).

Peirce's own theory of evolution was philosophical, designed to account for the origin and development of the cosmos. He meant to model his philosophical theory on the best scientific information and theories available. There were three main theories of the evolution of organic species current in his day: Darwinism, Lamarckism, and cataclysmal evolution (1.104; 6.14–17).

First, the theory of Darwin, according to which the entire interval from Moner to Man has been traversed by successive purely fortuitous and insensible variations *in reproduction*. The changes on the whole follow a determinate course simply because a certain amount of change in certain directions destroys the species altogether, as the final result

Rather if natural selection is generalized into a philosophical thesis man's *summum bonum* can only be the continuance of the stock regardless of the happiness of individual men. The individual is of no account except insofar as he can reproduce. And since there is no happiness except that of individuals, Darwinism has nothing to do with happiness at all (8.133–136). The only thing that motivates scientific inquiry is desire to know the truth. Furthermore, Peirce does not think that there is the slightest reason to believe that man's highest good consists in procreating, and consequently it is just absurd to extend Darwinism into ethics.

of successive weakenings of its reproductive power. Second, the theory of Lamarck, according to which the whole interval has been traversed by a succession of very minute changes. But these have not taken place in reproduction, which has absolutely nothing to do with the business, except to keep the average individuals plastic by their youth. The changes have not been fortuitous but wholly the result of strivings of the individuals. Third, the theory of cataclysmal evolution, according to which the changes have not been small and have not been fortuitous; but they have taken place chiefly in reproduction. According to this view, sudden changes of the environment have taken place from time to time. These changes have put certain organs at a disadvantage, and there has been an effort to use them in new ways. Such organs are particularly apt to sport in reproduction and to change in the way which adapts them better to their recent mode of exercise. (1.104)

Peirce is convinced, despite Weismann's attack on Lamarck, that most probably all three modes of evolution have acted to produce species, and further, he thinks it probable that the third mode has been most efficient (1.105).[5]

[5] The controversy concerning the inheritance of acquired characteristics went on until much after Peirce's death. With the great strides made in genetics the importance of the controversy gradually subsided because most biologists considered the question misplaced. Gene mutation was the real mechanism at work in the transformation of species. Peirce's instinct, then, seems to have been correct, namely, that there is much more to organic evolution than Darwin's hypothesis provided. Furthermore, since Peirce's philosophical evolutionism meant to account for all sorts of development—of ideas, of mind, of institutions, of history—there was no reason why he should restrict his speculation to one scientific model even if only one model should turn out to be correct for biological development. He was interested in the biological theories for their structures, that is, insofar as they were suggestive of how things *might* have developed. He then considered various phenomena to see which mechanism was more likely to be the sort of thing needed. Thus he tried a Darwinian and a Lamarckian model to explain the historical development of weights and measures (1.106). He did the same with regard to the development of our opinions and beliefs (1.107). He thought that the cataclysmal model was more appropriate for an understanding of the development of science (science

On Peirce's view these theories of evolution are complementary. Lamarckian theory only explains the developments of characters for which individuals strive, while the Darwinian theory only explains the production of characters really beneficial to the race, though these may be fatal to the individuals (6.16). Geological and paleontological evidence seems to require cataclysmal evolution. The data seems to indicate that species are not very greatly modified under normal circumstances, but are rapidly altered after cataclysms or rapid geological changes (6.17). On this assumption, then, Darwin and Lamarck would account for the insensible variation of species during the millenia between the geological ages when some drastic alteration of environment broke up established patterns of life abruptly, thereby bringing about drastic and rapid adaptive changes in the species which survived (6.17). Considered more philosophically, these sorts of evolution may be interpreted respectively as evolution by chance, evolution by habit and effort, and evolution by breaking up of habits and formation of new ones. And with this foreshadowing of Peirce's own developed philosophical position, let us turn to consider his analysis of various philosophical theories of evolution and their interrelations.

Peirce's classification of philosophical evolutionism is rather complex, and, as is his wont, he has devised a very unusual vocabulary to designate the divisions.[6] The main divisions of Peirce's classifications are (1) elements of evolution, (2) modes of evolution, (3) doctrines of evolution. Each of these divisions is subdivided into three parts.

grows by leaps) (1.109). His own general theory of evolution, however, must also explain these various mechanisms themselves—how they developed and how the laws which govern them came about. Cf. T. A. Goudge, "Peirce's Evolutionism—After Half a Century," *Studies*, Moore and Robin, pp. 323–341.

[6] Peirce coined unusual technical terms deliberately in accordance with the principles of his "Ethics of Terminology." New ideas should have new words to express them. If old words are made do, he thought, only confusion results. Since the old, familiar words retain some of their old meaning, a person seeing them quickly assumes that he knows how they are being used in the new context. Hence he runs the risk of missing the new meaning. Peirce would prefer to use obscure and unfamiliar words in such a case than familiar but ambiguous ones. It forces the reader's attention on the novelty of the idea expressed and makes him work to grasp it.

The terms for these subdivisions are ingeniously contrived out of the stems of three Greek words with appropriate suffixes indicating the main division in question. The Greek words are *tyché* (chance), *anangké* (necessity), and *agapé* (love of friendship). The classification is as follows (6.302):

1. PROPOSITIONS ABOUT THE MODES:
   a) *tychism* affirms that as a matter of fact chance plays a role;
   b) *anancism* affirms that as a matter of fact necessity plays a role;
   c) *agapism* affirms that as a matter of fact creative love plays a role.
2. MODES OF EVOLUTION:
   a) *tychastic* evolution (tychasm) designates any evolutionary process which involves the action of fortuitous variation;
   b) *anancastic* evolution (anancasm) designates any evolutionary process which takes place by mechanical necessity;
   c) *agapastic* evolution (agapasm) designates any evolutionary process which takes place by creative love.
3. DOCTRINES OF EVOLUTION:
   a) *tychasticism*, according to which fortuitous variation plays the principal if not the only role in evolution;
   b) *anancasticism*, according to which mechanical necessity plays the principal if not the only role in evolution;
   c) *agapasticism*, according to which creative love plays the principal if not the only role in evolution.

The point of this rather elaborate scheme is to help the reader understand the dialectical synthesis Peirce sketches. As one might suspect there is a connection between Peirce's evolutionary scheme and his categorial scheme. The structure of both analyses is too strikingly similar to be merely coincidental. Certainly it is not when we recall that he explicitly applied the "triad" to Darwinian evolution in his paper "A Guess at the Riddle" (1.395). The first division cited above corresponds to a phenomenological affirmation. At this point the only claim made is that these elements are to be accounted for in any scheme. The second division, on the other hand, introduces the notion of discrimination and ordering. Modes look to the inter-relation of the elements at work in evolution. One could not hold just one mode of evolution to the exclusion of the others, just as one could not hold one category only. Furthermore, the interdependence of the modes of evolution follows a definite order which cannot be altered, just as the interrelation of the categories does. Finally, the third division introduces the synthetic doctrines resulting from the ordering of the modes. One could not consistently be a tychasticist, an anancasticist, and an agapasticist.

It is clear that Peirce has Darwinism in mind as an example of tychastic evolution (6.298; 6.304). Evidently, the Darwinism to which Peirce is willing to give a place in the development of the universe is not that of the mechanists who tried to make it shore up a collapsing *a priori* principle.[7] Authentic Darwinism accounts for evolution in terms of two factors: heredity and natural selection. These factors are capable of great generalization (6.15).

> Wherever there are large numbers of objects having a
> tendency to retain certain characters unaltered, this
> tendency, however, not being absolute but giving room for
> chance variations [thus a mechanistic interpretation is not
> legitimate], then, if the amount of variation is absolutely
> limited in certain directions by the destruction of everything
> which reaches those limits, there will be a gradual tendency
> to change in directions of departure from them. (6.15)

The clearest illustration of this sort of evolution is that of gamblers betting at an even game. As one after the other is ruined, the average wealth of those left in the game continually increases (6.15; 1.396 ff.).

> Here is indubitably a genuine formula of possible evolution,
> whether its operation accounts for much or little in the
> development of animal and vegetable species. (6.15)

Diametrically opposed to tychastic evolution is anancastic. Peirce has in mind such men as Hegel, Spencer, and others (6.298, 6.14, 6.305). Evolution by mechanical necessity, whether that necessity is external or internal, is plainly absurd on Peirce's view for reasons

---

[7] Peirce has in mind among others Chauncey Wright and Herbert Spencer. Cf. 6.14 and E. H. Madden, *op. cit.*, Ch. 1 and Ch. 4 *passim*.

already sufficiently considered. Absolute mechanical necessity would be the death of evolution. It would be hell freezing over. There simply is no reign of absolute and exact law in the universe. Such a frozen state of things might be posited as a theoretical limit toward which the growth of law and order tends, just as absolute chaos might be posited as the opposite limit. But neither limit is ever reached. Speculation approaches them only asymptotically. The kernel of truth in back of mechanism is simply the presence of law in the cosmos, but mechanism itself is an exaggeration. The kernel of truth present in tychastic evolution is that chance is really ingredient in things, but a denial of law amid the chance is equally an exaggeration.

Tychasm and anancasm, therefore, are conceptions at odds with one another. They are at opposite poles, as it were, and the only hope of reconciliation is through a third party, a mediator. If the kernels of truth in them both are to be preserved, a synthetic view must be taken. Obviously Peirce is using the same strategy he did in the analysis of the categories: Firstness and Secondness can be reconciled only through Thirdness. Agapasm, of course, fills the bill.

Among the scientific theories, Lamarckism most closely resembles agapasm. Peirce believed that enwrapped in Lamarck's theory was a third position which supersedes the strife between the other two (6.299). What attracted him to a theory of development through effort and striving was its likeness to habit-taking, the great law of mind.

> Such a transmission of acquired characters is of the general nature of habit-taking, and this is the representative and derivative within the physiological domain of the law of mind. (6.299)

Furthermore the very notion of striving and endeavor means end-directed activity and consequently is essentially psychical, even though not necessarily conscious. New forms are created by spontaneity ("energetic projaculation") and habit forces them to take practical shapes compatible with the structures which the new forms affect; further, habit gradually replaces the spontaneous energy which sustains those forms.

> Thus, habit plays a double part; it serves to establish the new features, and also to bring them into harmony with the

general morphology and function of the animals and plants
to which they belong. (6.300)

Peirce sees in this account of evolution what he calls the "action of love."

> The movement of love is circular, at one and the same
> impulse projecting creations into independency and drawing
> them into harmony. This seems complicated when stated so;
> but it is fully summed up in the simple formula we call the
> Golden Rule. (6.288)

And he attributes these views to St. John, "the ontological gospeller," who made "the One Supreme Being, by whom all things have been made out of nothing, to be cherishing-love" (6.287). Be it understood, however, that for all the religious overtones in this conception, Peirce looked upon it as strictly philosophical.

> The philosophy we draw from John's gospel is that this is
> the way [i.e. by creative love] mind develops; and as for the
> cosmos, only so far as it yet is mind, and so has life, is it
> capable of further evolution. Love, recognizing germs of
> loveliness in the hateful, gradually warms it into life, and
> makes it lovely. That is the sort of evolution which every
> careful student of my essay "The Law of Mind" must see that
> *synechism* calls for. (6.289)[8]

So far Peirce has said very little about the place of cataclysmal evolution, the third scientific hypothesis, as a model for his philosophical interpretation. Where would it fit in the tripartite division: tychasm, anancasm, and agapasm? In one place he groups the defenders of cataclysmal evolution with those who make mechanical necessity the chief factor in the process (6.298). But he seems to think that this is merely an erroneous interpretation of scientific data in the same way that a necessitarian interpretation of Darwinism is a mistake.

---

[8] Peirce seems to have been very much impressed with the doctrines of Swedenborg just becoming widely known in his day. Henry James, Sr. did much to make them known in this country through his book *Substance and Shadow*. For the influence of Swedenborg and James on Peirce see M. G. Murphey, *op. cit.*, pp. 350–352, and W. P. Krolikowski, "The Peircean Vir," *Studies*, Moore and Robin, pp. 257–270.

Thus, naming Nägeli, Kölliker, and Weismann as mechanists, he remarks:

> It is very noticeable that all these different sectaries seek to import into their science a mechanical necessity to which the facts that come under their observation do not point. (6.298)

He adds in the very next sentence:

> Those geologists who think that the variation of species is due to cataclysmic alterations of climate or of the chemical constitution of the air and water are also making mechanical necessity chief factor of evolution.

The mistakes are always the same: (1) cocksureness which closes the mind to other possibilities and other facets of the evidence, resulting in sweeping generalization and exclusivity; (2) failure to realize that the mechanism (efficient cause) proposed as the "explanation" of evolution is efficient only because its force is under the guidance and control of law (final cause), and that it is precisely law which needs an explanation.

We suggest that the counterpart to cataclysmic evolution in Peirce's theory is the sometimes violent breakup of habits. Strictly speaking Lamarckian theory only accounts for the acquisition of habits through effort. It does not account for change of habit. Surprise and shock bring about the destruction of certain habits of thought in a manner very much like the sudden changes in environment which produced, according to some scientists, the rapid adaptation of species, say at the beginning of the glacial period. Something brute takes place which upsets established patterns. Either those patterns are given up or extinction ensues. Only those things develop which remain plastic enough in their habits to change them in the face of experience. In the development of science, for instance, it is true that it advances through cooperation and common effort of a community of inquirers (e.g. 2.157), and that there is continuity in scientific results even when those results come out of a theory later found deficient (2.150). But that does not necessarily deny that science makes its great strides forward by leaps (1.109). Today we would say that scientific advances depend upon the ability of men to look at the data afresh and so conceive a whole new framework in which to theorize. Once the new framework is established scientists cooperate in working out its implications and in testing its results. Furthermore, what has been verified in the whole framework is not abandoned. It remains a true acquisition within the system and many times has its counterpart in the new framework, although perhaps couched in very different terms and/or formulas. When Peirce thought of the community of inquirers, he had in mind primarily an ideal group of dedicated men pursuing a correct method of research. Now precisely the point of fallibilism in men of science is to expect and to welcome new conceptual frameworks. The new frameworks, of course, rarely come out of the blue. Usually they are "in the air" when someone formulates them. The very fact that scientists are working on a certain set of problems with unsatisfactory results paves the way for a new look. Evolution, or development, along Lamarckian lines, therefore, is not so incompatible with development by leaps and bounds.[9]

Peirce, then, believed that agapasm incorporated the best in tychasm and anancasm. These latter are only degenerate types of the former (6.303). Tychastic evolution alone could not handle the notion of positive sympathy among created things springing from continuity of mind (6.304). Anancastic evolution alone might do if it worked, but Peirce was convinced that without a good dash of tychism to relieve the atrophy of necessitarianism it was all a Hegelian dream (6.305). Only agapasticism satisfactorily accounts for all the various sorts of development going on in the universe by admitting both chance and law, but uniting them in and through habit.

Peirce was very much aware of the difficulty in keeping the lines of demarcation between these modes of evolution as sharp as is desired. Indeed such sharp delineation is impossible due to the nature of things—reality is continuous, not discrete. If all three modes are operative in the process of growth, they will be found to a greater or lesser degree in all such processes (6.306). Of course, this observation does not take anything away from the fact that the three are different. This way of looking at things reflects Peirce's thinking about the universal categories. Peirce saw that things may be distinguished

[9] Contrary to P. P. Wiener, "Peirce's Evolutionary Interpretations of the History of Science," *Studies*, Wiener and Young, pp. 144–145.

although not in fact separable. The modes of evolution can indeed be distinguished but cannot be separated in any adequate account of the real evolutionary process. Before bringing this chapter to a close therefore, let us consider these modes of evolutionary development in relation to the categories.

Peirce definitely thought of the three evolutionary modes and their interrelations along the lines of the three categories and their interrelations. This is just what one would expect, since the categories are universal. We would also expect that Peirce's peculiar contribution will have to do with what corresponds to the category of Thirdness since he was convinced that practically all philosophers of his day except himself had fallen into the nominalistic error of denying the reality of that category. We have already seen that Peirce refuses to do away with any of the evolutionary modes, just as he refused to do away with any of the categories.

Tychastic evolution corresponds to Firstness. It is pure spontaneity. It is lawless and aboriginal, therefore requiring no explanation. It is what it is without reference to anything else. For that very reason, it cannot be the only factor at work in this world of *existents*. Anything that exists requires interaction with an environment and hence Secondness. Anancastic evolution corresponds to Secondness. It is the brute element in development. It is the blind interaction of objects supplying the force after the manner of the sheriff. Finally, agapastic evolution corresponds to Thirdness, mediating between chance and brute force and so producing order, law and the reasonableness of the court.

If there could be any doubt about Peirce's mind in this matter a long passage in the paper "Evolutionary Love" removes it. He remarks that there is only one variety of tychastic evolution, but two of anancastic and three of agapastic. This is exactly the way in which the categories are analyzed: Firstness can have no degenerate form, Secondness can have two, Thirdness three (6.307).[10]

Here is how Peirce works out the variety of modes in the evolution of human thought:

1) *tychastic* development (Firstness): new ideas arise through

[10] Cf. Part I, Ch. 1.

purposeless and purely spontaneous departures from habitual ideas;

2) *anancastic* development (Secondness): new ideas are adopted without seeing whither they tend but whose character is determined either

   a) by *external* causes such as environmental changes (genuine), or

   b) by *internal* causes such as logical development (degenerate);

3) *agapastic* development (Thirdness): new ideas are adopted neither heedlessly nor blindly, but by an immediate attraction for the idea itself, divined even before the mind consciously possesses the idea by the power of sympathy or affinity (continuity of mind) either

   a) by the community possessing the idea in its collective personality and then passing it on to individuals otherwise incapable of attaining it, or

   b) by an individual discovering the idea for himself but only because he is in sympathy with a community and this sympathy allowed him to experience the idea's attractiveness, or

   c) by an individual discovering the idea for himself independently of his human affections simply by virtue of the attractiveness of the idea itself.

These subdivisions of agapasm seem to correspond to the genuine (c) and two degenerate (a, b) forms of Thirdness. When Peirce talks of the "attractiveness" of the idea one is reminded of what we saw in Part I about the normative sciences. Indeed it was just about the time when he wrote "Evolutionary Love" (ca. 1893) that he became convinced that ethics is connected in some important way with logic. He had not yet taken up a serious study of the relation between logic, practics, and esthetics, but it is clear that his cosmological speculations prepared the way for the investigation. Certainly the work he did on evolutionary theory foreshadowed what he finally said about man's ultimate good.

A paragraph from the paper "The Architecture of Theories" is worth reproducing here because in it Peirce explicitly applies the notions of First, Second and Third to what we have been considering.

> The origin of things, considered not as leading to anything, but in itself, contains the idea of First, the end of things that of Second, the process mediating between them that of Third. A philosophy which emphasizes the idea of the One is generally a dualistic philosophy in which the conception of Second receives exaggerated attention; for this One (thought of course involving the idea of First) is always the other of a manifold which is not one. The idea of the Many, because variety is arbitrariness and arbitrariness is repudiation of any Secondness, has for its principal component the conception of First. . . . In biology, the idea of arbitrary sporting is First, heredity is Second, the process whereby the accidental characters become fixed is Third. Chance is first, Law is Second, the tendency to take habits is Third. Mind is First, Matter is Second, Evolution is Third. (6.32)

In another place, he developed the same idea in a slightly different way, relating the notions of absolute first and absolute last to the Christian conception of God as Alpha and Omega.

> The starting-point of the universe, God the Creator, is the Absolute First; the terminus of the universe, God completely revealed, is the Absolute Second; every state of the universe at a measureable point of time is the third. (1.362)

If one holds that all there is to the universe is what is measureable with no absolute first or last, with no definite tendency whence or whither, he is an Epicurean; if one holds that the definite drift of nature's course is cyclic so that the absolute end is only a return to the nothingness of the absolute beginning, he is a pessimist (6.363). On Peirce's view, the only conception of the universe compatible with Christian theology is an evolutionism which admits that the absolute First is distinct from the absolute Second, and that the state of things in the end has a general character different from the state of things in the beginning (1.362, n. 1).[11]

[11] Although Peirce was a deeply religious man, he did not give religious conceptions much philosophic standing. Religion for him was not the specu-

In summary, then, Peirce's evolutionary cosmology is best characterized as "hyperbolic" (8.317). It begins in the world as it is—a
world in which there is life and growth everywhere. Spontaneity and
variety abound amid regularity and order. His world view looks in
both directions: backward toward the origins of this growing cosmos,
and forward toward the development yet to be realized. As man
looks in each of these directions he only approaches the limits indefinitely. To have reached the limits in either direction, even in
thought, would be to transcend the space-time order to which man is
bound. At best man can only speculate as to the how of the origins
and of the outcome. Peirce's idea of evolution, then, can be thought
of as an hyperbolic curve indefinitely approaching the x-axis of origin
and the y-axis of end.

In a letter to Christine Ladd-Franklin (August 29, 1891) Peirce
described these axes like this:

> The state of things in the infinite past is chaos, tohu bohu,
> the nothingness of which consists in the total absence of
> regularity. The state of things in the infinite future is death,

lations of theologians and philosophers. It was a personal conviction based
on one's direct (if mediate) experience of God. God was not to enter into
metaphysics as an explanatory hypothesis. Still, he is not willing to con-
demn all philosophers who have used the term God to designate some part
of their system. Thus he thinks that those philosophers who speak of "ideas
in God's mind" are on the right track, but are using figures of speech which
are more ludicrous than false (6.199). In another place, in a more indulgent
tone, he concedes that those who must think of the universe as having an
adequate cause are justified in thinking of that cause as God (5.536). We
must remark in passing that the greatest weakness in Peirce's treatment of
religion is his studied neglect of its cognitive or interpretative element. In
particular if he had been more aware of the cognitive claims of Christian
theology he would have better understood the gigantic intellectual efforts
put into the problems of analogous predication by the great scholastics.
To our knowledge, Peirce, despite his familiarity with the scholastic tradition, never takes up the question of whether there are any distinctions to
be made between sorts of analogy. He lumps them all together under the
heading of anthropomorphisms. Cf. J. E. Smith, "Religion and Theology in
Peirce," *Studies*, Wiener and Young, pp. 266–267. For a representative
presentation of the problems of analogy taken up by the great scholastics,
cf. G. P. Klubertanz, *Introduction to the Philosophy of Being*, 2nd ed.
(New York: Appleton-Century-Crofts, 1963), *passim*.

the nothingness of which consists in the complete triumph of law and absence of all spontaneity. (8.317)

Between these two different sorts of nothingness

... we have on *our* side a state of things in which there is some absolute spontaneity counter to all law, and some degree of conformity to law, which is constantly on the increase owing to the growth of *habit*. (8.317)

The tendency to form habits, to generalize, grows by its own action.

Its first germs arose from pure chance. There were slight tendencies to obey rules that had been followed, and these tendencies were rules which were more and more obeyed by their own action. There were also slight tendencies to do otherwise than previously, and these destroyed themselves. (8.317)

Finally, the law of habit is the law of mind and hence the growing cosmos is "alive." Matter is merely mind deadened by the development of habit to the point where the breaking up of those habits is very difficult. Consequently, the universe is not as the mechanistic philosophers would have it. It is not governed solely nor principally by the laws of dynamics. It is governed by reasonableness working itself out in the concrete. It has an intrinsic and immanent finality which cannot be reduced to the interaction of blind forces. All that remains for us to consider is Peirce's speculations about the universe's beginning and end.

3. *The Beginning & the End*

An hyperbola determines two limits, its asymptotes, which are indefinitely approached but never reached. Since Peirce uses this analogy to characterize the evolutionary process, one is not surprised that he gives an account of its limits, that is, of the universe's beginning and end. Man, of course, cannot experience these limits, and yet they are logically required if evolution takes an hyperbolic course. Since this is speculation about the infinite, although he used all the logic and mathematics at his disposal, Peirce himself had to admit his account of universe's origin must seem to his reader "wildly confused" (6.203).[1] For all the obscurity, however, we must consider the limiting cases for completeness.

Peirce says relatively little about the universe's end and a good deal about its origin. This is not to imply that the cosmos' outcome is any less important than its beginning. In some respects the outcome is more important for Peirce since so much of his logical theory depends upon the "long run" and since he frequently defines reality in terms of the ultimate agreement of the community of researchers. But since there are two papers which deal with the beginnings in some detail, it is best to start there and consider the universe's end later.

The two papers we are about to consider were written about 1898. By this time Peirce's cosmology had taken definite shape and he was seriously engaged in thought about the normative sciences. One paper is called "The Logic of Continuity" and the other "The Logic of Events." The editors of the *Collected Papers* have given the sections considered here the titles "The Logic of the Universe" and "Objective Logic," respectively. Since the papers complement each other we will discuss them together.

---

[1] See 6.419 ff. for an early expression of the importance of determining whether the universe is finite or infinite in age and extent. See 1.273 ff. for a much more developed mathematical approach to the same sort of question.

The question of origins is metaphysical rather than cosmological because it deals with the universe as a whole.

> Metaphysics has to account for the whole universe of being. It has, therefore, to do something like supposing a state of things in which that universe did not exist, and consider how it could have arisen. (6.214)

But because the question of the universe's origin is metaphysical, it is logical since, for Peirce, logical principles are principles of being. Such an investigation, then, must consider the objective logical sequence of the world's origin. There can be no question of temporal sequence since time itself, as an organized something, only began with the cosmos.[2]

With this fundamental distinction in mind, let us consider the strategy of Peirce's reasoning. He states that the basic supposition back of every attempt to understand something is "that the very objects of study themselves are subject to a logic more or less identical with that which we employ" (6.189). In other words, science is realistic and not nominalistic.[3] The "logic of the universe," therefore, governs ours. Our logic aspires to the universe's and not the other way round. Thus, the universe's own intelligibility is normative of our thinking. Whatever theory we entertain must submit itself to our experience of how things are and not dictate how things must be.

Consequently, with the modesty befitting a scientific man, Peirce begins by ascertaining as nearly as possible how things are in the world of our experience. According to him, logic shows that continuity is simply a higher type of generality. It is in fact relational generality (6.190). Our experience tells us that there is at least some

---

[2] This is an answer to Kant's fourth antinomy (A452–B480; A453–B481). To think of the cosmos as beginning *in* time leads to an absurdity, but to think of the beginning of the cosmos as the beginning *of* time does not.

[3] Peirce says that science "supposes" or "at least *hopes*" that the world is intelligible. It would be hasty to conclude from this reservation that Peirce thought any less of the arguments he gave elsewhere in support of realism. All he needs for the passage under consideration is the lesser claim. Besides, humble fallibilism requires the elimination of "cocksureness" even where one is convinced that one holds the best hypothesis so far offered. It could and should be altered if the evidence warrants a change.

continuity and generality in the world, since there are real laws of nature. As a matter of fact, we *know* the world only to the extent that we discover these laws. According to the logic of explanation (see Part III, Chapter 1), it is precisely the regularity of the universe which must be accounted for. Our world is one of variety and uniformity[4] in which, as far as we can tell, there is a definite movement from lesser to greater organization. Variety and diversity cannot be explained in terms of uniformity, but uniformity can be explained in terms of variety and diversity through the mediation of habit. So the universe is evolving from chaos to order.[5]

Granted, then, that the uniformity of our universe is the thing to be explained, the question Peirce puts to himself is whether one ought to look upon that order as the result of welding together discrete entities or not (6.191). On the one hand, Peirce's logic of explanation seems to demand something like that, since it must account for order rising out of chaos. On the other hand, our logic, as the reflected image of the universe's, seems to indicate that human reasoning always moves from the vague to the definite, from the homogeneous to the heterogeneous (6.191). Apparently, then, the uniformity of our universe ought to be explained in terms of something still more homogeneous and vague, or, in Peirce's words, in terms of a still higher sort of continuum. But in that case, how can we claim to be explaining uniformity in terms of variety?

The inconsistency is only apparent, but before we show why it is, let us try to understand what led Peirce to argue for an original and primordial continuum of pure indeterminacy as the beginning-limit of our world's evolution. There were two reasons: (1) since he took seriously the proposition that our logic reflects the universe's, he was forced to admit "in Spencer's phrase [that] the undifferentiated differentiates itself" (6.191), that is, evolution proceeds from

---

[4] See 6.88–101. Peirce analyzes four or five positions concerning how much variety and uniformity we are to admit.

[5] Peirce was convinced that the hypothesis most in line with science is the one which supposes that there is some progress and development in the universe, that is, which holds that the cosmos goes from somewhere to somewhere. He could not admit either the "Epicurean" or the "cyclic" conceptions of time (1.363). It is not that he thinks them foolish or inconceivable but simply that experience favors evolution (1.273).

the vague to the definite; (2) if all continua are made up of discrete units (individuals or collections or entities in one-to-one correspondence with either), Peirce thought that he could deduce a contradiction (Cantor's paradox of the greatest cardinal)[6] and to resolve the paradox he denied that the greatest multitude has any discrete or actual parts at all. This greatest multitude which has no parts Peirce called a potential aggregate (6.185 ff).

> When I say that the series of abnumeral multitudes has no limit, I mean that it has no limit among multitudes of distinct individuals. It will have a limit if there is properly speaking, any meaning in saying that something that is *not* a multitude of distinct individuals is *more* than every multitude of distinct individuals. . . . That which is possible is in so far *general*, and, as general, it ceases to be individual. Hence, remembering that the word "potential" means *indeterminate yet capable of determination in any special case*, there may be a *potential* aggregate of all the possibilities that are consistent with certain general conditions; and this may be such that given any collection of distinct individuals whatsoever, out of that potential aggregate there may be actualized a more multitudinous collection than the given collection. Thus the potential aggregate is, with the strictest exactitude, greater in multitude than any possible multitude of individuals. But being a potential aggregate only, it does not contain any individuals at all. It only contains general conditions which *permit* the determination of individuals. (6.185)

Peirce might have tried to resolve the paradox of the greatest

---

[6] Cf. M. G. Murphey, *op. cit.*, pp. 263 ff. Murphey's careful analysis shows that in fact Peirce failed to prove his paradox because he failed to produce a genuine case in which $2^n = n$. Still Peirce's formulation of the paradox is correct and Cantor himself proved it in 1899. Cantor showed that the power-set of any set is always greater than that set ($2^n > n$). He also showed that the set of all sets, M, must include, or be equal to 2^M, since 2^M is the set of sub-sets of M. Peirce's solution to the paradox, therefore, is of genuine interest.

cardinal after the manner of Russell's theory of types.[7] We are inclined to think that he did not because of his ultrarealistic contention that all logical processes reflect nature's. The vague and indefinite are real for Peirce. So he had no difficulty in admitting a pure and absolute indeterminacy at the beginning of everything and out of which everything arose. His solution did escape the contradiction of the greatest cardinal and at the same time avoided Russell's conclusion that there can be no meaningful self-referential propositions.[8]

Just how does Peirce characterize the initial condition of the universe?

> The initial condition, before the universe existed, was not a state of pure abstract being. On the contrary it was a state of just nothing at all, not even a state of emptiness, for even emptiness is something.
>
> If we are to proceed in a logical and scientific manner, we must, in order to account for the whole universe, suppose an initial condition in which the whole universe was non-existent, and therefore a state of absolute nothing. (6.215)[9]

But there are two sorts of nothingness, that of negation and that of complete indeterminacy. The nothingness of negation is really *otherness* and "other than" is a relation which can be applied only where there is some degree of definiteness and discreteness. The nothing of negation is only a synonym for the ordinal number *second* and as such implies a First (6.217). The nothingness of the "pure zero," or indeterminacy, is prior to any First. Pushed to its extreme, the nothingness of negation would be the nothingness of death; it would be the state of absolute Secondness in which everything would be

---

[7] Cf. Murphey, *op. cit.*, p. 274; S. Körner, *The Philosophy of Mathematics* (London: Hutchinson University Press, 1960), pp. 45–47; 62–66.

[8] Russell's solution is not entirely satisfactory either. It declares meaningless any statement which refers to itself. F. B. Fitch, for one, argues forcefully for the need of self-reference in philosophy. Cf. *Symbolic Logic: An Introduction* (New York: Ronald Press Co., 1952), pp. 217–225.

[9] W. Wallace (transl.), *The Logic of Hegel* (London: Oxford University Press, 1959), nos. 86–87, pp. 158–163.

frozen solid. The nothingness of "pure zero" is the nothingness of not having been born.

> There is no individual thing, no compulsion, outward nor
> inward, no law. It is the germinal nothing, in which the
> whole universe is involved or foreshadowed. As such, it
> is absolutely undefined and unlimited possibility —
> boundless possibility. There is no compulsion and no
> law. It is boundless freedom. (6.217)

Peirce likened this initial state to Aristotle's prime matter (6.206). Prime matter is *nec quid nec quale nec quantum*. Peirce's potential aggregate, however, has one property, spontaneity. For Aristotle, prime matter functioned as an individuating and limiting principle which has no reality at all apart from a relation to some form. It has no spontaneity apart from act. Peirce, then, seems to endow Aristotle's prime matter with a little *energeia* or act.[10]

From pure indeterminacy nothing in particular necessarily results. Here Peirce departs from Hegel.

> In this proposition lies the prime difference between my
> objective logic and that of Hegel. He says, if there is any
> sense in philosophy at all, the whole universe and every
> feature of it, however minute, is rational, and was
> constrained to be as it is by the logic of events, so that there
> is no principle of action in the universe but reason. But I
> reply, this line of thought, though it begins rightly, is not
> exact. A logical slip is committed; and the conclusion
> reached is manifestly at variance with observation. (6.218)

Hegel's slip was to think that because the universe is rational it is *constrained* to be as it is. According to Peirce, then, Hegel fell into the error of all necessitarians. He supposed the logic of evolution to

---

[10] The schoolmen disputed over how prime matter should be conceived. Thomists generally held that it could not have any act whatsoever not even an act proper to itself. Suarezians generally held that prime matter has its own act. The difference is not a mere quibble. It determines to a large extent how these schools analyzed the notion of being and so affects their metaphysics at almost every point. Although the terms "act" and "potency" appear in both they do not have precisely the same meaning.

be "of that wooden kind that absolutely constrains a given conclusion" (6.218). Peirce points out that the universe's logic of development may be that of inductive or hypothetic inference. Hegel's mistake forced him to deny "the fundamental character of two elements of experience which cannot result from deductive logic"— spontaneity (Firstness) and arbitrariness (Secondness).

Although nothing in particular necessarily resulted from the "tohu bohu," something or other had to, simply because it is boundless spontaneity and freedom.

> I say that nothing *necessarily* resulted from the Nothing of boundless freedom. That is, nothing according to deductive logic. But such is not the logic of freedom or possibility. The logic of freedom, or possibility, is that it shall annul itself. For if it does not annul itself, it remains a completely idle and do-nothing potentiality; and a completely idle potentiality is annulled by its complete idleness. (6.219)

There can be no potentiality which would never, somewhere and sometime, have the occasion to be actualized. To say that there were such a do-nothing potentiality would be to confuse potentiality with mere logical possibility. It would be to deprive potentiality of all its power and dynamism.[11] There is, then, a kind of necessity in the first step in evolution but not that sort of necessity required by the determinists. For Peirce there must be some move or other (*necessitas quoad exercitium*), but no one in particular (*necessitas quoad specificationem*). Strict necessitarians would require that the specification be also determined.[12]

Something or other, then, had to come from the original pure spontaneity just because it is pure spontaneity. But again, because

---

[11] Aristotle and Thomas would agree, but they would say that the power and dynamism of real potentiality comes from some act with which it is associated. If this is what Peirce means, he is not very clear about it.

[12] See T. A. Goudge, *op. cit.*, pp. 172 ff., for a discussion of an ambiguity in Peirce's use of the term "probable deduction." Sometimes it refers to necessary inferences about probabilities; sometimes to conclusions which are only probable. Our distinction between kinds of necessity might throw some light on this ambiguity.

pure spontaneity has no order, nothing in particular had to appear —neither this, nor that, nor the other. Whatever did appear, appeared by pure chance. We are beginning to see that Peirce saw no inconsistency in saying that uniformity resulted from variety and that the original chaos had a certain uniformity about it. Clearly Peirce has in mind two quite different sorts of uniformity. The uniformity which requires explanation is that manifested in laws of nature. That sort of uniformity is manifested amid an actual multiplicity of instances. The uniformity of the original vague potentiality is a unity without any actual multiplicity at all. It is not the sort of thing which would lead us to expect from it anything in particular. Therefore, it would not cause any surprises and so would not lead us to ask questions. The sort of unity which raises questions is that which we find in multiplicity. The original continuum has only that unity which comes from lacking every determination. It has a unity, as it were, by default. As Peirce pointed out to Dr. Carus, this sort of "law" is entirely different from the rigid law of the determinists. It is the "law of freedom" and the basis of the law of mind.

When we think of chance we are apt to think of a random distribution of discrete units governed only by the laws of probability. Peirce once remarked that a world of chance in this sense would not be totally lawless. A random distribution of discrete entities, then, would not be entirely without order. Of course that order would only be accidental to the collection. The units in the collection could have been distributed some other way without affecting the collection. Nevertheless, Peirce seems to have thought the collection would have some order. Now as far as we can tell, the random distribution of a discrete collection is what Peirce meant by "quasi-chance." The limit case of "randomness" is what Peirce calls "absolute chance" and it has no order whatsoever because it has no discrete parts. Quasi-chance simulates the indeterminacy of absolute chance and

> . . . in a broad view of the universe a simulation of a given elementary mode of action can hardly be explained except by supposing the genuine mode of action somewhere has place. (6.613)

Peirce, then, takes the potential aggregate as the limit from which the evolutionary process began back in the infinitely distant past. Once we have grasped this difficult notion, the rest of Peirce's logical account is not too hard to follow. We must not forget, however, that it is a question of logical, not temporal, sequence. All our thinking is bounded by temporal conditions and so we must ever be correcting the tendency to transpose the temporality of our mental processes into the atemporal ordering of logical relations.

Peirce's logical studies, of course, provided him with a set of ordered logical relations: Firstness, Secondness, and Thirdness. And, as we have seen, to these categories roughly correspond the modes of being: qualitative possibility, actuality, and law. Peirce can make use of these notions in his account of the origin of our existing universe. The spontaneity of the original vague potentiality assured that something or other would be actualized. Logic assures that the first articulation of that vague potentiality must be "Firstnesses" or qualitative possibilities.

> Thus the zero of bare possibility, by evolutionary logic,
> leapt into the *unit* of some quality. This was hypothetic
> inference. Its form was: something is possible; red is
> something; therefore, red is possible. (6.220; cf. 6.194 ff.)

The first evolutionary move away from complete indeterminacy, therefore, was the emergence of the "World of Platonic Forms" by their inherent Firstness (6.198). Potentiality in general became particular potentialities.

It would be a mistake, Peirce insists, to think that these qualitative possibilities arose separately and only afterwards came into relation (6.199). If they had appeared on the scene in complete isolation there would be no way in which they could ever be related, since in themselves they are what they are independently of anything else. Once in isolation they would forever remain so, and then the "Platonic World" would be atomic and static. No further development would be possible (cf. 6.222–237). Consequently, we must assume that they sprang up already reacting upon one another. In that case, Peirce can say that they have a sort of existence (6.199), something like the existence our ideas have in our minds.

Logic further requires that every potentiality have actual instances at some time or other, somewhere or other. Peirce can argue, therefore, that a necessary condition for the move from vague potentiality to definite potentialities is that these definite potentialities have at some time actual instances. Our existing world is one locus of the actual instances of some of the "Platonic forms." Concrete actuals, however, in our world at least, never exhibit only one quality. Each is an actual instance of several potentialities. The instances, then, can be thought of as at the intersection, or points of interaction, of the forms. We may conclude that the springing up of potentialities in reaction one to another is a condition for there being concrete instances, just as concrete instances are a necessary condition for real potentiality. The universes of potentiality and of actuality, therefore, are interdependent although distinct in the same way as Firstness and Secondness.

If we recall what Peirce had to say about law, we see that the relationship between potentialities and their actual cases defines law. Brute interaction can be conceived as taking place between individuals, but not between individual and type. The only way in which an individual can come under a type is by a law. Thus the universe of law is a logical condition for the other two. All the universes, then, are inseparably bound up although distinct, just as are the categories. They can be prescinded one from another in a definite logical sequence. Notice, however, that the order of involution and that of evolution are just the opposite. Thirdness or law involves Secondness or actuality and Firstness or potentiality; but potentiality evolves actuality and these two together evolve law. As far as temporal sequence is concerned all three universes appeared at once since time itself arose with them.

We must now say something about the limit toward which our universe is evolving. It must be a state in which the reign of law is at a maximum. This does not mean that the universe will ever grind to a halt or become frozen in a "heat-death." When Peirce does describe the limit in these terms (cf. e.g. 8.317), he knows it will never be reached. In one place he characterizes this ultimate condition as the Absolute Second and likens it to "God completely revealed" (1.362), thinking perhaps of Hegel's Absolute Spirit absolutely articulated. At this limit, there would be no spontaneity and so no mind. The Absolute Second is the antithesis of the Absolute First.

There are several reasons why the Absolute Second will never be reached. First, since the primordial potentiality can never be exhausted, all spontaneity cannot cease (1.615). Second, no general can ever be completely embodied by actuals. Third, perhaps not entirely distinct from the other two reasons, the law of mind cannot be self-destructive (6.148), for if it were, the very growth of concrete reasonableness would be its undoing. Reason would destroy itself in and through the very process of its development. Reason would, then, be acting in a most unreasonable way.

Peirce's criticism of absolute determinism really comes down to saying that such a view admits that the Absolute Second will be reached. More accurately perhaps, it says that the universe is always in a state of absolute Secondness. According to Peirce, the absolute determinist cannot, consistently with his own principles, admit growth, variety, and diversity, and so he charges that observational data not only do not support such a position but are against it.

As we have seen in an earlier chapter, Peirce does not claim that a sudden end of everything is inconceivable, but again there is no positive evidence to support such an hypothesis (4.547). He told us that there might be material laws of nature against everything coming to a halt tomorrow, but that the notion itself is not self-contradictory. It is conceivable, for instance, that some force transcending our world might destroy it. Still, mere logical possibility is not a sufficient ground upon which to base an hypothesis. Consequently, Peirce is convinced that tomorrow is destined to come—and another tomorrow and another into the indefinite future.

Between the limits of vague potentiality and absolute fixity evolution goes on. Through the tendency to generalize, the universe is growing and developing. It is becoming more and more organized and subject to the law of mind. Evolution is Reason progressively manifesting itself. Reason, for Peirce, *consists* in its governing individual events and without those actual facts it would have no reality at all. It consists in being continually embodied in fact. It follows, then, that Reason can never be fully embodied since no number of events of actual facts can ever fulfill its potentiality.

So, then, the essence of Reason is such that its being never can have been completely perfected. It always must be in a state of incipiency, of growth. It is like the character of a man which consists in the ideas that he will conceive

> and in the efforts that he will make, and which only develops
> as the occasions actually arise. Yet in all his life no son of
> Adam has ever fully manifested what there was in him.
> So, then, the development of Reason requires as a part of it
> the occurrence of more individual events than ever can
> occur. It requires, too, all the coloring of all qualities of
> feeling, including pleasure, in its proper place among the
> rest. (1.615)

Reason, then, is the working out of ideas in the world. And for Peirce
the growth of concrete reasonableness is the admirable in itself.

Peirce's cosmological speculations and his pragmaticism come
together in a striking way in his evolutionary ideal. The course of
evolution itself, the growth of concrete reasonableness, becomes the
summum bonum, the highest norm. He has found the object of
esthetics, and through contemplation of it, he feels that man can deliberately form habits of feeling in accord with it. In terms of this
highest good, man can determine what are to be his ideals of conduct,
for he has found his place in the universe.

Man, then, holds a privileged and unique place in this evolving
world. Although he himself is a product of that process of development and still is in great measure subject to it, he has reached a stage
where he is capable of a very high degree of self-control. It is this
superior degree of control which sets him apart from other animals;

> . . . it is by the indefinite replication of self-control upon
> self-control that the *vir* is begotten, and by action, through
> thought, he grows an esthetic ideal . . . as the share
> which God permits him to have in the work of creation.
> (5.403, n. 3)

Man has evolved to a point where he now can cooperate in the process of evolution itself, since he can deliberately control his own actions and influence the community of which he is a member. He may
choose to further as best he can the growth of concrete reasonableness
in the world and so fulfill himself, or he may decide to act perversely
and so succeed in destroying himself. He cannot completely frustrate
Nature for he is still subject to her. Reason will continue to embody
itself with or without him, but he is privileged to cooperate in that

process consciously and willingly. Man needs norms to guide his deliberate conduct and those norms he finds in and through the universe which he knows and experiences—the universe which he knows and experiences because he arose out of it and is a part of it.

> I do not see how one can have a more satisfying ideal of the admirable than the development of Reason so understood. The one thing whose admirableness is not due to an ulterior reason is Reason itself comprehended in all its fulness, so far as we can comprehend it. Under this conception, the ideal of conduct will be to execute our little function in the operation of the creation by giving a hand toward rendering the world more reasonable whenever, as the slang is, it is "up to us" to do so. (1.615)[13]

[13] Peirce came to acknowledge the embodiment of Reason as the *summum bonum* through a contemplation of the universe's structure. The interplay of the modes of being bringing about the cosmos' development struck him as something admirable in itself. We wonder whether or not this is the sort of thing he had in mind when he spoke of "musement" through which, he thought, one would be convinced of God's reality. In any case, he certainly held that "musement" on the interrelation of the "three Universes" would bring one to that hypothesis, which ". . . the more he ponders it, the more it will find response in every part of his mind, for its beauty, for its supplying an ideal of life, and for its thoroughly satisfactory explanation of his whole threefold environment" (6.465; cf. 6.452–493).

Appendices

Appendix I

In the "Minute Logic" written shortly before the 1903 Harvard lectures, that is, about 1902, Peirce writes:

> The science which Berkeley, Kant, and others have developed, and which goes by the name of the theory of cognition, is an experiential, or positive science. It learns and teaches that certain things exist. It even makes special observations. But the experiential element in logic is all but nil. No doubt it is an observational science, in some sense; every science is that. Even pure mathematics observes its diagrams. But logic contents itself almost entirely, like mathematics, with considering what would be the case in hypothetical states of things. Unlike the special sciences, it is not obliged to resort to experience for the support of the laws it discovers and enunciates, for the reason that *those laws are merely conditional, not categorical.* The normative character of the science consists, precisely, in that condition attached to its laws. (2.65, emphasis added)

It certainly seems that here Peirce contradicts what he said about normative science in 5.39 (quoted in Part I, Chapter 2), namely, that its truth is *categorical.* In any case it is difficult to reconcile these passages. In conversations with colleagues, however, a number of things have been suggested to diminish the conflict. (1) In the passage quoted in this note Peirce is interested in distinguishing logic from any *Erkenntnislehre* which makes psychology its basis. Psychology might tell us how we must think—what are the uncontrollable processes therein involved, but logic as a normative science must deal with reasoning precisely from the point where it can be controlled. Logic, then, is not a positive science in the same way that psychology is, and in this respect is closer to mathematics. (2) When Peirce says that the conditional character of logic's laws is precisely what makes logic normative, he means to stress that logic lays down rules for right thinking, and rules, since they refer to ends to be achieved, are most appropriately expressed in conditional, not categorical, propositions. He certainly has in mind formal rules of thinking which would be valid in any universe of rational creatures, but does not necessarily restrict normative logic to formal considerations. Thus he admits that logic does need at least that experience necessary to motivate its research, and in another place tells us that all true laws, true generals, formal as well as material, are characterized by conditional necessity only. While logic is like mathematics, it is still distinguished from it in that it also must take into consideration the processes of thinking and the nature of the object thought as they actually are, not just as they might be. (3) Peirce makes the laws of logic the laws of being. Normative logic looked at in this way might conceivably be thought of as making categorical statements of positive fact about reality, and still one could hold that the norms, rules, or laws which it enunciates are to be put in the form of conditional, not categorical propositions. Considered precisely as norms or laws for right thinking they ought to take the form, "If you want X, do Y." Considered as laws of being, general facts about reality, they might be expressed in categorical form, perhaps something like this: "It is a general fact or law of nature that if you want X, do Y." These suggestions are offered for what they are worth. At least we are working on the principle that before a man's thinking is pronounced inconsistent every effort to save it ought to be made. Cf. R. S. Robin, "Peirce's Doctrine of the Normative Sciences," *Studies in the Philosophy of Charles Sanders Peirce,* ed., by E. C. Moore and R. S. Robin (Amherst: University of Massachusetts Press, 1964), pp. 275 ff. for a perceptive discussion of this difficulty.

Appendix II

IN A LONG FRAGMENT (*ca.* 1906) Peirce expounds in some detail his doctrine of "interpretants" (5.475–493). He tells us that the "meaning" of an intellectual concept requires a study of interpretants, that is, of the "proper significate effects" of signs. There are three general classes of interpretants (corresponding to the three universal categories): (1) the emotional interpretant, or feeling produced by a sign, (2) the energetic interpretant, or effort, physical or mental, elicited by a sign, and (3) the logical interpretant, or rational purport of a sign (5.475–476). Peirce sets himself the difficult task of explicating the logical interpretant. The *first* logical interpretant is a conjecture or hypothesis suggested by involuntary experience (5.480). Such a conjecture stimulates voluntary performances or "experiments" in the "inner world," that is, one considers the consequences of the conjecture and weighs alternatives. The logical interpretant, then, is seen to refer to the future, not to the future which as a matter of fact "will be," but to what "would be" on certain assumptions. The logical interpretant, therefore, has the character of a general (5.481–483). But what categories of mental facts are of general reference? Peirce lists only four possibilities: (1) conceptions, (2) desires, (3) expectations, and (4) habits.

> Now it is no explanation of the nature of the logical
> interpretant (which, we already know, is a concept) to say
> that it is a concept. This objection applies also to desire and
> expectation . . . since neither of these is general otherwise
> than through connection with a concept. Besides, as to desire,
> it would be easy to show . . . , that the logical interpretant
> is an effect of the energetic interpretant, in the sense in which
> the latter is an effect of the emotional interpretant. Desire,
> however, is cause, not effect, of effort. As to expectation, it
> is excluded by the fact that it is not conditional. For that
> which might be mistaken for a conditional expectation is
> nothing but a judgment that, under certain conditions, there

would be an expectation: there is no conditionality in the expectation itself, such as there is in the logical interpretant after it is actually produced. (5.486)

By elimination, therefore, Peirce concludes that the essence of the logical interpretant is habit.

In every case, after some preliminaries, the activity takes the form of experimentation in the inner world; and the conclusion (if it comes to a definite conclusion), is that under given conditions, the interpreter will have formed the habit of acting in a given way whenever he may desire a given kind of result. The real and living logical conclusion *is* that habit; the verbal formulation merely expresses it. (5.491)

Peirce, of course, admits that another concept, or proposition, or argument can be *a* logical interpretant of a concept, but it cannot be the *final* logical interpretant, "for the reason that it is itself a sign of that very kind that has itself a logical interpretant." Only the habit can be the final logical interpretant because, although it too is a sign, it is not a sign like the concept of which it is the logical interpretant is a sign. What interprets habit considered as a sign (together with motive and circumstances) is *action*. But action is an energetic not a logical interpretant precisely because it lacks generality.

The deliberately formed, self-analyzing habit—self-analyzing because formed by the aid of analysis of the exercises that nourished it—is the living definition, the veritable and final logical interpretant. Consequently, the most perfect account of a concept that words can convey will consist in a description of the habit which that concept is calculated to produce. (5.491)

Peirce concluded this important paragraph with a rhetorical question.

But how otherwise can a habit be described than by a description of the kind of action to which it gives rise, with the specification of the conditions and of the motive?

This is but another expression of the scholastic maxim "*agere sequitur esse*," the medieval counterpart of the pragmatic maxim. To know what a thing is, you must see what it does! Cf. J. E. Smith, *The Spirit of American Philosophy* (New York: Oxford University Press, 1963), pp. 8–9. Yet cf. 4.536 for a slightly different arrangement:

Immediate interpretant = the interpretant as revealed in the right understanding of the sign itself, and it is ordinarily called sign's *meaning*.

Dynamical interpretant = actual effect which sign determines.

Final interpretant = refers to the manner in which sign tends to represent itself to be related to its object.

Bibliography

Bibliography

WORKS BY PEIRCE

Charles S. Peirce's Letters to Lady Welby. Edited by I. C. Lieb. New Haven: Whitlock's, 1953.

Charles S. Peirce Papers. Houghton Library, Harvard University (Manuscripts).

Collected Papers of Charles Sanders Peirce, Vols. I–VI. Edited by C. Hartshorne and P. Weiss. Cambridge: Harvard University Press, 1931–1935. Vols. VII, VIII. Edited by A. W. Burks. Cambridge: Harvard University Press, 1958.

Values in a Universe of Change: Selected Writings of Charles S. Peirce. Edited with introduction and notes by P. P. Wiener. New York: Doubleday Anchor Books, 1958. Reprinted, New York: Dover Publications, Inc., 1966.

WORKS ABOUT PEIRCE

Bernstein, R. J. "Peirce's Theory of Perception," *Studies in the Philosophy of Charles Sanders Peirce,* Second Series. Edited by E. C. Moore and R. S. Robin. Amherst: University of Massachusetts Press, 1964, pp. 165–189.

————. *Perspectives on Peirce: Critical Essays on Charles Sanders Peirce.* Edited by R. J. Bernstein. New Haven: Yale University Press, 1965.

Boler, J. F. *Charles Peirce and Scholastic Realism.* Seattle: University of Washington Press, 1963.

Dewey, J. "Peirce's Theory of Quality," *John Dewey on Experience, Nature, and Freedom.* Edited by R. J. Bernstein. New York: Liberal Arts Press, 1960, pp. 199–210.

Feibleman, J. *An Introduction to Peirce's Philosophy, Interpreted as a System.* New York: Harper and Bros., 1946.

Fitzgerald, J. J. *Peirce's Theory of Signs as Foundation for Pragmatism.* (Studies in Philosophy, XI.) The Hague: Mouton and Co., 1966.

Freeman, E. *The Categories of Charles Peirce.* Chicago: Open Court, 1934.

Gallie, W. B. *Peirce and Pragmatism.* Harmondsworth, Middlesex: Penguin Books, 1952.

Goudge, T. A. *The Thought of C. S. Peirce.* Toronto: University of Toronto Press, 1950.

————. "Peirce's Evolutionism—After Half a Century," *Studies in the Philosophy of Charles Sanders Peirce,* Second Series. Edited by E. C. Moore and R. S. Robin. Amherst: University of Massachusetts Press, 1964, pp. 323–341.

Haas, W. P. *The Conception of Law and the Unity of Peirce's Philosophy.* Studia Friburgensia, New Series, No. 38. Fribourg: University Press, and Notre Dame: University of Notre Dame Press, 1964.

Hartshorne, C. "The Relativity of Nonrelativity," *Studies in the Philosophy of Charles Sanders Peirce.* Edited by P. P. Wiener and F. H. Young. Cambridge: Harvard University Press, 1952, pp. 215–224.

————. "Charles Peirce's 'One Contribution to Philosophy' and His Most Serious Mistake," *Studies in the Philosophy of Charles Sanders Peirce,* Second Series. Edited by E. C. Moore and R. S. Robin. Amherst: University of Massachusetts Press, 1964, pp. 455–474.

Knight, T. S. *Charles Peirce.* New York: Washington Square Press, 1965.

Krolikowski, W. P. "The Peircean Vir," *Studies in the Philosophy of Charles Sanders Peirce,* Second Series. Edited by E. C. Moore and R. S. Robin. Amherst: University of Massachusetts Press, 1964, pp. 257–270.

Lenz, J. W. "Induction as Self-Corrective," *Studies in the Philosophy of Charles Sanders Peirce,* Second Series. Edited by E. C. Moore and R. S. Robin. Amherst: University of Massachusetts Press, 1964, pp. 151–162.

Madden, E. H. *Chauncey Wright and the Foundations of Pragmatism.* Seattle: University of Washington Press, 1961.

Murphey, M. G. *The Development of Peirce's Philosophy.* Cambridge: Harvard University Press, 1961.

Oliver, W. D. "The Final Cause and Agapasm in Peirce's Philosophy," *Studies in the Philosophy of Charles Sanders Peirce,* Second

Series. Edited by E. C. Moore and R. S. Robin. Amherst: University of Massachusetts Press, 1964, pp. 289–303.

Reese, W. "Philosophic Realism: A Study in the Modality of Being," *Studies in the Philosophy of Charles Sanders Peirce*. Edited by P. P. Wiener and F. H. Young. Cambridge: Harvard University Press, 1952, pp. 225–237.

Robin, R. S. *Annotated Catalogue of the Papers of Charles S. Peirce*. Amherst: University of Massachusetts Press, 1967.

———. "Peirce's Doctrine of the Normative Sciences," *Studies in the Philosophy of Charles Sanders Peirce*, Second Series. Edited by E. C. Moore and R. S. Robin. Amherst: University of Massachusetts Press, 1964, pp. 271–288.

Schneider, H. W. "Fourthness," *Studies in the Philosophy of Charles Sanders Peirce*. Edited by P. P. Wiener and F. H. Young. Cambridge: Harvard University Press, 1952, pp. 209–214.

Smith, J. E. *The Spirit of American Philosophy*. New York: Oxford University Press, 1963.

———. "Religion and Theology in Peirce," *Studies in the Philosophy of Charles Sanders Peirce*. Edited by P. P. Wiener and F. H. Young. Cambridge: Harvard University Press, 1952, pp. 251–267.

Thompson, M. *The Pragmatic Philosophy of C. S. Peirce*. Chicago: Phoenix Books, 1963.

Weiss, P. "Charles Sanders Peirce," *Dictionary of American Biography*, 14 (1934), pp. 398–403.

———. "The Essence of Peirce's System," *Journal of Philosophy*, 37 (1940), pp. 253–264.

Wells, R. "The True Nature of Peirce's Evolutionism," *Studies in the Philosophy of Charles Sanders Peirce*, Second Series. Edited by E. C. Moore and R. S. Robin. Amherst: University of Massachusetts Press, 1964, pp. 304–322.

Wennerberg, H. *The Pragmatism of C. S. Peirce: An Analytical Study*. Library of Theoria, No. 9. Lund: C. W. K. Gleerup, and Copenhagen: E. Munksgaard, 1962.

Wiener, P. P. *Evolution and the Founders of Pragmatism*. Cambridge: Harvard University Press, 1949.

———. "Peirce's Evolutionary Interpretations of the History of Science," *Studies in the Philosophy of Charles Sanders Peirce*.

Edited by P. P. Wiener and F. H. Young. Cambridge: Harvard University Press, 1952, pp. 143–152.

————. *Values in a Universe of Chance: Selected Writings of Charles S. Peirce.* Edited with introduction and notes by Philip P. Wiener. New York: Doubleday Anchor Books, 1958. Reprinted, New York: Dover Publications, Inc., 1966.

Workman, R. "Pragmatism and Realism," *Studies in the Philosophy of Charles Sanders Peirce,* Second Series. Edited by E. C. Moore and R. S. Robin. Amherst: University of Massachusetts Press, 1964, pp. 242–253.

MISCELLANEOUS WORKS CITED IN THE TEXT

Abbot, F. E. *Scientific Theism; or, The Philosophy of Free Religion.* Boston: Little, Brown and Co., 1885.

Bettoni, E. *Duns Scotus: The Basic Principles of his Philosophy.* Translated by B. Bonansea, O.F.M. Washington, D.C.: The Catholic University of America, 1961.

Einstein, A., and Infeld, L. *The Evolution of Physics.* New York: Simon and Schuster, 1961.

Fitch, F. B. *Symbolic Logic: An Introduction.* New York: The Ronald Press Co., 1952.

Hegel, G. F. W. *The Logic,* Translated by W. Wallace. Second edition. London: Oxford University Press, 1892.

Hertz, H. *The Principles of Mechanics.* New York: Dover Books, 1956.

James, W. *Pragmatism and Other Essays.* Introduction by J. L. Blau. New York: Washington Square Press, 1963.

Jammer, M. *Concepts of Force.* New York: Harper Torchbooks, 1962.

Kant, I. *Anthropologie in pragmatischer Hinsicht.* In Vol. 10 of *Immanuel Kant's Werke.* Leipzig: Modes und Baumann, 1839, pp. 113–377.

————. *Critique of Pure Reason.* Translated by N. K. Smith. New York: St. Martin's Press, 1961.

Klubertanz, G. P. *Introduction to the Philosophy of Being.* Second edition. New York: Appleton-Century-Crofts, 1963.

Körner, S. *The Philosophy of Mathematics.* London: Hutchinson University Press, 1960.

Pearson, K. *The Grammar of Science.* Everyman's Library, edited by E. Rhys. London: J. M. Dent & Sons, 1937. (First published in

1892, then in 1900, and again in 1911, each with modifications. Peirce reviewed both the first and second editions.)

Perry, R. B. *The Thought and Character of William James*, Vol. II. Boston: Little, Brown and Co., 1935.

Ross, Sir David. *Aristotle*. New York: Barnes and Noble (University Paperback), 1964.

Teilhard de Chardin, P. *The Phenomenon of Man*. New York: Harper Torchbooks, 1961.

Weiss, P. *Modes of Being*. Carbondale: Southern Illinois University Press, 1958.

Whittaker, Sir Edmund. *A History of the Theories of Aether and Electricity*. New York: Harper Torchbooks, 1960.

Indices

Index of Names*

* The author wishes to thank his students at Loyola Seminary for their invaluable help in compiling these indices.

Index of Subjects

ABSTRACTION, 9n, 83, 84, 94, 131
ACT-POTENCY, 23, 196n
ACTION, viii, 4, 5, 6, 19, 21, 33, 45, 48, 50, 53–55, 59–61, 63, 64, 65, 66, 80, 114, 125, 130, 134, 138, 140, 166, 190, 196, 198, 210; chance, 136n, 140, 143; conservative, 134, 139, 142, 166 (*see also* force); controlled, 19, 34, 48, 125 (*see also* control); and habit, 55; human, 34, 120; of love, 183; mechanical, 142; nonconservative, 139, 140, 166, 173; and thought, 39, 53ff., 62, 66, 67; ultimate end of, 47
ACTUALITY, 11, 12, 17, 56, 64, 97, 98, 100, 199, 200; and Secondness, 12, 13
ADMIRABLE IN ITSELF (*per se*), 33, 34, 37, 40, 44n, 46, 50, 127, 202, 203n. *See also* summum bonum
AFFINITY OF MIND TO NATURE, 121, 130, 187
AGAPASM, 180, 182, 183, 185, 187
AGAPASTICISM, 180, 185
AGAPISM, 180
AGGREGATE, POTENTIAL, 194, 196, 198
ANANCASM, 180, 182, 183, 185
ANANCASTICISM, 180
ANANCISM, 180
ANTHROPOMORPHISM, 120, 121, 189n
ARCHITECTONIC, ix, 3, 20, 23, 161n

CATEGORIES, x, xii, 4–12, 23, 32, 36, 38n, 42–44, 75n, 87, 97n, 104, 113, 127n, 136, 181, 182, 185, 186, 199, 200, 209; and act-potency, 23, 196n; and division of philosophy, 18–22; and evolution, 180–189; genuine degenerate grades, 16; interdependence of, 14–18, 91, 94; and normative science, 8–24, 94; transcendental and predicamental, 38n. *See also* Firstness, Secondness, and Thirdness
CAUSATION, 138, 139, 170; efficient, 112–117, 119, 128, 132, 136, 184; final, 55, 63n, 112–121, 126, 128, 132, 136, 140, 142, 184, 190
CHANCE, 84, 103, 104, 106, 134–136, 140–145, 152, 157, 164, 166, 167, 174, 179, 185, 186, 188, 190, 198; absolute, 135, 136, 141, 161, 162, 165, 166, 168, 170, 198. *See also* spontaneity
CLASSES, NATURAL OR REAL, 116, 117, 125
"COCKSURENESS," 57, 177, 184, 192n
"COMMON NATURE" (*natura communis*), 80, 81, 93
COMMUNITY OF INQUIRERS, 63, 184, 185, 187, 191, 202
COMPULSION, 16, 17, 25, 27, 28, 72, 102, 108, 112, 113, 196
CONDITIONALS, 57, 58, 64, 66, 82, 94, 96–98, 101, 102, 108, 109, 207–209
CONDUCT, 4n, 5n, 6n, 19, 20, 25, 26, 30, 32, 34, 38n, 39, 40, 48, 50, 58, 59, 61, 64, 65, 66, 89, 102, 120–124, 126, 128, 129, 134n, 203; habits of, 127; ideals of, 121, 122, 124, 202, 203; rules of, 122
CONSCIOUSNESS, 6, 12, 13, 30, 43, 55n, 100n, 104, 112, 118, 119n, 123, 125, 129–136, 153, 165, 169; direct, 129, 131; grades of, 145; physiological basis of, 131; reflexive, 129, 131; rudimentary, 140, 145; three degrees of, 131
CONSEQUENCES, 59, 97, 99, 121, 136n, 164, 209
CONSISTENCY OF PEIRCE'S PHILOSOPHY, viii–ix, 24, 34ff., 87